DAVID MEETS SOME VERY TOXIC PEOPLE.

(YOU MAY NOT BE RESPONSIBLE FOR BEING DOWN, BUT YOU ARE RESPONSIBLE FOR GETTING BACK UP AGAIN).

Written by David L Jackson. MA. BSc (Hons). So-GFY (Hons)

Editing, design, typesetting and publishing by UK Book Publishing

www.ukbookpublishing.com

ISBN: 978-1-912183-73-9

FOREWORD

This book is dedicated to, and in recognition of, some of those major 'Oi You Fucker' moments experienced during the course of a fully-fledged, institutional life, during the 1960s and 1970s. The system was called 'childcare' but it was, in reality, a system of brutally horrific regimes, founded upon extraordinary levels of inhumanity, cruelty, violence, fear, and intimidation, propagated against some of the most vulnerable people in society. It was, and in many ways remains, both a depressive, and oppressively dysfunctional system that requires a tolerance for perpetual physical suffering and mental hardship. Survival – and life outcomes – operated on a perverted logic that declared to children: 'You are worthless, you have no value, you cannot achieve; therefore, we can brutalise you with impunity, as it is no loss to society'. When a child rebelled against the rigidity of this generic 'care model', the care model itself was then judged to have been correct and validated in its continuation of ritualised systematic abuse.

This was the environment that the 'Unfortunates' found themselves embedded in during the 1960s. It was a system that lacked care, thought, and all things humane. A system where the imposition of brutal physical and sexual abuse had been normalised, legitimised, embraced and accepted, as perfectly reasonable tools, for the control and 'care' of children in local authority homes.

These were the homes of 'the Damned', hidden behind austere facades, in relatively normal, suburban streets. A catalogue of daily horrors was rigidly imposed at the personal pleasure of those charged with the care of this hidden, and often forgotten, sub-culture of children who, through no fault of their own, would be forced to embrace these traumas as they became normalised, daily occurrences. It was simply, and often, the case that, as little Johnny from one end of the street happily kicked his ball against the garden fence, proudly watched by his loving parents little Chloe, a few doors away, was being sexually abused by her 'carer', which, as time revealed, nobody cared about, because little Chloe was one of 'the Damned'. Chloe didn't count, and it was unlikely, under this regime, she ever would count.

Within this environment, a black child emerged to face the marauding hordes of abusers and their invited friends. Isolated, abused, brutalised and afraid, his fledgling sense of self was being violently torn apart, as he stood against the overwhelming, all-embracing and seemingly unstoppable forces of neglect and evil, that were as pervasive as they were ruthlessly brutal.

There was, however, a solitary driving force that took a daily surge through his fledgling mind, one pre-developed goal that defied the reasoning of both age and intellect. This single objective that kept him moving forward day-by-day, week-by-week, month-by-month, and year-by-year. It was an instinct to survive, to live, to be free from the tyranny that had enveloped his childhood. That boy was called Snowball, and this is his story.

FRUIT SALADS, BLACK JACKS AND GRAPES (THE LATE 1960s)

Fruit Salads, Black Jacks and grapes. These were the only reasons Snowball liked going to school every morning. This love for the sweets and grapes meant that he would secretly curse the advent of all, and any, school holidays, as they came around in the annual calendar, that was both tactically and annoyingly positioned on the kitchen fridge at home. He had a short journey home from school; alone, on foot, yet he was watched closely by an innumerable amount of community eyes, ensuring his timely, safe and unimpeded progress. Fruit Salads, Black Jacks and grapes were the mini feast that invariably would come his way, being in plentiful supply, from numerous sources, as he meandered past the community lookouts, and friendly faces, that watched over his childhood frivolities and homeward bound dalliances on a daily basis.

It was a friendly, caring community, that took a direct interest and responsibility in ensuring that the children were raised in the 'right way'. Every pair of adult eyes were perceived as those of his parents. Every word spoken, and instruction given, carried the same, if not greater weight, as those given by Mum and Dad, who waited patiently at home for his imminent arrival. And there was always an omnipresent threat, that any cheek, challenge or rebellion to the wrong person, or that landed in the wrong set of ears, would result in a sharper slap around the back of his stocky brown legs, than what he would expect to receive from Mum or Dad for a similar offence.

Whenever it did occur, it was a slap that, for good reason, he would inevitably neglect to mention upon arrival at his own front door. The shame felt by his foster mum or dad would inevitably lead to his being frog-marched down the street in humiliation, to apologise under the threat of a spanking, that he knew only too well was coming anyway. The desire to demonstrate that your kids were decent, good kids, and that Mum and Dad were decent, good parents, outweighed the true gravity of any offence he had unwittingly caused. It was a disciplined, structured life in many ways. A life designed to ensure that he and his siblings grew up the right way, and became responsible adults, who respected the right people and institutions, and always chose to do the right thing.

The downside of having a thousand eyes watching your every move was far outweighed by the care and consideration routinely displayed throughout the community, and it was something that could often be taken for granted. Snowball felt safe on these streets. These were familiar surroundings that he had grown to love and appreciate. He knew nearly every face, every front door, who lived where, and where to go when he needed help. These were the streets he had grown up in, and they were *his* streets.

At roughly six-years-old, it always seemed like a long, albeit uncomplicated, walk home from school. But it was a welcome walk that brought him into contact with many of his favourite local characters and often saw him line his pockets with sweets and pennies, as his familiar and popular, smiling brown face softened the hearts of the many he passed. There were clear and present advantages of being the only black child in the town, and he had long ago learned how to take maximum advantage of this.

Snowball found school an aggressively disciplined environment that he cared little for. He had a form teacher who, clearly unloved by all her own family during childhood, had taken it upon herself to ensure that every child under her care suffered an equally miserable time while she held the reins. She was a tall, stern-faced, gangly woman, as unpretty as she was ruthless, and she held sway by a hedonistic mixture of enforced detentions during break times, and ritualised beatings at the end of each day. These would see the unfortunate culprits of real or imagined offences lined up in front of the remainder of the class, placed across her knee and beaten to tears.

Snowball had learned to cry sooner rather than later, though not too soon, as it was commonly understood that it was the tears that floated her boat, and she wasn't going to stop until she had elicited them. He found it was also prudent to position himself at the back of the queue on a Friday, as this was the day that every child was ritually beaten before the weekend commenced, on the premise that if you had not been smacked for something during the week, it was because you had not been caught, as opposed to a prolonged period of good behaviour. But the walk home each day washed away all that misery. As his mother reminded him on numerous occasions, missing school was not an option, so he had adjusted himself mentally to the daily challenge, and sought to focus on the positives, such as walking home and collecting goodies.

Long straight roads were punctuated by the odd left or right turn, intimidating canines, and overly friendly felines. It was pretty much as simplistic as it could get, even for a six-year-old, and as all roads led to the mount by the sea, there was infinite scope for distraction into unfamiliar territories, without the risk of becoming painfully lost. But the Fylde Coast harboured some harsh winter weather at times, weather that would brutally batter and bruise all but the physically hard, and strong of mind, and the direct way home was always the best way home for a child that suffered the cold with utter disdain, as Snowball did. The simplicity of the walk, however, given the often wintery conditions, was constantly overshadowed by the tactical considerations that needed to be taken, in order to avoid the worst of the weather.

The key was knowing which side of the road harboured you most from the piercing wind. But the worst of the nasty dogs were where the pleasant cats hung out. You had to know where the dazzling morning sun would break between the chimneys, momentarily blinding you, as well as which doorways and alleys offered the greatest refuge from the driving rain, and occasional snowfalls. It was all about positioning yourself in the most advantageous place, at the most appropriate time, compounded only by the necessity to be within the proximity of certain gates, at certain times, so that his pockets were replenished with his favourite sweets and occasional pennies. It was a game of jaywalk chess, and he was a Grand Master in the making. He knew the rules, and where every piece went on the street board. That was why he was the kid with the sweets, and his siblings were the kids with a cold, runny nose.

He knew that by the time he had traversed the myriad small, pretty Northern terraced streets between school and his front door, with their lazy maze ways, broken flags, occasionally disjointed cobbles, and regular mounded deposits from man's best friend the deep winter chill would have taken a huge bite out of him. His resolve would waver, and he would undoubtedly welcome the warm broth that often came part and parcel with his timely, welcomed arrival home.

His mother always welcomed him with a broad, beaming smile. It was a smile which confused him, as much as it warmed him, because he was unsure if it signalled that she had not expected him to make it home, and was pleased he had, or that she was just happy to see him again, in the same way she was happy to see his siblings. It didn't really matter, but he was a child who hated ambiguity, so it played momentarily on his mind, until he was ushered away to stow his coat on the hangers behind the door, and change from his school clothes into those he played in.

The routine was as simple as his everyday walk. Having hastily changed, the grapes he had amassed on the way home now eaten, he deposited his Black Jacks and Fruit Salads in plain view on the kitchen table. He would eagerly await the warm winter offering, simmering on the stove. He knew better than to eat the sweets before he had eaten his tea because, in that household, sweets were a treat for clean plates and happy faces. As long as they remained in plain sight and away from the nefarious intentions of his soon-to-be-home siblings, he cared little for the ruling; he knew his plate would always be clean, and his face was always smiling.

But the streets were where his mind wandered. These were his streets. He was familiar with their slow, constant meanderings and the pungent, lingering odour of the recently landed fish, from the daily trawler runs that began each morning, long before he had ever arisen, and ended just as he was on his outbound journey to school. He would occasionally get a pleasant and well-intentioned stream of "Good mornings!" from the trawlermen who were making their way home, sea-battered, work weary and covered in the blood of the gutted morning's catch, a 'lifted' fish wrapped in white, blood-stained paper in one hand, and an edition of the early morning newspaper in the other.

The crisp morning air was overpowered by the pungent odour of burning Old Holborn. Small, green tobacco and rizla packed tins gave way to fag tip embers glowing below runny noses, held by yellow hands mimicked in the yellow stained teeth of every smoker that passed him. These were toughened, worldly men who commanded respect for their daily endeavours, but little did he know at such a young and tender age that most of his morning 'friends' would pass early, having succumbed to the natural forces of the seas, or the lingering deposits that their chain-smoking addictions were secretly secreting in their powerful lungs.

Every now and again, they would call at his front door with their fishy offerings on display for his financially-pinched parents. They were conscious that she, who had lovingly opened her door and her heart to twelve foster children, would likely be pre-dispositioned to avail herself of some cheap fish to feed her growing brood. Freshly caught that morning, it was better than the occasional weekend trips to the chip shop with his father, who would buy battered fish over the counter for their Saturday night treat.

He knew the streets well. Through the small strip of local shops, the newsagents and the grocers, to the knitwear shop on the corner, and the chip shop and café plumb in the middle of the lot. He knew Mrs Marreste, a delightful little French lady, who owned the cake shop close to home. She would occasionally furnish him with a leftover treat if she was preparing to close early, before watching him go on his way, up to and past the hardware shop, managed by Mr Jones and his ailing mother, Miriam. He rarely saw her these days as she had become increasingly bed ridden, but he remembered her for her overbearing kindness and generosity towards him and his siblings, on the many occasions they had visited with his father.

These were happy, carefree times for 'Grandad's Little Snowball', as he was affectionately known amongst family and friends. Love was in abundance. He was well-nurtured and tended to. He felt wanted, a far cry from how he had felt at the start of his life.

Life for Snowball could not possibly be any better than this. He had everything he needed, and most of what he wanted. He was at home and comfortable in his surroundings, valued and respected. He was part of a huge family, his only family as he knew it. He knew the layout and the scheme of things as he wandered with carefree abandon through the streets and onwards towards home, a hundred hidden eyes ensuring that as he travelled from street to street, no harm or ill-intent befell him. This was his manor. Everybody knew him, where he was from, and where he was going. He could not get up to any mischief, nor could he come to any harm. It was a Fairtrade deal, long before Fairtrade deals were ever thought of, and he revelled in and grew beneath this blanket of security.

He knew the route, and what to expect better than he knew anything else. Large stone gate posts were followed by a wrought iron gate, followed by another large stone gate post. There was a dwarf brick wall, topped with a painted concrete cornice, a half-post denoting the boundary of one front garden and the beginning of another, with an even smaller dwarf wall running the breadth of the garden inwards, terminating to the righthand side, just below the living room window. His route continued. Gate post, gate, gate post, gate, dwarf wall. Row after row, street after street. Endless rows of mandatory conformity, maintained as pristinely as time, social expectation and finances would allow, with an added and welcome dash of communal care and responsibility from those who resided there.

Snowball was unique in his hometown. In the days when his near perfect brown skin was something of a local oddity, Snowball stood out amongst the vast array of skin shades and tones, generically termed as 'white', despite being anything but. He had never seen another black face during those few short years, nor did he imagine he ever would. He knew he was different but had no idea why. He was the most recognisable child in any crowd, much to his chagrin, but it was something of a blessing for his mother, who often sat and watched in awe as this hurricane of enthusiastic and bumptious activity appeared to cover ground, time and space like no other child she had ever cared for, or had indeed seen. He was a child of short stature, with curly black hair in a centre parting, with a beaming smile that displayed an array of well-tended to, developing white teeth. These were punctuated by only the odd gap that had been recognised and rewarded by the financially challenged Tooth Fairy.

Everything about him drew curious attention. People would prod and poke him to see if the colour came off. They wanted to know if he would sunburn in the summer or turn white in the winter. They wanted to know where he was from, and seemed startled when the answer was Manchester, as opposed to Mombasa or Harare. It was ignorance, but an amusing ignorance, that often saw him furnished with pennies of embarrassment, as the enquirer suddenly became aware of their own profound degree of isolation and unfamiliarity and were consumed by a need to redress any potential offence to his mother, or embarrassment to the child.

Ladies envied his eyelashes, which curled outwards, up and round, almost to where they were back in contact with their original point of origin. They shielded his big brown eyes from all manner of intrusion and held in rapture envious females of all ages. It was his eyes that caught the attention of most people, bar his overtly dark skin. They drew people in. They held them in their gaze, sapped their attention, and warmed even the coldest of hearts. By all accounts relayed by his mother, you could wallow in them for hours, and Snowball knew exactly how to use them to his own advantage, and he often did with Aunty Margaret, his favourite victim. She plied him with attention and sweets every time she called, or as he passed the small café she owned near the seafront. These eyes were housed in an almost perfect little head, supported by a short but relatively broad, muscular neck for a six-year-old. Perched aloft, this neck connected to a short expanse of shoulders, short strong arms, and a puffy chest that eluded to and tentatively informed of the never-ending whirlwind of childish activity that supplemented his daily routine.

To the backdrop of being the only black kid in town and the pleasant attention that brought, he developed a confident gait, almost a swagger, supported by stocky brown legs, born of the attention this 'unique' status had afforded him. Powerful calves, firm thighs, and a small but developing torso supported his bounding walk. It was a far cry from the days when the professional opinion was that he would never walk again, if he did indeed manage to survive. This bundle of joy was a hurricane. Always well-dressed, intellectually smarter than his years, quirky and inquisitive; an eclectic mix of characteristics that demanded attention. He was a talker. He was a listener. He was a wide-eyed dreamer. He was an artist, an actor, and an engineer. He was a little professor in the making, proffering the occasional gallic shrug as the conversation was heard but in no way understood. In his fledgling mind, he could do and be anything he wanted, and he thrived. He was unique. He was his very own 'Mr Benn', constrained from day-to-day only by the limits of his forever roaming and developing mind. A bright and happy individual, he was about to have his entire world shattered in a solitary blow.

It would not always be so, but Snowball came from what was a very good home. There were two loving parents, and on occasion, more than ten children crammed into a two-storey terraced house on the edge of the town, close to the beach and chilly waters of the Irish Sea. They had their biological children, then the foster children who had been placed in their care because of an array of unhappy, but long forgotten and never discussed reasons.

Their foster parents loved them all equally, although to the casual observer, it was apparent that Snowball, with his unusual ethnicity for the time, garnered a little more attention from his adoring foster mother. Some would argue that they were loved too much, but it mattered not to any of them or their parents, as once the doors to the house were closed to the outside world, the joy of the tight knit family unit and all the love and security it offered came into full force, consuming everybody and everything within those walls. They were well-loved children, each and every one of them, and they knew it. They appeared to outside eyes as a strong, well-balanced family, built on a foundation of love, respect, discipline and joy. And so, it was.

In the main, it was an extremely happy home. It was a typical Sixties household; his father was a strong-willed, hardworking patriarch, who could turn his hand to anything in pursuit of an income, and who provided for his family through hard, manly toil, dirty hands, healthy beads of sweat, and a less overt, but nonetheless loving, concern for his charges. His mother was an even stronger matriarch, responsible for making family life happen. They were clean kids, they were well-fed kids, they were happy kids. They were respectful, polite, disciplined, and mutually tolerant of each other, and to those they encountered in the world outside. His mother was the person who glued them all together and made it happen. She created the loving bond that existed between them all, ensuring that respect and discipline flourished, and, in the main, that everybody lived a happy, carefree life that they deserved. They were creditworthy mini adults in the making, forming a strong familial bond that made for a bright, happy household which they all came to cherish. These were happy times, long before the burden of administration, regulation and accountability turned child protection into a synonym for career and self-protection.

It was a well-structured and disciplined household that operated and succeeded on a clearly defined set of rules, rewards and occasional punishments, when the good life got taken for granted. Rewards came in the form of a large sweet jar that sat perched, ever so close but oh so far away, on the living room table. It was one of those Sixties sweetshop jars, plastic in design with a bright red screw-top. Broad and tall, it contained a plentiful supply of everyone's favourite candy, from foamy flying saucers to sticks of liquorice, gobstoppers, and chewing gum. Sweets could be gained for getting dressed on time in the morning, having a bath on Sunday without making a fuss, doing up one's own shoelaces, getting dressed or undressed when asked, washing your hands after going to the toilet, helping with the pots, and a whole host of other chores and expectations, succinctly aligned with age-related expectations and development.

The sweet jar meant everything to Snowball. It was at the centre of daily life, an ever-present reminder that there was a system in operation, even if you did not always recognise it as such. Snowball knew the system. He knew what was rewarded, and what was not, allowing him to align his behaviour accordingly. He knew when the rewards were due, and when they were not. He also knew exactly when the jar would be replenished and timed his best and most compliant behaviour accordingly. Amongst all else and regardless of the good and the bad he had encountered in his short years, he was a fast learner, and where the sweet jar was concerned, his potential for learning was epic.

The sweet jar helped immensely with discipline in the household. The dreaded phrase "No sweets" served as a constant reminder that life, inside and outside the home, included responsibilities that had to be met. His father would most often handle discipline where the older boys were concerned, and the lure of the sweets was far less potent. His softened, well-worn leather belt made occasional and unwelcome visits to the backsides of the ungrateful and errant instead. Snowball came under his mother's disciplinary domain, too young and too small to be belted. He had the age-related 'luxury' of short painful visits across her knee, followed by long periods of reflection in his bedroom while the rest of his siblings roamed outside, playing with the neighbours' children, all within sight and earshot. It all seemed so cruel at the time but had the desired, remorse-inducing effect that was needed, so that it was never too long before a gingerly cant downstairs towards his mother's awaiting arms, and an oratory of pre-planned sorrow, saw him reunited in mischief with family and friends alike. As somewhat of a deep thinker, the entire process caused him a disproportionate degree of vexation, and a considerable dose of humiliation, amusing his siblings and distressing himself in equal measure.

Snowball lived in a house where there was a constant stream of regular, friendly visitors. At times, it appeared that half of the town were there inside, if not in the immediate vicinity, and beyond. It was a popular household. There were not that many ten-person households in the town, and it seemed like everyone was there to help, either with advice – which clearly his mother needed none of – or bags of donated clothes and occasionally food which she was always immensely grateful for. It was a happy house, busy, full of life, joy and laughter. There were grandparents, uncles and aunties (real, and by virtue of their age) and there were friends, lots of them. Everyone called in, and often; each and every visitor bringing with them their own brand of character, care, attention and a hint of communal discipline that reinforced that expected degree of appropriate respect. This typified the 'In it Together' attitude that pervaded the time, which would, for political expediency and economic failure, be alluded to decades later, as politicians strived to justify taking the country back to the austere economic realities of the time in which he currently lived.

It was an environment in which children were loved and could thrive; and thrive they did. Each and every one of them, each and every day. Life for Snowball was free from all worldly concern, as much as it could be for a Sixties child. He was insulated, well-insulated from all that was harmful, and which he had encountered during his earlier life. It was a time when communities provided everything that a child needed, and most of what they wanted, so within this context, he was an extremely well-looked after child. Attention, love, warmth and guidance, occasionally disguised by a harsh frown, or tough words, though nevertheless well-intentioned, were a staple diet. These were times when children had a place in society, and for their own well-being, they were taught that place early in their formative years. This was how Snowball and his siblings learned to thrive, and as a result of this powerful and pervasive sense of community, he had grown to know most, if not all, the faces that he ever bumped into as he meandered and played in the local streets and parks.

Most, of course, knew him by name, though what he failed to appreciate at the time was that remembering the only black face in the town was probably a lot easier than he imagined. Nevertheless, he drew comfort from the constant stream of 'Hello David's as he played in the back streets with his football, built sandcastles on the beach, wandered alone through the nearby park, or navigated his weekly trip to the sweet shop, his 'good boy' pocket money in hand, to buy his two-penny bag of goodies, and a drink. He had even learned how to occasionally take advantage of this popularity, and would, when the opportunity arose, visit the sweet shop with nothing but plastic toy coins in his hand. He would immediately go through the process of selecting his favourite sweets from the penny tray, before furnishing a handful of plastic coins to the shopkeeper. This would inevitably mean returning many of the sweets to the tray, but invariably he knew that, providing the shopkeeper was unaware of the cunning ruse, he would get to keep some of the sweets out of sympathy, as feigned tears of emotional distress trickled down his face.

The 'pain' of the conditions attached to earning his 'good boy' pocket money only ever slowly diminished as he drew closer and closer to Mr Garner's newsagents. The daily chores he and his siblings were assigned were not at all difficult, but a lesson in contribution and responsibility that was decidedly unwelcome at his tender young age. There was the morning routine of washing and dressing; the communal Sunday night bath that ensured everyone at least started the week looking clean and healthy. The pain of eating 'all' his porridge each morning, which he had a pervasive and peculiar love/hate relationship with, directly linked to whether it was jam or honey that had been ladled into the centre of it. Then there was the toast that was laid out on the table for breakfast, often cold and soggy by the time he reached the table, but which needed to be eaten regardless. It was a household where nobody went hungry, but little, especially food, went to waste in as economically challenging a time as this. It was largely a case of eat the breakfast or take an all-expenses paid excursion over his mother's knee *then* eat the breakfast, so it didn't take much working out. As he was often told, it was all for his own good.

He also had to tie his own shoelaces, don and buckle his own duffle coat, and as time marched on, learn to fasten his own tie. How he hated trying to make his bed and put his dirty clothes in the massive laundry basket, secreted away at the back of the kitchen in a cold dank room referred to as the wash house. All this in the name of earning enough merits to warrant his pocket money every Saturday morning. His life subsequently became more troublesome when his mother saw fit to eat his jelly in front of him, as punishment for his lack of cooperation one morning. How he had hoped she would choke on every mouthful and succumb to an agonising death, preferably before she had finished his dessert, for obvious reasons!

But at least his pocket money remained intact in the main, although on occasion he would find his access to the only television restricted for transgressing the rules or coming up short on merits. Gone for days were episodes of *The Flintstones*, *The Jetsons* and *Blue Peter*. *The Magic Roundabout* could easily have become a thing of memory, and *Play School* was consigned to immediate history, along with *Mr Benn*, *Thunderbirds*, and many more of his favourites. It seemed ever so harsh, but in the cold light of day, it did the trick, as it was clearly easier to comply and enjoy life than spend countless hours with his ears pressed against the bedroom floor, struggling to hear the latest episodes of his favourite programmes, played out in the living room downstairs.

Yes, it all seemed quite onerous to this well-cared-for infant, until that moment he caught sight of the goodies Mr Garner had to offer, and then it all made perfect and reasonable sense. Sherbet filled Flying Saucers sat next to aniseed balls, which in turn gave way to long thin laces of liquorice, and liquorice Catherine wheels. Alongside this came the penny tray, filled with pink bubble-gum, Black Jacks, Fruit Salads, Love Hearts, Parma Violets, Fizzers, traffic light lollies and confectionery cigarettes. Mr Garner stocked them all, and the pennies in Snowball's pocket facilitated a tasting spree every Saturday morning, which he cherished and looked forward to.

He knew his parents were not his natural ones. History had conspired in a strange way during his few short years, and although he was much loved, he knew by the very nature of his brown skin, that 'Mum and Dad' as he knew them, were, in fact, not his own. It was not as if it really mattered, and he had never been led to believe it did; it was just so strikingly obvious. It was a quandary that had often crossed his young mind as he sought to develop kinship and identity, culminating one warm summer's day in a skin tone experiment, involving a large paintbrush, a tin of pink emulsion, and an overly eager application of paint from head to toe. Problem and solution, a strategy that would serve him well in later years. If nothing else, Snowball was a problem solver. If only his mother had seen it that way.

He was the one brown face amongst a host of white family, friends, teachers, shopkeepers, callers and all other manner of people who came and went, crossing his path with a happiness he had come to enjoy, and a love he had grown to depend on. A far cry from the days of pain and anguish that had wracked his earlier years, and very nearly cost him his life. And it was in this cocoon of happiness that he made his way home that fateful day. Not that he had avoided significant or fateful days in the past, but this sharp turn of events would, in fact, mark a significant departure from the life that he would probably have mapped out for himself, but for his infant years and worldly naivety.

On William Smith Street, he passed the ageing Mr Ashcroft. A man who seemed to always be flirting with an uncomfortable close proximity to death, he spent his days either domicile in his bay-windowed lounge, or casually strolling through the terraced streets of Farm Wood, calling in on friends and casual acquaintances with an air of senile indifference to the busyness of their day. He was a man of sturdy build, with a pungent odour to him that seemed to linger in the air long after his presence had departed. Snowball imagined him to be a 'powerful' man in his younger years (a term he had heard his father use many times), a man with a power matched only by the pungent bodily aroma he chose to cultivate in later years. A man with hands that appeared bigger than the coal shovels he watched his father heave nuggets of black gold onto the family fire with. Yes, Mr Ashcroft was not a man to be trifled with, but as the familiar "Hello David" echoed through the crisp winter air, and the lingering waft of stale sweat descended, he realised trifling with Mr Ashcroft was not something that had recently crossed his mind anyway.

Balme Street, with its continuous flow of yet more typically regional terrace houses, complete with fake Tudor facades, was where he frequently bumped into the familiar, albeit slight, figure of Mrs Swarecki. She was a short, thin woman, but with a sharp, vocal rasp that seemed to echo through the streets when she called your name. You never got away with anything when Mrs Swarecki was around because after the ritualised mumblings of her daily "Hello" in a somewhat foreign tongue, her iconic rasp had clearly signified to every resident in the street that you were, in fact, around and thus ripe to be blamed for any mischief that ensued in the coming minutes, whether you were guilty or not.

There were two notable things about Mrs Swarecki that Snowball always remembered. Firstly, she had a clearly foreign name and tone. He had heard stories that she had been in a refugee camp during the war, and that she had been allowed to settle in the United Kingdom when it had ended. Whether it was true or not he had no idea, but it made for a plethora of other war-related tales that were most likely either flights of fantasy about her, or the legitimate recantation regarding the 'deeds of derring-do'.

The second, and most prevalent, characteristic about Mrs Swarecki was that she always had and would freely distribute to passing children who caught her beady squinting eye, a pocketful of sweets (Gobstoppers, Fruits Salads and Black Jacks), which she bought daily from Mr Garner's newsagents further down the street. This simple fact alone was enough to justify walking the long way round when heading home, and occasionally slowing your walk to almost a crawl if Mrs Swarecki had not appeared at the due time when school was out, and the kids in 'the know' were heading home. Her house was the most easily identified in the entire row. Just about everybody had conformed to the implanted norm and painted their facades black and white, in keeping with the visual amenity of the area, but Mrs Swarecki was a little bit different and had chosen a bright red paint with which to drench the front of her house. It proved an unsightly annoyance to most of the residents, but Snowball quite liked it. His mother had relayed a story from Mrs Swarecki, who had asserted that it was a memorial, of sorts, to a relative who had survived the Holocaust, and whose last memory before walking from the train into the camp, was a solitary, bright red flower, blooming out of sync with the muddied fields and green grass that surrounded it. Some believed that Mrs Swarecki was, in fact, that very survivor of whom she talked, but nobody really knew for sure, and she was unlikely to be forthcoming with any further details, preferring instead to tantalise and tease with a patchwork of details that could never quite be sewn together.

Mrs Swarecki was a daily ritual to which Snowball would gladly conform. Dainty in stature, she was nevertheless the strong matriarch that typified so many households. Women ruled the day, Dads ruled the TV and the car, and the children (or at least those with any sense) concentrated only on those things that children should, whilst maintaining a discreet absence from sight and sound that was expected in just about every household and establishment they would ever frequent. Snowball would often think, 'What a great mum Mrs Swarecki would be, giving out sweets every day!' For as much as he loved his own mum and dad, sweets every day was a dream too far in a household with ten or so hungry mouths to feed. He mused that, perhaps, one day, he could run away and stay with Mrs Swarecki, if only for a short while.

In Rothman Place, Snowball often bumped into the Smithers twins, who were the human manifestation of mumps and measles. They were an odious pair, who lived only to manifest the criminal intent that had been instilled in them by their equally nefarious parents. It was never the most pleasant, nor eagerly anticipated of his daily encounters, as they too had noted the difference in skin tones and would regularly foist abuse upon him because of it. Nor did they have sweets to offer, which basically added injury to their insults. They were two socially awkward and poor young boys, even by the standards of the somewhat austere times in which they all lived. Nor were they the brightest of children, though both were significantly older than he was. In their zeal to be offensive, it seemed to have escaped them both that the language they were using was way beyond Snowball's infant comprehension, and it was, in fact, the non-verbal cues, gestures and hostile demeanour they elicited that caused his apprehension they had so eagerly sought through verbal slight.

In many ways, he mentally contrived to pity them. They never appeared to have an outwardly happy disposition; they were always angry, hostile, never with friends, and there was an overt absence of any parental love or guidance. Indeed, to the extent he could understand it, they had it tough. All they had was each other, and a preceding reputation that encouraged most of the local grown-ups to treat them with disdain and contempt. Simply put, they were two ostensibly ignorant boys who, in years to come, would likely be found on Spanish shores, complaining in a tapas bar that the gazpacho was cold, and that the restaurants in Lloret de Mar were rubbish, because they did not sell English grub and were full of foreigners.

He knew that one of the boys had been in an approved school as he had heard his mother talking to a neighbour about it, though its definition was not something he was coherently aware of. However, it was obvious from his mother's tone, and the fact that she would occasionally threaten to send him there as a punishment, that it was not something to be proud of. However, the one thing he always remembered with envy about the Smithers boys was food. Yes, food; the Smithers boys always seemed to have it. They were always seen eating it, wasting it, kicking it around the floor when they were done with it. In the absence of love, comfort, discipline, safety and security, food had emerged as their constant companion, their friend, their saviour and master. Never had he seen anywhere else food in such abundance. It was in seemingly never-ending supply. It was food for food's sake, a substitute parent, grandmother, teacher and friend. Food, food, food and more food.

Passing Garner's Newsagents-cum-General Store was always a treat. It was an old-fashioned emporium, with row upon row of jarred sweets, a counter to one side where he stacked his newspapers and laid out a penny tray that was full of tooth-rotting goodies, and a wall of tidy shelves that was home to every conceivable thing a budding cook or housewife could ever need in the kitchen or home. Mr Garner was a jovial man, of jovial proportions. He was a big, bulbous, and somewhat portly man. Dominant in stature, he invaded and controlled the personal space of all around him. Lacking in cranial hair, this was more than compensated for by his firm, woven beard that jutted out at almost ninety degrees in places. He was a strange combination of a facially un-ageing but greying, almost hairless man. He clearly had a follicle challenge on his hands but was showing few other signs of his extensive time on the planet.

Though Mr Garner's primary business was his newsagents, he also did a natty line in what could only be described as semi-fresh fruit and veg on a good day – cheap and in abundance. Women would fill their brown wicker shopping baskets with vegetables and turn his dodgy offerings into tasty soups and teatime accompaniments. For Snowball, however, it was the fruit that was of interest. In particular, the bright green grapes in the small flimsy wooden boxes that Mr Garner stacked closest to the counter, away from the door, as they were considered a 'desirable item' and as such, ripe for light-fingered children and adults alike. Mr Garner's counter was in direct line of sight of the doorway. He could see everyone who passed, everyone who entered, and most importantly to him and to Snowball, everyone who paused in the vicinity of his treasured fruit pile.

Mr Garner and Snowball had established an almost comical routine, in which they engaged daily as he made his way home from school. As he meandered home, he would slowly approach Mr Garner's shopfront, always cautious to allow enough time for any potential customers to finish their business and leave. As he drew level with the shop, he would approach the door, peering through the dirty, stained glass up at the counter where Mr Garner stood, awaiting his next caller. The air of expectation at this point was tangible. It was unclear who enjoyed the game most, Mr Garner or the little black face, a novelty face in those days, that peered through the glass; half in expectation of seeing nothing, then disappointment that would ensue, and half in expectation of seeing a smiling Mr

Garner, who would point to the grapes and nod his head enthusiastically with a beaming smile that lit up the day.

Today he was in luck. Not only was Mr Garner there, his face also beamed brighter, and as he nodded and pointed to the grapes, he noticed the ripe and fresh greenness of today's batch. "Great!" he thought. Snowball grasped the permitted small handful from the stem's fallen fruit, smiled back appreciatively at Mr Garner, and bounded away with an added skip in his step. It may have been cold, but Snowball cherished these little touches. Mr Garner was running a close second to Mrs Swarecki in his mind, and as he had been made aware, as he grew so would his hands, and thus he could alleviate Mr Garner of even more grapes.

And so into Blackwell Street he bounded, carefree in his final approach to home. He was cold on the outside but warm on the inside, with a heady mixture of Fruit Salads and fresh grapes swirling around in his stomach. Yes, life for this young boy was good. Mr and Mrs Hall were halfway down the street and often greeted him warmly as he passed their gate, grinning like a Cheshire cat and waving frantically at Mr Hall to grab his attention. He always smiled back, and Snowball would stop briefly to engage in infantile chatter. Mr Hall had a strange way of talking to him, slow and deliberate, with great emphasis on almost every word and syllable he uttered. Snowball would learn later in life that this trait, along with a raised voice and enhanced inflection, was the British way of speaking to foreigners, something Mr Hall clearly thought he was because of his dark skin.

Pleasantries concluded, he bid farewell to the Halls, and headed onwards toward the mid-row terrace that was his home. His happy home, his place of safety and sanctuary. A place where he was loved and pandered. Home was where he always wanted to be. School was a venue he tolerated; it kept him in sweets and all manner of goodies. The requirement, the necessity. But home was where he was always at his utmost happiest.

There was something unusual as Snowball turned into the street, one of those inexplicable sensations you get when some strange sixth sense kicks in, and you become all too aware of something abnormal, but cannot quite put your finger on it. There was a peculiar feel to the air, it rested heavier upon his shoulders, and it was as plain as the grapes in his tiny hands that something was not quite right. Mr Jenkins at number twenty-seven refrained from his usually bumptious greeting, and chose instead to simply nod, with an air of knowing, in Snowball's direction as he slowly passed his gated front garden. He could see his Aunty Margaret midway up the street, and it was clear that she was upset, and in some distress. The inquisitive spectre of Mrs Amery, propped up against her garden fence with a mug of tea in hand and bemusement across her face, was the clearest sign yet that something abnormal was going on. All was not right, as he casually perused the sights and sounds laid out before him. Yes, the smart row of northern terraces was as it always was. His home was still plumb in the middle of the row, just as he had left it that morning. Dad's car was there, in the frequently disputed parking space. The Jones' house was still there. Mr Wilson was pottering in his garden as usual for that time of day, still wrapped up like an Eskimo just as he had been all week. So much was as it should be and where it should be, but something wasn't right. His mind began to race, his senses began to fail him at the very moment he needed them most. Synaptic clefts synchronised in a flurry of neural activity but producing nothing of substance from which he could make immediate sense of his surroundings. 'What was it? What the hell was it?' he repeatedly asked, talking to himself. He paused briefly to take it all in. Eyes shooting first to the top of the street, then to the mid ground, and then back to the top. It simply wasn't right. 'What in God's name is going on?' he thought, the words his mother had so often used in anger from the bottom of the stairs, ringing through his head. 'Yes! Yes! It is the cars. Yes, the cars. Why so many?'

He had never seen so many cars in the street. Sure, one or two of the neighbours had them. Mum and Dad had an ageing Cortina that could barely move from the kerb when they were all crammed inside, but never had the street outside his door been blighted by so many cars. He even recalled the times his father had argued over the space directly in front of the house, only for his mother to point out to him and the neighbour the silliness of arguing, when the street was mostly empty of cars for almost twenty-four hours a day, and that they were arguing over a very small piece of that street. Oh, the importance of parking directly outside your own front door had not eluded him. 'So, why so many cars today?' he wondered. His dad would not be happy. He meandered slowly towards home. Too much was out of place for him to be happy, but nothing had yet presented itself for him to be anything but. And then it began. The doors of hell swung open, and out came the four horsemen of the Apocalypse. Conquest, War, Famine and Death were about to ride roughshod through his entire life, and little did Snowball realise, as the four powerful steads raced towards him, things would never quite be the same again.

INNOCENT KIDS

Simultaneously, Snowball heard the first scream and saw the front door suddenly burst open. He knew that scream all too well. He had heard it so often, and knew immediately that it was Sarah, one of his foster sisters. Sarah was a perpetual screamer. She screamed when she talked, she screamed when she was unhappy, and she also screamed when she was happy. She would even scream when she was indifferent, or when others were indifferent to her. She screamed when she was in trouble, and often she would scream simply at the prospect of being in trouble. Sarah was a girl with one volume on her dial, and it was loud, very loud. She was tolerated because she was family, and loved and cherished for the same reason. But this time it was different. Her wail was frantic and distraught. Something had clearly happened, and for once in all the years that he had known Sarah, she could be excused her histrionics. These were screams of fear, and Sarah clearly believed that she was in danger.

Snowball noticed that she was being held tightly, physically restrained by a grotesque, brusque looking woman, who seemed to care little for her tears and protestations, as she dragged her unwillingly towards the cars parked almost directly outside the front gate. Snowball's heart pounded, missed a few beats, and then pounded some more. What was happening? He could feel an uncontrollable shiver in his legs, which flirted with the idea of collapsing beneath him. It was a reaction to fear, a fear he had only ever experienced on his frequent visits to hospital, where the benefits of the treatment he was receiving were always nullified by the roughshod manner they seemed to manhandle him in the process. Why was his sister so distraught? Who the hell was that dumpy, rotund monstrosity with the double-rimmed glasses and Hitler Youth look about her, who had so inelegantly waddled from his garden, bereft of grace and poise?

Why had she bundled Sarah into the back of the car? Oi, YOU FUCKER, who the hell are you?

Snowball froze as the second set of wailing began, Sarah sitting petrified in the back seat of a blue Austin Maxi in which she was now entombed. His eyes flashed first to Sarah, then back to the front door, where Monica was now present, crying uncontrollably as she was brutally ripped from her mother's arms. The proverbial shit was hitting the fan, and the girls were stood on the wrong side of the extraction. His eyes briefly met Monica's as her hand and her last vestiges of hope parted company with her mothers, flopping limply to her side in a sign of reluctant resignation at the fate which had beset her. She probably did not see him, such was her distress, and she became a rapidly blurring memory as his own eyes began to fill slowly from the bottom upwards, the drama unfolding in front of him. Of all the girls, it was Monica to whom he was most attached. She was the one who always had time to play, the one who always smiled when he walked into the room. She shared her toys, and happily played with his, and more importantly, she shared her sweets. They were brother and sister in almost every sense, regardless of the absence of a biological link. 'What the hell were they doing with Monica?' he wondered, fear ripping into his stomach, and he wobbled awkwardly on his now feeble legs.

Through his rapidly welling eyes, he could now see his mother racing frantically toward him. Fear and anguish were etched on her face, and tears streamed from her eyes. His Aunt Margaret was by her side, and as he stared at them both, he realised that something dreadful had happened, and that they were not in any way in control of it. His mother was torn between reaching him first and standing her ground, as the remainder of her children were callously ripped from the once happy family home and bundled into waiting cars. She scooped him into her arms and turned, just in time, to see two small bags of clothing placed in each car, and the boots slammed shut.

"We will be in touch once they are settled," exhaled the brusque overweight woman in a grey coat. She seemed to have taken on an aura of authority, almost relishing the power and control as, upon those words, the car engines started in unison and slowly began to pull away from the kerbside. He stood in the street with his mother crying, as Sarah and Monica were driven away, never to be seen again. Margaret broke down and slumped to the floor. Snowball wanted to go to her, but his mother held him too tightly, knowing he was next to be ripped from her grasp and driven away to an uncertain and unknown future.

His mother, tearful and resigned to the loss of the two girls, carried Snowball inside, closely followed by Margaret and her great friend, Christine. He could see there was a house full of strangers, alongside the formidable presence of PC Robert Allen, whom he was familiar with from his frequent visits to the school. He came in to talk to the young children about what is right and wrong, and to regale them with his tales of good conquering villainy, and of the perpetual war against the rising tide of nefarious activity on the Fylde Coast. Nobody believed his stories, and they were not intended to be believed, but they did get his point across and they entertained in the process of doing so. Though massive of frame and brutal in looks, PC Allen was a kindly, gentle man. All the children liked him, and he liked them. He was a respected and highly visible member of the community, and every child in the nearby streets had been taught that he was the man to go to if ever they needed help. But today was different. Today there was no smile, no welcome, no gentle pat on the head as he acknowledged Snowball's presence. Today was business, bad business, and he was clearly in a state of unease, alongside his good friends and neighbours, as the drama unfolded and futures were being slowly shattered, one life at a time.

They were all tightly crammed into the small living room that was normally reserved for special occasions and was adults only. It was a kind of sanctuary for Dad most of the time, an early evening escape from the hardships of good, honest daily toil, and the constant daily demands of an ever-burgeoning family at home. It was somewhere people could be entertained, without the need to step over children, their toys, and any other paraphernalia that came with them.

"Go upstairs and sit with your brothers," his mother pleaded. "Go on, I will be up in a minute." She tried to place him on the bottom rung of the stairs, but Snowball was too frightened to let go. Fear gripped him, and so she beckoned his elder brother downstairs, and ushered them together. "I will be up in a minute," she asserted as Tony took Snowball to the first floor bedroom the boys shared.

Harry was sat on the bed when they entered. Tears streamed down his cheeks, and he had a look of guilt running deep into every facial crevice. What had he done? What could possibly have warranted all this havoc and upset? They had all witnessed that look on his face before, and it only ever meant one thing. Harry had been indulging in mischief, and it was only a matter of time before, burdened with guilt and under the threat of chastisement, he would duly confess. Snowball set off crying again, and Tony whisked him up quickly and sat him on his knee. It felt like his entire world was collapsing around him, and unbeknownst to him, it was. They could hear a heated debate ensuing downstairs. His foster mother was crying loudly, wailing almost. He could hear his father vehemently protesting some theme of innocence on Harry's behalf, and a mixture of strange voices punctuating the occasional silence as they discussed what his mother would always describe as 'adult business'.

Margaret was the calming influence. She could be heard imploring everyone to settle down, and to think of the children upstairs, and what they might be going through. His much-loved Aunty Christine could also be heard demanding consideration for the children in the house, and he even heard her mention his name, as requiring consideration, due to his age and sensitivities. She had always been the calming influence, in many ways the rock upon which they all depended, and she had saved Snowball from more than one spanking after his wayward behaviour had exceeded his mother's patience. He would spend a few hours or a sleepover under her protective wing while his mother's frayed nerves and frustrations calmed.

The winter light was fading when the bedroom door finally swung open, and he was confronted by his tearful mother, eyes reddened, face drawn, and defeat written all over her. She had spent a lot of time crying that day. Snowball had seen nothing like it from her in the past and was distraught at the sight of her tears and anxiety. She looked like she had shrunk at least a foot from the turmoil, and it appeared that her hair had greyed in the few short hours that separated his current predicament from his departure from school. She was broken, in distress, and clearly struggling.

She brought them all together, sat Snowball on her lap, then wept as she declared, "You all have to go away for a short while, but don't worry, I am going to come and get you as soon as I can." In unison, the three boys broke out into tears, and she held them all tightly, while the floodgates opened. "I can't explain right now, but one day, it will all be alright again," she asserted. They were words that she no doubt believed in her own mind, but they fell upon deaf ears in the main. With that, she led all three of them down the stairs, Snowball in her arms, Tony slowly creeping behind her, and Harry held tightly with her free hand. It was both a memorable and fateful day. Heart-breaking for all concerned. The day had started like so many before it. Full of laughter. Full of the noise of happy children and frustrated parents ringing from every room as they prepared themselves for the day's events that would see them separate in the early hours, re-converging in the latter part of the day, as a family, to share the stories the day had brought. To laugh as a family, eat as a family, play as a family and be merry. This day would end so differently from those gone by. Today, the house would fall silent. There would be no laughter, only tears. There would be an overhanging deathly silence, a darkness that could not be penetrated, and a cessation of mirth. The small, plastic paddling pool in the rear yard would remain empty that night. There would be no fighting over who rode the wooden horse in the living room, and for how long. The wooden dolls' house, so painstakingly constructed with handcrafted furniture, would go without admiration as day turned to night. Everything would change, and it would change forever.

There were three more social workers in the lounge. Three more bags of clothes. Three more cars waiting outside, one for each child placed inside. And so it passed, the cars pulled away, and they were gone, forever. His foster mother never did come back for Snowball. He would come to wait up, night after night, expecting her imminent arrival, but she never came. Too many mornings he would awake slumped across the window sill, hidden by the long, hanging curtains and chilled to the bone, ever expectant, ever disappointed. He never understood why. Life had just turned sour, and there was nothing he could do to stop it.

Sat smack in the middle of the green Avenger, Snowball calmed down enough to think. What was happening? What was this all about? Where were they taking him? Was this one of those frequently explained occasions Harry had talked about, where it was okay to use an expletive as long as their mother was not around? Surely this qualified? Snowball briefly reminisced about how Harry could be so grown up at times. The solitary female figure in the front seat said nothing. Her eyes focussed on the road in front as the early evening winter light dropped, and the realisation dawned upon her contorted, screwed up face and squinting eyes, that in the dark lanes of the Fylde Coast, her headlights were wholly inadequate for the time of year. But that, in all honesty, was the least of her problems. The manifest problem that was truly hers was the plotting little banshee in the back of her car, who had developed a 'compromise' strategy all his own that he hoped would see him returned to his mother, literally that night.

Snowball took a sudden lunge forward and grabbed a handful of her neatly groomed auburn hair in his left hand. By the time a scream of surprise had left her mouth, he had, through previously unknown stealth, also grabbed a handful of hair in his right hand and proceeded to pull it with everything he could muster. The car screamed to a sudden halt in the darkened lane and he was violently catapulted forward into the front, spinning almost 180 degrees in her lap, leg trapped between the handbrake and the floor as he steadfastly refused to relinquish his grip, screaming like the possessed child he had now become. It was game on, and unbeknownst to Snowball, he was about to lose without the need for extra time or a penalty shootout. He could hear the words Tony had spoken to him and Harry on numerous occasions echo in his mind: "You might not win the fight, but always let them know you were in it." Always let them know you were in it. These were indeed words of wisdom, and the height of reasonable expectation to a young and extremely impressionable Snowball, even if he did not really understand what it meant exactly. After all, it is not like there could be a downside!

He had never been called a 'little bastard' before, but face down and feeling the full might of her right hand land hard across his upturned backside three or four times, he figured that was not a compliment. Reassessing his strategy, he promptly let go of her hair, in an act of overt contrition. He was not sure if she knew she had been in a fight, but capitulation seemed at worst like a score draw at the time, and there was no harm done. However, with the realisation that defeat was potentially imminent rather than in the balance, he instigated Plan B, which largely involved crying loudly, professing remorse and hugging her tightly. It had always worked with his mother, and there was no reason why it could not work here, if only she could forget the handful of her hair he had ripped from her scalp and was now wiping from his hands behind her back. He hoped she would, as he had never been afforded the need for a Plan C, such was the manner and ease in which he could often bring his mother round to his way of thinking. He knew that if she did not, he was fucked. And fucked he was.

It would be decades before Snowball came to understand what had happened that day, the day that shook and shifted his happy, joyous life forever. The day that had brutally, without compassion or remorse, ripped him and his brothers and sisters apart. It had all started, as usual, with Harry. He was a lovable child according to his mother, but he had a propensity for stupidity, a special kind of stupidity. Harry was one of those children that never learned from his mistakes. He had been caught stealing from Mr Garner's shop, was punished by their father, then caught again sometime later. He was regularly punished at school for his misdemeanours, only to be found complicit in recurrent acts and infringements, and punished again. Whatever the underlying reason, people simply could not get through to Harry, and it had brought with it concern for the other children in his mother's care.

The final straw came one winter's night, when Harry had chosen to ignore the age old and well-intentioned advice that all children receive and played with the matches. With his brother, he had erected one of the family's tents in the boy's bedroom, and duly set about lighting candles to illuminate the interior. As evening turned to night and the children retired to their beds, the candles were forgotten and so ensued the bedroom fire that endangered them all. It was the final act in Harry's play of defiance, an act that was the death knell for the idyllic life they had all come to enjoy and thrive in. The house was evacuated, the fire dealt with, and a few days later they all returned and resumed as normal. Harry was punished, but that was not enough in some quarters and plans had been set in motion that would see the children 'rescued' from the clear and present danger they were in and scattered, far and wide, across the country.

A once happy home with a doting mother and father, loving siblings, and an abundance of family and friends on hand, was ripped apart at the seams. Hung, drawn and quartered at the altar of 'child protectionists', with a greater irony yet to unfold, as the passage of time would declare they would all have been safer left where they were.

Whether Harry ever came to understand the real impact of his actions, devastating an entire family and tearing it limb from limb, destroying it and the lives it contained beyond all recognition, all for the sake of a few juvenile rebellions, would never be known. This once happy household that thronged to the sound of infants playing, laughter, fun, love, care and attention was gone forever, at the behest of his adolescent impulses for infraction. Gone were the monthly birthdays that were celebrated as if they were the only thing happening in the world that day. Never again would the dining room table be filled with an abundance of chocolate eggs at Easter. The sweet jar on the table would remain half full and untouched. The excitement of Christmas Day, paling to a quiet, unremarkable awakening in an almost silent house, bereft of the childish, seasonal joys that it once struggled to contain.

It was the final ringing of the bell during a mixture of Sunday night fun and chaos that saw everyone in the household bathed and their hair washed, clean and ready for school the following week. The daily fight over positions in the car were over. Never again would Tony lick his fingers before sticking them in the cake Mother had so lovingly baked to indicate the slice he was now claiming as his own. Snowball would never again fight with Sarah over the remaining Fruit Salads in the jar, nor Tony with Harry over the diminishing number of liquorice sticks. Never again would they all attack their father in front of the coal fire on the living room floor, nor, after running their mother ragged with mischief, would the boys have to queue, solemn faced and hands on head, awaiting the spanking that she decided they all needed. Family life was now a shattered set of memories, thrown into the winds of winter, and blown to all corners of the country. Love, care and attention had been replaced by tyranny, abuse and mistreatment. An array of young lives had been transformed into a living nightmare. Beaten, abused, starved and neglected. Brutally punished for the sins of others. They would never be the same again.

And so, it came to pass that Snowball's life at the Fylde Coast was done and dusted. Love, care and attention, happiness, growth, safety and security, his school, his friends, Mr Garner and Mrs Swarecki, Aunty Christine, Grandad and Nana, his siblings, the church, the playgrounds and the parks. All were consigned to the refuse tip of life and lost to Snowball forever. How could things ever be the same? The girls were gone, his brothers were gone, his parents and extended family, all gone. The pain and suffering of that final day would be etched into the memories of many, far beyond those who were immediately impaled with the torment. The tears of a mother drowned only by those of her children, as each and every one of them were torn mercilessly from her care, crammed into the rear seats of separate cars and driven away to a destiny that for her would remain unknown, untried, untested.

There would be many a night spent gazing blankly into the sky, as Snowball pondered what life had become. Life for him, his siblings, his beloved mother and his father. Where were they? What were they doing? Did they know where he was, and where he was going? Were they even thinking about him at all? What had he done to deserve this living hell, this perversion of everything good that his mother had done for him? There would be days of internalised grief and misappropriated guilt that would seamlessly turn into weeks, then months and finally years. Troublesome times until the memories of those happy, carefree, safe, and secure days began to fade, so that they could never be recovered, never be relived, never be treasured as they once had been. Life had begun with an abusive start, and the abuse would sustain. As the years would pass, the hatred would grow and fester. The memories of what was torn from him fuelling a hate he would struggle to quell.

And so this was the backdrop to when life truly turned sour, his world fractured and ripped apart at the seams. Everything and everyone he had known and loved had been torn brutally from his tenuous grasp. Life had once been so full of brightness. There were no shadows, no darkness. He had been lavished in love, in care and in attention. The warmth and kindness of his foster mother ensuring that he had never grown to understand the meaning of need, nor hunger. He had never been cold in his own home, never lacked the warmth of a cuddle, or the wrap of a blanket, nor been deprived of attention when he needed it most. He had been well-dressed and well tended. Life, as he could recall it, had been idyllic. He had an abundance of family around him, and extended family of unfathomable size; he had friends, siblings, and everything he could ever want and need. Fruit Salads, Black Jacks and grapes, the things that memories are made of.

FUCK ME THAT WAS A ROUGH START, SNOWBALL (THE BEGINNING IN 1965)

Well, that escalated quickly. These were the only words Snowball would have uttered if he had been in the mood, and capable. He, however, lay there, still, quiet, cold, and hungry. The greasy, grime covered linoleum floor had been his home for the preceding weeks. He had rolled and turned in his own urine and faeces, his brittle, spindly legs and taut skin carrying the sores of his prolonged contact with the dirty floor. The old newspapers, which had been strewn around him, were passed off as some pathetic excuse for a comfortable bed. He was weak, exhausted and close to death. His heart could be seen pounding through the visibly taut skin around his rib cage. Weak and irregular, it was the only visible sign that this tiny body was still living. Skin pulled tight over brittle bones, legs abnormally bent in a foetal curl, arms outwardly flayed and head held precariously on a short, stubby, pencil-thin neck. There he lay, waiting for the almost inevitable liberation that death would bring from his pain and suffering.

The roar of running water could be heard in the background as steam bellowed upwards towards the ceiling, clinging first to the bare-walled interior of the bathroom, before circling like a rolling thunder cloud across the tiled ceiling, and back down to the floor. The embrace of the tepid moisture providing the only sense of comfort he had felt in a long time, though the horrors belied it, were to feature heavily in his immediate future. The constant thunder of the water and the ever-increasing envelope of grey steam was punctuated occasionally by the solitary voice coming from the nearby bedroom. It was the voice of his mother. She had spent the night alongside his father in the relative comforts of the only maintained room in the maisonette. It was by all known accounts their getaway, a place of solitude and privacy, their sanctuary. He had a heightened sense of fear as he heard heavy footsteps approaching, before the bathroom door closed, muffling the sound of his cries as, once again, she liberated herself from all sense of parental responsibility and any innate sense of humanity. There he lay, hollowed, haunted, darkened eyes staring up at the solitary bare bulb, which swung gently in the slight breeze that permeated the room through the poorly-fitted window frame to his right-hand side. His naked body contorted in pain, his feeble cries no longer heard, and completely uncared for. The blessing of a quick death eluded him with every minute that passed.

The bathroom door suddenly swung open and a blurred figure filled the space, upright but somehow disfigured with contortion. Just the shadow of an outline passed his eyes. Bulbous bodied, short in stature, naked with hair pulled back in a tight, wiry bob; this murky, obtuse figure was his mother, and she came and went without so much as a touch or a glance. Still the water cascaded down into the bathtub. The steam rose and encased his frame in its warm, damp residue. He remained where he was, unattended, crying, unable to move. At twelve months old, this was his plight. What had he done in a previous life to deserve all this? Through the heavy steam, and out on the landing, he sensed movement. There was no rhyme, logic or reason to his thoughts, he could just sense it. There was clearly more than one person out there, and the sudden and raised voices confirmed this eerie perception. The argument was fierce and went back and forth several times as the quest for dominance swung first to his mother, then to his father. Back and forth it went for several minutes as he lay there on the bare floor, his anxiety heightened, and his pulse racing.

His complete lack of verbal comprehension was vastly compensated by his intense understanding of intonation. It was a household where voices were often violently raised and then lowered, only to erupt in anger again, before fading into silence once more as apparent calm took hold of the house. They were the interactions he had come to know so well. Inevitably, they resulted in some form of physical attack, either upon his mother, or indeed upon himself, which seemed to be the only satiating requirement for the issue to be deemed dead. However, quite suddenly, there was a flurry of activity from the landing to the bedroom and back again before a finale of aggressive shouting, wall-banging, and the slamming of the fragile timber of the front door, followed by a shattering of glass. He could hear his mother's tears. Tears of frustration. Was it the loss of the argument, loss of her man, the thought of paying for the shattered front door, or the daily drudge of life itself that caused her tears? Only she really knew. Nobody else cared, perhaps because care was the last thing she deserved.

His mother was now alone, except for the child lying naked and close to death on her bathroom floor. It was a rather surreal sight. A woman in tears over the life she had, and an infant in tears over the life that was being taken. If only they could come together, maybe the whole thing would have turned out alright. The child she had not fed, washed, clothed or tended to for days, the child that was too weak to cry and too stubborn to die, lay at her feet with all expectation of maternal protection torn from his body and mind.

Once again, he could hear her footsteps, but could see nothing in the thickening steam that consumed the room. He winced as her foot caught a glancing blow against his, before the gush of the running water suddenly ceased, throwing the bathroom into complete silence. Her invisible presence looming large to his senses, he knew all too well she was there, right there, and yet still she remained invisible. The silence was as lingering as it was intimidating. An ominous silence had descended that would characteristically precede the pain and torment that she frequently rained down upon his fragile body. Devoid of all maternal instinct, she had not fared well as a mother, and today her failings were epic in fashion. She had lost her husband, lost her livelihood in many respects, had most certainly lost her front door, and had lost her self-respect and dignity many moons before. Yet still, eyes and ears wide open, he could see and hear nothing at all. His alcohol soaked, and drug-addled mother was nowhere to be seen, nor heard. She seemed to have just vanished, and his racing heart slowed into a steady rhythmic pound, painfully pushing against his taut skin and ribs, and threatening to explode violently from his fragile body. Potentially, the grand finale to his life, or signalling to the world that life was not yet extinct, and with life, as the saying goes, the last thing to die, is hope.

Then suddenly from nowhere she loomed. Face contorted and dripping in a steamy sweat and flushed with anger. There was pain in her eyes, ill-intent and malice in her heart. She had a mission, and he was clearly part of it. Her hands loomed above his tiny frame, painfully sweeping him up in her grasp, and holding him firmly aloft in front of her face. He could see her mouth move, though he had no understanding of the words she spoke. It was all reminiscent of those early silent movies, where the context provided all the clues for the words, that you simply could not hear. All he knew was that the pain of her grip was becoming unbearable, and he let out another feeble whimper in protest at that pain, repeatedly flashing through his tiny body as she shook him violently, before dropping him to the floor like the limp and lifeless rag-doll he had become. She had entered her end game. His head bounced from the lino. The pain rushed through his fragile frame, and he passed into semi-consciousness. He felt her foot come crashing down on first his right leg, then his left. He regurgitated a scream. A hollow scream. A worthless scream. His reward was short and swift. A solitary kick to his swollen, air-filled stomach before the agony of her grasp once again wracked him with pain. Oi, You Fucker!

So, there he was. Held aloft above a steaming bath of boiling water, as once again he stared his callous mother in the face. God, she was ugly. The angry, pain riddled contortions of her face were matched only by the fevered, alcohol-fuelled, incomprehensible bile she spewed from her mouth in such hate-filled anger. And then it began, the Oi You Fucker moment that would have to be lived with from that day onwards, and into ever-lasting eternity. She lowered him feet first into the scalding water, before pulling him out as the searing pain shot through his feet, legs and tiny body. The shock being too much to handle, he could only offer a barely perceivable, wincing gasp before he passed into unconsciousness, she once again lowering him into the boiling abyss. Raised and lowered, raised and lowered, the unbearable pain searing the skin, flesh and nails from his tiny feet, legs and buttocks. His limp, lifeless, unconscious body then tossed to the floor of the adjacent airing cupboards, she ran from the scene of horror that she had instigated, both callously and coldly. If he was lucky, death would consume him quickly. If she was lucky, death would consume her slowly. And that was where she left him to be found. Near to death, starved beyond all reasonable expectation of survival, hanging onto life by a tenuous thread of stubbornness that defied all logic and reason. Oh, the fuckery of it all.

NO INVITE REQUIRED

It was here that Snowball came to lay. Prone, exhausted, weak, malnourished and close to death on a cold, rickety, old ambulance trolley. How his life expectancy must have seemed so much brighter, that cold February night back in 1964, when he had entered into a vicious, cruel world not of his making and cared little for his comfort or safety. His mother was a mixes-race woman of UK and Caribbean descent. She was born into an era when the very concept of a mixed marriage was as unthinkable to many of the 'enlightened' indigenous population as eating fish on a Thursday instead of a Friday. They were cool with Nazi-era concentration camps, the KKK, white serial killers burying kids on the moors, and the possibility of a nuclear holocaust if the Kennedy Clan did not get it right – that was just life. But the idea of a black man marrying a white woman was a step too far in the tombola of Christianity. So the fact that she had been born in wedlock to a black father and white mother pretty much made her and her mother about as welcome in the south of England as a leprosy infection in an African village recovering from a Cholera outbreak.

To her only credit, his grandmother Dorothy had, against all advice and prevailing common sense, rejected all the protestations, character slurs, prospect of being ostracised, and physical intimidation in the South, and moved lock, stock and barrel, to a reasonably affluent area of North Manchester to give birth to her. She had struggled against a tide of prejudice, loneliness, unemployment and uncertainty. A small savings account kept the family going, but times were indeed hard, and as they inevitably got harder, she found herself slowly pulled into the murky underbelly of criminal life in Manchester, and the unwelcome attentions of the police soon followed. For Snowball's grandmother, it turned out to be a prosperous, albeit dangerous transition from the right side of the tracks and brought with it a level of protection to the family that unfortunately never found its way as far down the tree as Snowball would have liked.

His mother was an unremarkable woman in herself. Typical of the day. Bumptious, confident beyond any demonstrable ability, poorly educated, but with a gift of the gab, and always willing to work hard for a crust, if only people were willing to give her the opportunity to demonstrate her work ethic. She had drifted somewhat casually between destructive relationships, where violence and intimidation had ruled her world, before landing herself with two older children in the preceding four years, then conceiving Snowball. It was the same with work. Numerous jobs interspersed with bouts of unemployment that she mitigated by running 'errands' for local criminals and drug dealers, as a means of keeping food on the table, booze in the fridge and drugs running through her veins. Life had given her chances, and she had spurned them all. So, this was how she survived.

Snowball was unplanned, unwanted and unwelcome, but the prospect of an abortion compounding the already unimaginable burden of family shame meant she had been forced by her mother to carry him full term, whether willing and welcome or not. Little was known about his father, other than that he was of Nigerian heritage. By all accounts, he was a man with a long arm, and a Casio sunburn, and could turn himself pretty much to anything as long as it involved payment and little work and was devolved of parental responsibility of any kind. He had always been extremely standoffish from the family, and had little, if any, input into daily life, with Snowball's unwelcome appearance into his world being the catalyst for one final act of paternal cowardice, as he callously disappeared into the night and was never seen again, unless he needed money, food, sex, or all three. Snowball's older siblings had seen little of their father since birth, and the reality was that his mother neither expected nor wanted him around. Their father was a shadow that crept along the landing at night, and occasionally made physical contact by punching the older brother or taking a strap to his sister. As a consequence, life seemed oh so complicated, and his mother found the struggle was significantly easier, though no less troublesome, if she was alone and without him, as she fought for some semblance of a normality in the dark days that seemed to conspire against her.

Snowball could momentarily feel the breeze of the cold, outside evening air sweep across his face. It was a pleasant interjection from the warm but intimidating environment from which he had hailed the night previous. His big brown eyes, now seemingly dimmed by the horrors he had endured, momentarily opened as the clatter and vibration of the hospital trolley being hastily lowered to the ground shook him back into his wretched life one more time. Hope had not died, after all, the night before. It had merely taken a siesta. The trolley, attended by a growing number of people, rumbled uncomfortably across the short expanse of uncovered concrete walkway, before a shallow bump and a bang saw it ushered into the long, well-lit, vinyl floored sloping corridor that led directly to the Accident and Emergency Wards of the Royal Infirmary.

He could hear the panic-stricken voices that surrounded him with a consuming and welcome level of attention he had never experienced before. He could see their faded outlines, blurred faces, arms stretching forwards toward him, and then back into the blurred light that surrounded his body. A ragged, soiled cloth was cut from his tiny frame, as the fluorescent lights above flickered periodically with a hypnotic charm that lulled him into a state of further relaxation, while the trolley continued on its hasty journey into the bowels of the hospital. The trolley rumbled onwards, closer and closer to the help he so desperately needed. The help that would save his life and become the catalyst to a mysterious journey that inevitably would take a lifetime to complete.

There was a searing pain in his lower body, an unbearable pain, which worsened as the protective blanket they had wrapped him in was unceremoniously pulled from around his body. Such was the force, it almost catapulted his weakened body to the floor, but they hastily tipped him back, and set to work. There were more panicked voices, more rumbling wheels, more flashing lights above his head. The sensory rush became too much as the hive of activity continued unabated around him. He closed his eyes one more time and decided to simply let it be. Yet still he felt the rumble of the trolley beneath him. He could hear the wheels rattle and slide, as the aluminium frame shook and wobbled. Every bump, ridge and undulation in the floor sent a vibration through his tiny, pain-wracked frame, which became more and more unbearable as his journey continued to its climax. Oh, how the release of death would be so much more preferable in the short term. Momentarily, he would notice the change in ambient temperature, as one corridor was exited, and another entered. More people joined the frenzied fray. Nurses, doctors, consultants and all. The National Health Service in full flow, and about to do what it did best: save people. It appeared that everyone was most welcome to gate-crash this party. No invite was required.

Another boom sounded the medical call to arms, as the heavy rubber doors first sprung open then flapped violently against each other upon closing. Awoken again, he could hear the frantic voices, feel the excruciating pain, and count the lights. Yes, he could now count the lights. He had arrived in theatre, and he was the only show in town. He was still, or at least the trolley was. He was rolled, pulled, pushed back and rolled forward the opposite way. It was a melee of activity, that while frantic, retained the appearance of a coordinated and controlled response to what was clearly a life-threatening situation unfolding. The pulling and pushing was a constant and painful reminder of the predicament he was in. He was on his front and then his back. On his left side and then his right. It was a whirl of activity, none of which he had the slightest bit of control over. The trolley had stopped, but the panic and the unfolding drama clearly had not.

By now, Snowball lacked the physical energy to cry. He could feel the desperate need, and it was all he wanted to do, all he knew how to do, and all that he understood, but he could not. The anguish would not subside, but the tears just would not flow. He was a withered, taut, emaciated and a near death semblance of the healthy infant he should have been. Nothing really worked bodily, bar the fact that, somehow, he was still breathing, still working internally, even if everything on the outside was near total, gangrenous collapse. He could hear the words around him but understood nothing of what was said. All he knew was that his tiny heart was still thumping hard against his ribs, and as long as it continued to do so, the fuckery of recent months would soon pale away into a depressing history, that he would one day be grateful he could recant.

"Jesus Christ, what's gone on here?"

"He's never going to make it."

"Poor thing."

"Who in their right mind could...?"

"He looks like something from Belsen."

"It's a ninety-eight percent chance he won't get through the night, folks, but let's do something." Ninety-eight percent. Things were on the up at last. There was a sudden rush of something warm, something calming, something welcomed, as his eyes slowly began to peacefully close. For the first time in his short and tormented life, Snowball felt no pain, no fear, no cold. He just closed his eyes and drifted into a deep anaesthetised coma, feeling the welcoming mummification of absolutely nothing.

For more than eight hours they treated him. They pumped blood into his veins, drugs into his tiny body. They washed his emaciated frame, coated him in antiseptic creams, and bandaged the horrific burns he had suffered. They grafted skin from one body part to another, removed his remaining toenails and amputated a toe before finally immobilising his mummified body in a mobile cot, and delivering him to Intensive Care.

There was no way for Snowball to understand how long he had slept, but the evenly spaced ticks from the black and white wall-mounted clock marked his waking arrival into the bacterial sterility of the Intensive Care Ward, when he finally came to. The frantic rumble of metal wheels on concrete that had signified his chaotic admittance to hospital was replaced with a dull, quiet rumble of rubber against linoleum, punctuated infrequently by the sudden rise and fall of the trolley mounting the raised rubber lip that separated one room from another, and rooms from corridors alike. The austere, germ-free, clinical haven would now become his home. His final home in the eyes of many. The eyes of the knowing, the clinically experienced, the medically educated and qualified. A short, miserable and tormented life. A pain-riddled life brought to a premature end, at the hands of the woman who, in the not too distant months past, had unwillingly brought his very life into the world.

The instructions were simply to watch and wait. If there was any mercy remaining in the world, his pulse would begin to fade, blood pressure and vital signs would begin to drop, internal organs would find the struggle overbearing, and he would die quickly, in a sedated, intravenous fed, pain-free slide into the afterlife. And so, they pulled up their chairs, made themselves comfortable, grabbed a cup of tea, and simply waited. And they waited. They changed shifts, and they waited some more. Guess they didn't know Snowball well at all. In this hallowed place of his, pain is sacred, pain is bliss. Endless torment, painful toil, pain of death, he strives to foil.

Many hours earlier, Snowball had been found after the police had raided the squalid maisonette in the heart of Manchester, where his mother had recently housed family, 'friends' and an assortment of nefarious ill-doers, societal misfits and drop-outs, who had been seen coming and going, and who had been anything but shy in letting nearby neighbours know of their arrival and departure. It had become a constant and ongoing theme of life in the block, and the police had been called out on many an occasion to find the house full of alcohol and steeped in drugged, limp adults, amongst an array of neglected children, who had often been bundled into a single upstairs room, while the adults below, had engaged in their nefarious frivolities. Times had become significantly harder than during their earlier arrival in the sprawling metropolis that was Manchester, and his mother's lack of maternal instincts had only deteriorated as a direct consequence. His grandmother had been forced to sell the detached family house in the leafy northern suburbs, partly through the need for hard liquidated cash to survive, and partly to feed the burgeoning addiction to alcohol and drugs that her daughter was cultivating.

A neighbour had tipped the police off about the baby boy, that sometime appeared to be the occasional, albeit feigned, focal point of family pride and attention, but who had not now been seen for a significant amount of time, despite claims from the household that he was okay and doing just fine. There had been a persistent period of neighbourly concern, and some extensive doorstep chatter, as the boy always seemed to be crying in what she had described knowingly, given that she was from a large Scottish family and raised four children of her own, as the "cry of a hungry bairn".

The police had entered the filthy maisonette to find his mother and an unconscious friend present in a downstairs room, both in a state of heavy drug and alcohol intoxication. The home was in a state of gross disrepair, and had a putrid, nasal closing stench about it, which had forced both constables, in unison, to raise their hands across their noses, before knowingly nodding at each other in open acknowledgment that something was clearly wrong. Wallpaper had been randomly torn in strips from various parts of the walls as if a maniacal child had been at play, or redecoration was imminent. The walls beneath were stained with dirt, as were the off-white skirting boards and magnolia rinsed ceiling, with the swirling mosaic of smoke staining clearly visible. The light-shade was ripped, and a smashed bulb lay directly below where it had fallen, left to be trampled into the off-coloured rug, where it had eventually turned to a fine powder. The windows were covered, both inside and out, with a thin veneer of grime and smeared fingerprints, and discarded food lay on the urine-stained floor, alongside cracked dirty plates, fish and chip wrappings, beer cans and empty spirit bottles. It was a sight to behold, and one no human could have been proud of, let alone a mother housing three children. The carpet was stained with faeces from the three cats that they had both subconsciously counted as they had entered, and there was a strong smell of cannabis, with the incumbent paraphernalia in plain sight on a three-legged coffee table adorned with a cheap, fading, white patterned tapestry cloth, designed ironically to either keep it clean, or hide the cracked mosaic tiles beneath it. Every room was the same.

There appeared to be nobody else present, and they were about to leave had it not been for the timely intervention of feminine intuition. The attendant young WPC had become duly concerned about what she was witnessing before her. Not so much about the state of the home, but the fact that there was a profusion of dirty nappies littering most areas of the house, and yet no sign of a baby. She joked briefly with her colleague about how it would take a woman to make such an observation, putting two and two together, and so before she left, she decided upon one last final look around. This was the point that Lady Luck made her first visit to Snowball's life, and he would hopefully get to thank her shortly afterwards.

Nothing was found on the ground floor of the maisonette, but the upper floor housed the three small bedrooms, and a bathroom. To the right of the bathroom was a small airing cupboard, a common enough feature in a common enough tenement block of the times, that typically housed a boiler and plenty of room to store clothes as they dried or awaited a timely intervention with an iron.

As the WPC passed inquisitively from bedroom to bedroom, before placing a tense foot on the first riser of the stairs, Snowball executed an almost perfect 'OI YOU FUCKER' moment, and delivered the most timely and fortuitous cry, a mixture of both pain and hunger, you could possibly imagine. By no means the best of cries, but it would do under the circumstances, and it would serve him well. The carpet under the airing cupboard door was tightly fitted, insulating all outside from most of the noise within, and vice-versa. But there was enough of a noise escaping for the emaciated mess that lay within to attract the right sort of attention, and that was all that was required. One small opening, and night had suddenly turned to day. And so, Snowball came to be, from urine and faeces covered cupboard floors, to the warm tender embrace of a Mancunian WPC, followed by a swift, hot-paced ride in an ambulance, and the rigours of the rickety hospital trolley and the imminent safety of a hospital ward. Life for Snowball had just begun. Goodbye Mother Dearest, and welcome to 1965, Snowball. You have a nice day now.

TREAT ME IN THE SLEEPING HOURS

Snowball spent an inescapably long time in hospital, for numerous reasons. There had been an initial period of almost a week, where the expectancy of survival had been so small that he simply remained largely untreated, bar the exception of that which needed immediate attention to be stable. Heading into week two, it became apparent that his chances were improving daily, and that maybe now was the time to reconsider the original prognosis, so survival and recovery treatment could start in earnest.

Still heavily bandaged, and largely overcome by pain-relieving drugs, Snowball was wheeled from ward to ward, consultation to consultation, operation to operation, and back around the repetitive cycle. Toes were amputated, skin peeled and grafted, bones reconstructed, and so much more. Plastic surgery followed plastic surgery, which followed operation after operation, and recuperation. The cycle seemed infinite. These were horrific days for Snowball. Days filled with mental trauma, physical pain and total discomfort. It was impossible for him to differentiate between the nefarious pains he had endured at the hands of Mother and the pains of good intent, inflicted at the hands of the caring medical professionals upon whom his very life now depended. It simply appeared that everyone was trying to hurt him. He spent weeks immobile while cast in plaster, as his grafted bones were given time to blend and heal. Then came the painful trauma of having stitches removed from feet and legs, as, one by one, they were snipped at the bridge, before being pulled out with a tweezer, the small specks of blood that betrayed their egress wiped clean and dabbed with a stinging antiseptic.

He recalled that day with horror. A nurse had arrived at his bedside that morning, bringing with her heavy duty scissors, a small cutting blade, towels, antiseptic, and bandages. It had struck an intense sense of fear into him as he knew that, yet again, another day would begin with pain and suffering as the previous one had ended, over which he had no control. He had cried uncontrollably, and despite the reassuring hand of his nurse, he was inconsolable. In the end, they had been forced to restrain him physically, as a nurse cut through the plaster casts that encased his left leg, washed down the withered limb, and then began the systematic removal of every stitch from his feet and thighs. All this was too much for his tiny frame and tortured mind, and he slipped slowly into a traumatised sleep, only to awaken sometime later, his legs lightly bandaged, and his body tightly wrapped beneath the sheets of his bed, encased like a mummy with just his head protruding from the sterile tomb that held him captive. Day after day, the pain and torment continued. Day after day, the fear of the waking hours tormented his infant mind.

Recovery was a long, slow and tortuous process. Days turned into weeks, which seamlessly turned into months. Before long, a year had passed with intermittent visits and residential stays in the hospital, and so it continued. Gradually, the malnourished waif began to fill out as legs and arms fattened, the protruding bones of his gaunt cheeks slowly disappeared, eyes once again regained their shine, hair grew, legs straightened, fingers uncurled, and the everyday pain began to subside. It was a long, hard battle that he was subtly winning. Snowball was on the mend.

Snowball would never forgive his mother for the events of that fateful night, a night that left him painfully scarred, both physically and emotionally. It was a night that would haunt him for the remainder of his life, and he hoped beyond all hope and beyond all reason, that it would be a haunting experience for the remainder of hers as well. Forgiveness would always remain the furthest thing from his mind. How could he possibly forgive the woman who was supposed to nurture him, love and educate him, turning him into a decent, caring, stable and honest man? How could he ever forgive what she had done, what she had betrayed, what she had chosen to sacrifice? He was supposed to be loved, to be cherished, but instead she tried to crush him. Survival had been by chance, not design, and he owed her nothing, bar a solitary "Thank you" for having brought him into the miserable world she had abandoned him in, and he would now strive to survive in, alone. She had set the tone for the abuse, neglect and violence that would follow, and so forgiveness, if it ever was a wish, was something that she would take to her own grave and the doors of hell.

Little did she realise that it would grow to be so much more than just the pain. There would be the years of guilt. The years of wondering: what had he done to deserve what she did to him? It would be the anguish of every single move, from one home to another, and the fresh torments and abuses that those moves would bring. It would be the agonising times he would stand by the school swimming pool, only to be ridiculed because of the burns, the amputations and the skin grafts. Every week of every school year would be the same. Every swimming session, every sports session, every time there was a need to strip down to bare feet or attend a school medical. It was always the same. There would be the questions, there would be the ridicule, there would be the burning hate and the inferno of desire to bring it all to an end, just for the sake of finally having some peace from the persistent realisation that he was different and would never be the same as everyone else.

In one night of brutally callous disregard, she had stripped him bare of so much life he would want to kill her for it. Every day would bring fresh torment. A fresh trial. A set of fresh obstacles to overcome. From the verbal abuse of his peers to the crippling effects of the ill-fitting shoes he was forced to wear in one home, down to the frequent and painful visits to chiropody services as they tried to heal the broken feet upon which he painfully stumbled from day to day. As the weeks, months and years came to pass, and he began to understand the gravity of what she had done, the hate would become all consuming. It would be a hate that would burn long and deep within him for years. Choking him physically, stifling him emotionally, arresting his development in more ways than he could imagine. It would steal every ounce of compassion that he might have developed, and channelled it into one painful, demonic belief that one day he could stand above her dying body, and simply smile. Revenge served as coldly as it could be, hate having been satiated. The years of pain expunged, and her, lying there in her dying moments, knowing that he had come for her personally and made her pay.

It was a hate so powerful that it would push him to the brink of insanity and pull him back for more. It would be a hate so strong, so dominant, so overwhelmingly powerful, that it was at times simply uncontrollable in his hands. He would want revenge, he would want her dead. He would want to burn her like she burned him. He would want every conceivable misfortune to befall her, and then he would pray, in her final moments, that there existed the chance to inflict just a little more before she slowly passed. In a world he would frequent, a world driven by relentless, inexcusable abuse and systematic violence, forgiveness was something that he would never dream of offering.

Snowball would quickly come to learn that the fight for survival was a physical one. It would be hands on, often brutal, pointless in many respects, but something that simply had to be done. Every kick and punch thrown or received was down to her. Every bloody nose endured or delivered, shin kicked, stomach punched, eye gouged, all because she could not, or refused to, cope. Every punch he ever threw would be in the face of his mother, such was the depth of hate and contempt that he grew to have for her. A hate and contempt that would only subside and disappear as news of her death eventually trickled through into his later life. The burden of carrying her and her guilt on his shoulders finally lifted for eternity and beyond, as he experienced new, emotional horizons, and finally started to become what is so commonly described as 'normal'. But once she was gone, he would feel cheated. Cheated because she had passed without his help. Cheated because she had enjoyed her life as she had wanted. Cheated because when push came to shove, she simply had not paid a high enough price for everything she had done and subjected him to.

He would often come to muse about how one solitary night of madness could have had such far-reaching consequences, beyond all imagination. How actions undertaken by others and totally out of his personal control could have had such a dramatic impact on every single waking moment that he experienced. How could it be that a mother could relinquish her own child to such an existence? How could she walk this earth and never once come looking for him? There were no birthdays, no Christmases, no family occasions or gatherings, nor special events. There would be no hugs or love. He would never fall asleep in her arms only to wake hours later, safely tucked up in a warm bed, knowing she had placed him there with one final kiss goodnight. There would be no school plays, annual parents' evenings, sports days or any other typical event in the life of a child. She would never stand on the side lines of a sports field, freezing cold, but proud that her boy was out there on the pitch, simply doing his best. Nor would she ever sit proudly amongst other proud parents, and watch him graduate, or pack his lunch as he headed off to his first job. There would be no sitting proudly at the head of a table as he brought a new daughter-in-law into the family, nor would she hold his own child in her arms on the day she finally became the doting grandmother he would have wanted her to be. Everything he thought he should have experienced, that should have been taken for granted or been expected, and the memories that he should have come to cherish and share, had been savagely torn from his grasp in one random act of sheer evil and lunacy, and it could never be returned.

In an unforgiving world, Snowball would learn never to forgive. It was a humanity that he would be deprived of for years. Painful, lonely years in an isolated world that cared nothing for the mental tumult that rolled around his head, like marbles in a baking tin. One bad memory or experience after another, crashing around and colliding with errant force around in his head, until the pain of remembering surpassed the pain of the cause. His unredacted hate for his mother and all that she embodied would be as corrosive as hate could be. It would be the acid that ran through his veins, fuelled his resilience, and blinded him to all that was possibly good, in a world that was experientially all bad.

OH, FOR FUCK'S SAKE RIPPED FROM THE BOSOM OF MY FAMILY FOR BLOODY PRESTON!

Farm Wood to Preston. Not exactly a long-haul flight, but for Snowball, it may as well have been, as he was far enough from everything and everyone he had ever known, loved and treasured. Gone was his beloved foster mother, his father, and his siblings. No more would he bounce on Grandad's knee, or raid Nana's tin for his favourite biscuits. The trauma of being torn from his family the day before was still ripe in his mind as he awoke in the unfamiliar, cold, austere surroundings of Melbourne House. He could still hear Sarah screaming, still see Monica's tears, and the look of anguish that had swept across his parents' faces as they came to realise the gravity of what was unfolding before them. It was a cold, dark morning, and as Snowball lay there momentarily staring up at the whitewashed ceiling, he could not help but wonder where everyone else was waking up that gloomy, rain-swept, trauma-filled morning.

He was suddenly and overwhelmingly gripped with a stomach-churning fear as, in a state of panic, he surveyed the brutally unfamiliar surroundings in which he now found himself. He could not remember when he had last eaten, but he felt like he could vomit right there where he lay, except for the fact that the only thing his stomach felt were the unfamiliar pangs of hunger. He had arrived the evening before in darkness and seen little of the home or the surrounding area as he approached.

The anti-Christ disguised as a social worker who had brought him the night before had not stayed long. 'Distance to travel home' apparently, so he had been hastily deposited in the foyer and left there with his few worldly possessions in a carrier bag, and a worried scowl etched across his face. He remained unhappy about the good hiding he had received in the car on the way over, but by now fear and fatigue had taken over and he cared little for the fact that he had been abandoned in a strange house with apparently nobody in attendance. His face still tear-stained, he had arrived traumatised, cold, hungry, wet and alone, a far cry from the happy times he had experienced at home, and a life changing moment from which he might never fully recover.

It had seemed like an eternity before the smiling face of a youthful looking lady called Miss Bradwell appeared. She was a young, somewhat statuesque, bright-faced looking woman, with an engaging smile that captivated him for the brief few moments it flashed in front of his swollen, tired eyes. To Snowball she appeared so tall, but at his age and size, so did everyone else he encountered. Heeled shoes and long, firm, tights-clad legs that disappeared up a dark blue knitted skirt, hemmed just a few inches above her knees. She wore an ill-fitting blouse, and a lightweight red cardigan, held together by two central buttons and what looked like a gold-plated trinket completed the image, immediately captivating her weary charge. She took him gently by the hand, picked up his dripping carrier bag, and led him into the heart of the building and onwards to the sprawling kitchen. She had a gentle touch and a calming effect, and the glass of warm milk she provided helped to ease the nervous shivers that were careering through his body.

"Don't worry, everything will be fine," she assured him. He would hear those words often in one guise or another. It was never fine in the end, but in the here and now, they were words of comfort, and they would suffice.

She sounded almost insistent in her certainty of this statement, but nevertheless, it was clearly something that she could not possibly know and was more an instinctive generic announcement than a statement of fact.

How could she possibly know it was all going to be fine? He had just been ripped from the only home he had ever known, from the only family he had ever really known. Everything he was cognitively aware of had been suddenly taken from his grasp, and yet here she stood, telling him that everything was going to be alright. What a fucker she was! He just wanted to go home, to be with his mother, his family and his friends. All that raced through his head, as he sat there with the cup of warm milk warming his frozen hands, was would his mother be coming up any time soon to see him, to take him home and show him that it was all going to be alright. He wanted his family, his toys, his own bedroom with his brothers. He wanted to see Mrs Swarecki, and to pick grapes from Mr Garner's fruit box. It was not bloody fine, and it was not going to be! It was indeed an 'Oi You Fucker moment' which he would remember for years to come.

Melbourne House was a large L-shaped building at the end of Laney Avenue, a long cul-de-sac located in the arse end of Penwortham in Preston. Preston was the 'chocolate starfish' of the North, the existence of which would have remained unknown to most people but for the North End, the local football team, that featured large and proud in the League and a well-known local character called Tom Finney. By all accounts, Finney had done rather well in the game, and was a regular feature in the then England setup, something that would eventually lead to him being knighted, placing Preston firmly on the national map.

Constructed in an era-modern brick, Melbourne House stood in an impressive piece of ground that had roaming fields to three sides (think Theresa May's 'fields of wheat' comment, and you are getting there), a nearby brook, free-roaming horses to one side, and farmed dairy cows the other. It was a taste of the countryside, on the edge of the city. Each side of the 'L' was equally proportionate to the other, and they were joined centrally on the inside by a two-storey glass-fronted foyer that housed a central stairway between upper and lower floors. Externally there was a sprawling garden, complete with a pond, driveway, climbing frame, and a carpark filled with an MG1100, two Ford Capris, several Ford Cortinas, a Vauxhall Victor Estate, a Ford Anglia, a Hillman Hunter and a Ford Escort MK1, which had been parked in such a way as to prevent the dilapidated-looking, green Leyland Minibus from reversing out of its parking place. This the minibus did infrequently, due to the long running saga of its mechanical malfunctions and general state of dilapidation.

Additional stairways were located at each end of the 'L', and a quarter of the way down one side was a glass-fronted entry, which acted as an occasional reception area for visitors and staff alike. To the rear was another sprawling lawn and a concrete based basketball court, which was corralled by a painted white wooden fence comprising driven posts, upon which three horizontal planks had been nailed, spaced in such a manner that they spanned in equal thirds the distance between the ground and the top of the posts that supported them. It sounded and looked almost idyllic, but Melbourne House was an Approved School for the criminally wayward, the generally unwanted, and the abused children of society who could not be placed anywhere else. It was supposed to be a place of care, but as Snowball would quickly come to learn, it was a violently oppressive place of incarceration, designed to subdue and break a child, rather than help to develop the unfortunate charges who came to reside there.

Rising from his bed, the first thing he noticed were the five other children who shared the room. They all looked at each other inquisitively. Who were they, and who was he, they no doubt pondered. Tears began to form in his eyes as he gingerly placed his feet on the floor and stood awkwardly, as the gazes of the other children cast over him.

"Do you want the toilet?" a voice sharply asked. He nodded politely. "It's out there, but you can't go out until Miss comes for us."

He promptly headed to the door, not fully comprehending what had just been said to him but certain that the last thing he was going to do was wet his pants in front of everyone. And who the fuck was this "Miss" anyway?

As he swung open the door, the remaining children looked upon him in what appeared to be a combination of awe and fear. He thought it was a strange look, but they were strange people, so it could all have been perfectly normal, and within their own framework of reality. He glanced down the long corridor in front of him, then back at the children in the bedroom, before taking a tentative step onto the wooden slatted floor that ran its full length, terminating only to turn right at the central stairway that joined the two upper floor wings.

"It's that way," a voice informatively commanded, and he headed midway down the corridor before turning sharply left into the open, sparsely fitted bathroom that housed an enamel toilet, sink, bath and towel rail.

There was a toilet roll holder drilled into the wall alongside the toilet. It cradled an old and unwelcome friend called IZAL, with whom he was well-acquainted. IZAL, an abrasive toilet paper, seemed quite deliberately and specifically designed not to undertake the job that it was engaged for. It was not the case that you could actually wipe your bottom with IZAL. It was more that you simply used it to gently slide your fingers around the slippery contents of your bottom cheeks with a fleeting momentary pretence to personal hygiene, whilst at the same time praying with all your might that you did not sustain a paper cut to either your finger or your buttocks. Task complete, you then had the ignominy of loitering around in the toilet while your lightly poo-stained endeavour took an eternity to soak up enough water to flush away, before you could leave. If ever there was a case of institutionalised child abuse on a national scale, IZAL was it. It was indeed a far cry from lavatorial opulence. He quickly finished with the toilet, and on tip-toes, washed his hands as he had been taught and headed back towards the bedroom.

He did not see the vicious swing of Mrs Rivers coming, nor could he prevent himself from stumbling violently into a plastered wall opposite as the impact threw him from one side of the corridor to the other. He was dazed, shocked and bewildered, all in one fleeting moment, before the searing sting from her palm sliced deep into his face, and he began to wail. He felt her tight grip around his arm as she dragged him across the floor, and into the bedroom, pulling him upwards onto his feet, before spinning him around, lowering his pants and striking him hard, in front of all those present as an additional warning. It was all such a blur that he barely had time to recognise one abuse before the next one commenced.

"We don't leave the bedroom until we are told," she bellowed, as each strike landed firmly across his exposed bottom. "We don't leave the bedroom until we are told." The message was loud and clear. Oi You Fucker, you only needed to say.

Suitably satiated, she casually threw him to the ground where his head collided with a sickening bang against the protruding frame of the bed opposite. Then she stormed out, muttering loudly, as the door to the stairwell slammed shut, and silence, barring Snowball's wailing tears, once again descended across the upper floor. He could hear the silent echo of what he now recognised as words of warning, ringing through his tingling ears.

"It's out there, but you can't go out until Miss comes for us." Direct, clear, chilling but misunderstood. 'I get it, I fucking get it,' he thought.

Mrs Rivers had a penchant for beating children. It was her hobby. She was an unattractive woman, both inside and out, who ran the home with her equally brutal and abusive husband. Her cruelty was matched only by her vanity, and she would often be seen parading around the home, in varying stages of undress, hair in rollers, make-up and mirror in hand. It came to be known that one of the few times you were relatively safe from her unwelcome and often brutal attentions, was when she found the need to attend to and preen herself, usurping the need to inflict mindless brutality upon the young charges placed in her care. Her brutality was only tempered by what she knew she could get away with, given the age range of those she wantonly abused. The open palm to bare skin was her chosen methodology for the younger ones, while straps, plimsolls and canes were used on the older children who, in her eyes and warped mind, were clearly capable of taking the physical impact. It was all rather cold, and extremely calculated, an environment that Snowball, by necessity, would need to rapidly adapt to.

The Rivers drove an old Ford Cortina, which often sat unused in the parking spaces at the front of the home. Despite clearly being in charge at the home, and presumably the better paid, fiscally and materially, they appeared to fare much worse than many of the staff who worked for them, which, according to rumour, was a surprising state of current affairs given that they used the home's petty cash tin as a personal slush fund for most of the family's spending. There was also plenty of talk about how the 'lucky' girls in the home got to ride with Mr Rivers on his 'trips and errands' out, while the 'lucky' boys were beaten and abused by Mrs Rivers in the family apartment they shared, located in the 'access prohibited' staff area of the building. There was no end of talk about that area of the home, and the abuse that took place there, out of sight from prying eyes and insulated from the attention of an uncaring, and apparently unknowing, outside world. They were the sort of couple who would have boded well managing a concentration camp, such was the pleasure they appeared to get from their own cruelties, and between them, they consciously chose to run the home with a camplike mentality and an iron fist.

They were equally feared amongst staff and children alike, which largely accounted for the apparent docility and complicity amongst the resident social workers, when they bore witness to the brutality of the regime that they were inflicting upon the defenceless children of Melbourne House. It was simply the case that many of them found it easier to stay quiet, and avoid the unwanted attention of the Rivers, than it was to speak up and face their wrath. Grown adults were prepared to tolerate the perpetual suffering of children in order to deflect unwanted attention from themselves. How the spirit of Dunkirk had faded in the arse end of Preston. The regime was cold, harsh, oppressive and brutal. Everything had a consequence, and with the Rivers, rarely was the outcome pleasant for child or adult alike.

By the time the 'official' moment to rise came around, the pain in Snowball's face had subsided, along with his anguish and tears. He followed the other children from the bedroom to the bathroom where each, in total silence, took turns to wash their faces, clean their teeth, and use the toilet, before returning to the bedroom to dress in the clothes that had been laid out in the interim. Many of the children appeared almost zombielike. They passively complied to the rigours of the regime in the desperate hope that they could circumnavigate the brutality that would be visited upon them, or someone else, if they faltered from the norm. It appeared that as life unfurled at Melbourne House, there always had to be an example made, a lesson taught, or a rule implemented. And at the centre of it all stood the Rivers.

On Snowball's bed lay short brown pants, a red and white striped shirt, white socks and underpants. He had also been left his own flannel, comb, small towel, toothbrush and a bar of soap.

"They are yours," a voice murmured.

"You have to put them in the drawer," informed another.

With a freshly instilled keenness to comply, he duly placed them in his drawer before getting dressed and waited quietly on his bed to see what the others would do next. Several children shared his room that morning. All appeared routine and extremely docile for their ages. It was as if the very life that they should have been enjoying, which should have been oozing from their young bodies, had been systematically sucked out of them. None of them, apart from a young girl called Anita, appeared to talk unnecessarily, and when they did find the courage, it was almost always in murmurs and whispers. There was a tangible fear embedded in their interactions, in their movements, and they appeared fretful and wary of every action in which they found themselves engaged. There was a marked absence of spirit. They had been brutally subdued.

Breakfast came and went. Cold porridge with a teaspoonful of jam or marmalade was the order of the day as Snowball would find most days. It was generally served onto the table at the same time the children were instructed to rise, alongside plates of buttered toast, and small dishes of marmalade. The idea was that those wanting a warm meal would consequently spend less time fooling around getting washed and dressed if they knew their breakfast was going cold on the table. It was a flawed logic in many ways, not least given that arriving in the dining area at any time before Mrs Rivers had personally told you to "Go to breakfast", would result in a caning or slippering that you did not really want. In all reasonable likelihood, no breakfast would be an additional punishment, just to satiate her craving for cruelty. Snowball would soon come to find that food deprivation was as much a tool of punishment as the beatings he would unfortunately suffer, and regularly witness. The pains of hunger supplemented with the pains of the rod.

He had been there less than twenty-four hours, but to Snowball, it felt like a lifetime. He already knew that Melbourne House was a place that he cared little for, and which cared nothing for him. He did not want to be there, and he clearly was not wanted. Time and time again, he naively wondered when his mother would come and collect him, how long would it take to get home, and would his 'brothers and sisters' be there waiting for him. Maybe she would bring his siblings with her, and perhaps Mrs Swarecki would try to be there as well, with a bag of his favourite Fruit Salads and Black Jacks in hand. Surely he would not be staying here long. After all, he did not belong here. He had a family.

The children in the home spanned an age range from roughly five years old, and upwards. Snowball was one of the youngest. A blessing in many ways, it spared him and others from some of the harsher extremes and rigours that the regime, and those who administered it, had to offer. Most were from broken homes, or were just simply unwanted by parents who, for a variety of reasons, felt that they could no longer care for their own children and had subsequently abandoned them to a fate unknown, amongst people unknown. Many had been physically and sexually abused at home and would fare no better at Melbourne House. Mothers, fathers, uncles, family and friends were all complicit, in one form or another. Many carried the physical scars of their abuse, and nearly all carried the mental ones.

There had been burns, breaks, bruises, cuts, rapes and sodomy. Every known form of child abuse was represented in one form or another and without exception, it appeared that the children themselves were being held to blame for everything that had happened to them, and punished accordingly. Bad children who had brought it all upon themselves, as the story often went. It was easier to blame the child than confront the abusers, and as so many in care found, the same justification was used for the continuation of the abuse once the local authorities had taken responsibility for their welfare. It was a sorry state of affairs but one which Snowball, like the remainder of the children, could do little about. It was not a case of grinning and bearing it, just bearing it. The irony was that they had been placed in 'care' for their own protection, and yet here, in this house of undeniable, overt and unbridled evil, they were being systematically abused by the very people charged with their upkeep and well-being. From one hell to another, the irony of the situation was not lost on many of them, even if they were unable to articulate it.

School and home life were separated by the wheat fields, cow fields, and the brook. A short, undulating walk, arid in summer and quagmire in winter, became a daily routine for Snowball, alongside many of his newfound 'brothers and sisters'. Separated though they were geographically, school and home life shared a united front in the rigidity of the regime they imposed, and the brutality and abuse that they routinely inflicted. The physical and sexual depravity of life in the home, cognitively separated and differentiated only by the tenacious way those responsible conspired to conceal their abuses from prying eyes. At the regulated and frequently visited school for the 'undesirable and untamed', abuse was less overt, though equally calculated, frequent and forthright. Teachers carried canes, plimsolls, long wooden rulers, paddles and straps as if they were fashion accessories, only for them to disappear into a locked cupboard at the first sight of anybody with an air of authority. Beatings were frequent, public and brutal, designed to harm, intimidate and humiliate. And it simply was not a case of *if* you would be punished, but when and with what frequency. Every child was beaten, every child was marked, and every child was a victim of this relentless oppression. How Snowball would often ponder, as the years drifted by, what he had done to deserve this outcome. Did he deserve it? Where had he gone wrong? Maybe he was just a bad child and was getting everything he deserved and more. After all, wasn't the fact they had been abused clearly their own fault?

BiG LEACHY, LiTTLE DARKiE

School was a daily trauma for Snowball. On the one hand, there was a sense of relief at leaving the home and the abuses hidden within its walls, but on the other, the short walk between home and school provided scant relief from the daily torment of his waking hours. His school life was as rigid as his home life. Everything had a time, and everything had a place. Every transgression was punishable in ever increasing, inventive and painful ways. It just seemed to be a life that revolved around dodging the attention of one set of abusers or another. Every teacher in the school carried an implement of punishment and used it frequently, with scant regard given to age, understanding, right and wrong. Punishment was summary and brutal. How could they call this 'child care', and keep a straight face? Why did no one do something to stop it? The only way he could possibly survive was with a little help from his friends, and that was where Big Leachy stepped in. Leachy was a huge lad, one of the so called 'Cocks of the School'. From a tough northern background that was made all the tougher by his long-term stay at the home, Leachy knew exactly how to look after himself, and fortunately for Snowball, he had taken such a liking to him that despite the environment they both shared, his protective instincts towards the kid he called his 'Little Darkie Friend' began to shine through.

However, Leachy had not been seen for some time over recent days, though he was there larger than life that morning and it was widely believed that he had done what was commonly referred to as 'a bunk', or in unromanticised layman terms, run away from the home. Leachy was an iconic presence at the school. Not many came bigger or harder than Leachy, and he was as revered as he was feared by most. His presence that day was ominous, and when they were all summoned and assembled in the school hall, it soon became apparent that Leachy was in serious trouble, although characteristically he showed little, if any, sign of fear or trepidation. He had apparently been caught by the police the night before, some miles away, loitering around the home of his estranged parents. It was a strange place to be found in the eyes of many, as it was his own parents who had originally placed him into care, abandoned him to the abuses from which he was actually running, and ultimately instigated his capture by the police. But such is the fuckery of this thing called life.

Having notified the police, his parents had sat back and watched as they duly attended to and found Leachy hiding in some bushes nearby. He was reputed to have been in possession of a bottle of beer, food and a large carving knife, which in hindsight for many in the know, had served to remove some of the puzzlement in regard to his location, but in turn, had added a greater deal of concern about his possible intentions. They had returned him to Melbourne House that night, and like the rest of kids, he was up and attending school that morning.

There were all sorts of rumours about the beating he had received from Mrs Rivers that night. Most of it was probably just speculation, but he was clearly subdued that morning, tired and with an apprehension that only subsided as they had all headed across the fields to school. He had confided in one friend that Mrs Rivers had stood him up against a wall while she slapped his face over and over, within minutes of the police leaving. He had been stripped naked and forced to stand in a corner of the corridor with his hands behind his back and a book on his head for several hours, and only when in a near state of collapse had she eventually sent him to bed, the threat of "more coming tomorrow" ringing in his ears. It was a punishment that was known to them all, and there was little surprise expressed when this ritualised abuse became widely known. The book had a sinister purpose. If the child started to fade and tire, their head would wobble. If the head wobbled, the book fell and if the book fell, the child was caned, before being placed back in the corner to start the ritual all over again. And so it was, that in the very early hours of the morning, nearing mental and physical collapse through fatigue, he had dropped the book, the sound of which had alerted Mrs Rivers, who had subsequently taken him into the office, placed him across a table, and viciously caned him.

As Leachy would find out to his cost, it was only the start of a campaign of punishment and intimidation, designed not only to deter him from thoughts of repeat behaviour, but to also send a clear and direct message to the rest of the children that there was no mileage in that type of behaviour. It would inevitably be met with a brutal response, no matter how big you were. Ironic really, as the real message for all capable of cognitive athletics was that you would be abused whether you stayed or not, and so any temporary respite, facilitated by a 'bunk' made perfect sense, despite the potential outcomes.

In front of the entire assembly, Leachy was summarily called to the front by the then headmaster, a fearsome man known only as 'fucking Hughes'. He was also referred to as a number of other derogatory terms, but 'fucking Hughes' was the most common of all and could be said with a slight intonation towards venom, that conveyed the appropriate degree of hate when required. Everybody knew what was coming, as the walk of the damned across the hall floor to the stage was a daily ritual that they had all taken part in, at one time or another.

Hughes was incandescent with faux outrage as he whipped up an atmosphere of collective fear that he thrived upon. He relished delivering the traditional reprise of outrage and contempt for the behaviour that had been reported and outlining the 'heinous' nature of the offences that were to be so brutally punished, followed by a eulogy on where that "form of behaviour" might lead the culprit later in life. They had all heard it before, and many wondered why the fuck he just did not get on with the beating, happy only in that they were not the unfortunate recipient on this occasion.

Leachy stood motionless and in fear for most of the verbal onslaught. He was not a boy that was easily intimidated, as many had unwittingly found out to their own expense, but Snowball guessed there was always an added apprehension when Hughes was up there, ranting and raving, and you were aware that you were the victim of his vitriolic attentions. Everyone stood motionless and in fear. Hughes remonstrated and gesticulated wildly. He was like a man possessed. It was nothing unusual, but somehow there appeared to be an added impetus to his vitriol. What the fuck had Mrs Rivers told him? He was the Al Sharpton of Preston when he went off on one, preaching at his pulpit, and watched by the unknowing, unwanted, unconvinced and the unwilling.

The assembled teachers behind him stood with canes and straps in hand, occasionally nodding as his histrionics continued for what seemed like an eternity, conscious not only of him but of the reactions of the congregated throng, over whom they wielded such outright control. Much of the language being used was flying at an altitude far above Snowball's head, but he had the general drift of what was being said and what was going on. His heart raced like everyone else's. He could hear it pounding inside, he could feel it banging against his ribs, as could the others who stood, transfixed on the scene that unfolded in front of them, awaiting the Martin Luther King-esque finale, when Hughes would, with great clarity and a deafening roar, declare that his eyes had indeed seen the "Glory of the Coming of the Lord", before wrapping up his sermon, and getting down to the business they were all assembled for. On cue and without apparent prompt, Leachy, his big bold friend and protector, stepped calmly forward. A sense of resignation had swept over him. He seemed resolute, he seemed strong, he seemed unfazed, but he was also resigned.

Hughes demanded he hold his right hand out, and Leachy duly obliged. Hughes adopted a power stance on the stage and to the right of Leachy, with his back to the watching assembly. The thick rattan tapped three times against Leachy's outstretched hand, before it was swiftly raised, then swiped viciously down onto the outstretched hand to which it had been measured. Leachy yelped, withdrew his hand sharply, before raising it once again in front of the waiting Hughes. Up and down went the rattan, each stroke measured in three short gentle taps, before viciously stinging the outstretched hands of the victim, and bringing ever more desperate squeals from Leachy, alongside seemingly approving glances from the assembled teachers at the back of the stage. The cruelty of it all, seemingly unacknowledged, as the craving to inflict both pain and humiliation was usurped. Any sense of decency and compassion that they once might have had fermented in the conscience of those who approved this treatment. Six strokes to each hand, and Leachy was left a defeated, humiliated, blubbering mess on the stage, in full view of the assembled masses. It was a clear lesson to all assembled. If you run or hide from our abuse, we will find you, and abuse you. If you speak of our abuse, we will silence you and abuse you. Nobody will help you, you are ours to abuse, and we will abuse you whenever we like. Lesson learned.

There were, however, occasional periods when life at Melbourne House and the school seemed to settle down, and run relatively 'normally', inasmuch as most of the unfortunate residents understood 'normal' to be. In many ways, the respite from fear was coordinated and timely in that it usually precipitated a visit from a local dignitary, or someone in authority in one capacity or another. These occasions were few and far between but given that apes share a DNA that is roughly only two percent different to humans, it would be remiss not to acknowledge that the staff occasionally had a human side, that in some instances, could be widely recognised as such.

The concrete basketball court at the back of Melbourne House had a large metal lighting post at each end that cast a radiating heat, as well as ambient lighting, across the entire court. These posts would double as a single, centralised goalpost, and many football matches were played there with the aim not of scoring a goal, but hitting the post with the ball. Hit the post, goal scored. Pretty simple in theory, significantly more difficult in practice, not least because of the sheer number of players taking part, often meaning that all they could hit was each other.

There was a standard format to organising the games. Two captains were chosen, usually the toughest two there, the owner of the ball, or the ones who shouted the loudest. In turn, they would choose a player each from the remaining participants, until all available players had been selected. An odd number of players resulted in a floating substitute who would be utilised as and when children were called away for various reasons, or simply chose to drop out of the game. Selection was a useful process for understanding where you stood in terms of footballing skill and usefulness. The most useful players were selected first, the least gifted later. The later you were selected, the shitter you were deemed to be with a ball. Some would take significant umbrage at this process; others, like Snowball, given that he could not hit an elephant's arse with a cricket bat, let alone the solitary goalpost, were just glad to be included in the game and accepted their status with an eagerness to both please and impress. Games would ensue without a time limit, and often on the basis of "first team to X wins", or until, characteristically, someone, usually an extremely bored member of staff, was heard shouting "NEXT GOAL WINS!", as either the light dimmed, or interest was waning to such an extent that the diminishing teams left too much ground to cover for the remaining players, and it got too tiring. By the time the games finished, nobody really knew what the score was and a fight would often break out as one member of the team attempted to assert their influence at score keeping over the others. It was another one of those occasions where it was handy to be on Leachy's team, as he was as handy with his fists as he was with a ball.

Snowball would often make use of the enormous cupboard of toys and sporting equipment that was in the home. It was more of a small room than a cupboard, locked at all times and only opened on request so that staff could monitor who had what, and it had just about everything you would need for most prevailing sports of the day. Cricket bats and balls, footballs, table tennis equipment, badminton and tennis rackets, lacrosse and hockey sticks, and much more. Nobody really understood how only two lacrosse sticks were of any use to anyone, but they had made the effort so it was best not to complain too loudly. It was, in fact, the one area of life in which they were probably better endowed than most of their home-reared peers, but even the toy cupboard had a sinister twist. There was a small, old gymnastics vaulting horse in the far corner. Dark varnished wooden slats formed the tapered, oblong sided structure, while a brown heavy padded removable top completed the overall school-inspired design.

It was common enough in most schools at the time, but perhaps a little unusual outside of that environment. It was well known by everyone in Melbourne House that the cupboard was where many of the random beatings would take place, providing another salient reason for controlled access. Children were taken there, stripped and placed across the vaulting horse before being beaten with canes at the whim of the staff. Snowball could be nothing but grateful that, although he had suffered awfully inside that dreadful room, his visits had been somewhat infrequent in comparison to many of his peers and counterparts. He had, however, like so many who passed through the system at Melbourne House, suffered nonetheless.

UNFORTUNATELY, WE'RE ALL GOING ON A SUMMER HOLIDAY (OKAY, A DAY TRIP)

There was one feature of life at Melbourne House that came around every year and provided both pleasure and pain, of the double-edged sword variety. It could be a time of great pleasure and great pain, and Snowball, like the rest of the children, would routinely experience his fair share of both. The problem was the long summer break as the schools broke up for what was a traditional six-week respite from the rigours of education, or the twattery of enduring teachers feigning attempts at education, as a mask for inflicting a daily diet of physical and mental abuse. This long break placed Snowball and his peers at the tender mercies of some of the most brutal staff in Melbourne House on a daily basis, and throughout the prolonged summer days, it often proved impossible to avoid regular skirmishes with trouble, and where it was avoided on the one hand it would, with surprising ease, find him on the other.

The other side to this pitiful sword of injustice was that summertime often brought with it some additional funding from social services, which was used invariably to take some of the children, usually the youngest and least troublesome, on various days out and excursions. The excursions themselves were enjoyable affairs, not least because of the excitement that was gained when the green Leyland Minibus chose to break down, and they were all deposited and fed in a local café while they awaited help. However, the trips would often result in someone finding trouble, and a beating being handed out to the culprit, or indeed every child, if the culprit thought better of admitting their guilt, and adopted the collective responsibility approach of 'selflessly' sharing their beating equally amongst their friends. The altruism of some was outstanding. It was on one such trip that Snowball's stock in life was elevated to near superstar status amongst his peers, though it resulted in a cessation of all further trips for him throughout the remainder of the summer break, and as was typically the case, landed him with another beating at the hands of the ever-willing, and insatiably sadistic Mrs Rivers.

The day of the eagerly awaited big trip had arrived, and after dutifully assisting with the preparation of their packed lunches, eight children, Miss Bradwell and Mrs Rivers loaded themselves into the minibus and set off for Haworth, into Bronte Country. All Snowball knew was that they were visiting some well-known museum and a house, and that Miss Bradwell had told him a semi-interesting story about a family who had lived there, in addition to the fact that the house itself was reputed to be haunted. Whether the house was haunted or not mattered little to Snowball in the general scheme of the regular bollocks that he was told, but the prospect of encountering a 'real-life' ghost was enough to capture Snowball's imagination, and it was more than enough to ensure that for the week leading up to the trip, he had somehow remained on his best behaviour and trouble-free in order to ensure that his place on the bus was secured.

The trip itself was well-planned, and they all arrived safely and without mechanical incident, for a change, shortly after lunchtime. Miss Bradwell parked the bus (she was doing it long before it became a popular strategy at Spurs) and announced that the first action of the day was to eat their lunches in the car park before being escorted around the house, and regaled with the house's history as it pertained to the Bronte family. It probably was not the most appropriate of trips for the age group, but it was supposed to be haunted for fuck's sake, so why not take them? Lunch turned out to be a feeding frenzy of piranha proportions, as the main objective was to get into the house as quickly as possible and begin the ghost hunt.

There was a dumpy looking, middle-aged woman on hand, who politely informed the group that she would be their guide, and that all they had to do was follow her and listen intently to every word she said. Following her? That was a clear yes. Listening to her? Really? And so, as Mrs Rivers and Miss Bradwell returned to wait in the minibus, the tour began in earnest, and they were away. Room after room was explored and explained by the enthusiastic guide with the peculiarly pungent odour, who did not seem to notice that nobody really gave a shit about who would sit and write stories at this table, and who had a penchant for baking buns. They wanted the fucking ghosts, and Snowball was the most impatient of all.

Eventually they arrived at one of the bedrooms and upon entry, were told everything that they wanted to hear. As history had apparently recorded it, one of the family had actually died in the very bed they were staring at, the very bed that stood without fanfare, thrill or commotion in the centre of the room. It was alleged that the room, and indeed the entire house, had been haunted by their ghost ever since. Numerous people, none of which could actually be named by Mrs Sweaty Pits, had seen the ghost and had been so frightened that they had been instantly struck dumb (which probably accounted for them not saying who they were). There was a large sign encased in plastic on the bed. It detailed the death and the various ghostly sightings, warning that those present in the house after the hours of darkness could expect a visit if they were unfortunate enough to keep late hours or sleep too lightly. It was an enthralling tale and was all the children could talk about as the tour subsequently continued on the upper floor. As time pressed on, the tour came to an end, and the guide led her captive audience outside, locked the front door behind her, and pointed them in the direction of the car park, and the waiting minibus that would return them home to the living hell from which they had come.

Miss Bradwell was first out of the bus, closely followed by Mrs Rivers, who flashed a rare and endearing smile in their direction as she joyously enquired as to whether they had enjoyed themselves or not. The smile turned out to be something of a false flag, in that they had not realised she had been drinking in their absence, and the broad grin across her face was in fact alcohol induced and not really meant for their benefit at all. There was fevered chatter as they were loaded onto the bus, recanting the tales they had been told by the guide before a stunned silence descended as Miss Bradwell realised they were missing one child. It was around this very moment that Snowball was crawling out from under the Bronte bed, and preparing himself for a night of ghost hunting in the house, safe in the knowledge that if the door was locked, the ghosts would not be able to flee, affording him the opportunity to go down in history as the only named living person who had encountered the ghosts and not been struck dumb in the process.

"Who is missing?" enquired Mrs Rivers.

"You probably don't want to know," replied a hesitant Miss Bradwell, as the questions were asked and a search ensued.

"Who saw David last?"

"Where did you see him?"

"What was he doing?"

It was all pretty pointless as none of them knew anything, but it was preliminary to the long search that lay ahead, before someone finally twigged that if he was not roaming freely anywhere in the grounds of the house, the only place he could reasonably now be expected to be found was actually still inside it. The guide was subsequently located, and she promptly returned to the house to unlock the front door. The sound of footsteps on the stairs alerted Snowball to the fact that the appearance of the ghost was imminent and after darting to apparent safety under the bed, he braced himself as the realisation that he had no real idea what a real ghost looked like sent a shiver of fear down his spine. The bedroom door cranked open, and as the long dark shadow of Mrs Rivers flashed across the floor, Snowball took a loud audible intake of breath as he realised that not only were ghosts real, but that they were, contrary to all the pictures he had seen, black as well. He squeezed his eyes tightly shut as fear got the better of him, only to reopen them confronted by a furious gin-soaked Mrs Rivers, who was now kneeling by the bed and peering directly at him. She communicated only with a crooked finger that beckoned him from his hiding place, then projected him onto the landing space and into the grip of a resigned but stern looking Miss Bradwell, who calmly shook her head, and pulled him towards the stairs. The shit had just hit the fan, and he was stood directly opposite on the other side. It was a long, slow trip back to Preston, one filled with more fear and trepidation than the Bronte ghost could ever have hoped to induce in him. It also turned out to be an early night and a painful one, but at the end of the day, he had seen a ghost of sorts, even if it was just the pale, nondescript features of a pissed-up Mrs Rivers.

NO SUCH THING AS
A FREE LUNCH (OR
PROLONGED HAPPINESS)

Mr Rivers was something of a nemesis to Snowball. It was a strange relationship that, on the one hand, saw him take Snowball into his small and somewhat fragile family fold on occasions, purely as a friend and companion to his own son and yet, on the other, saw him deliver bouts of sustained cruelty that were totally incomprehensible and, in fact, criminal had they been delivered to any child other than one in the care system. It was a dalliance with psychopathy that nobody, least of all Snowball, could understand and yet, it was a norm that he had come to accept.

Michael Rivers and Snowball had been happily playing in the family apartment together. They had been there most of the day, taken their lunch there courtesy of the preening Mrs Rivers, and even gone into town with Mr Rivers on an errand in their ageing Ford Cortina, before returning to play in the spacious gardens, front and rear. It had been an unexpected, rare but welcome day of idyllic pleasure and carefree abandon. The day had, quite literally, flown by and for once, Snowball was happy. It had been fun, and there was no sense of trepidation when, later that afternoon, he had been asked to go and see Mr Rivers in the small downstairs office. In a rare, carefree and unguarded moment, he had strolled into the office and beamed widely at the seated Rivers.

Rivers quickly rose from his seat and with the wave of a hand, intimated that Snowball should close the door behind him. Hand placed flat by the handle of the open door, Snowball pushed gently until he heard the characteristic click that signified the closure was complete, before slowly turning back towards Mr

Rivers. By this time, Rivers had silently traversed the room and was looming, larger than life over him. Right hand raised, he brought it down with a ferocity that saw Snowball's head spin violently one hundred and eighty degrees, with a force that sent him crashing face first into the wooden door behind him. His right eye socket smashed hard into the door handle, jolting his head and neck backwards at a right angle as he slumped limply to the floor. Barely had the pain registered when the second and third blow arrived, before the temporary respite was enough to afford him time to acknowledge the pain, feel the burgeoning flow of blood from his face, and recoil from the horror that was ensuing. Too shocked to cry, too fragile to fight, he just lay there staring upwards and awaiting the onslaught that would inevitably beset him.

He was awoken several hours later in his bedroom. He could see that it had gone dark outside; he had been stripped and redressed in pyjamas, placed into bed, and covered with a blanket. He had no recollection of how he had gotten there or who had tended to him, but there he was, hidden away from prying eyes and curious minds. His head and face had been lightly bandaged and his blood washed away. All he knew was that he was hurting. His last moments of recall were of a raging Mr Rivers raining blows down upon him before a blanket of unconsciousness had been draped over him, facilitating the passage of both pain and time to silently pass him by. He felt a warm hand across his brow and looked up, through the haze and the pain. It was Miss Bradwell, the one person to whom he had become attached and, over time, had come to trust. He liked her. She had never struck him, nor had he seen her strike another child. She had never really been harsh to him or others, she had never brutalised or humiliated him. She was the one and only person he could recall who appeared to care. Everyone liked Miss Bradwell. She was the go-to person for anything you needed, wanted or thought you deserved, if you could find her alone and had the courage (or temerity as she often and jokingly chastened) to ask. She was the one good cop, amongst a station of the corrupt. How he and others would often think to themselves, 'If only they were all like Miss Bradwell'.

"Are you ok?"

'You clearly mean well, but that's a stupid fucking question,' he thought.

Snowball remained silent, tears welling in his dimmed, swollen eyes. He just stared right back at her. She had brought him some food and helped him eat.

"What did you do?" she pried. Snowball offered up his now familiar gallic shrug. "OK, just eat your tea, and I will be back soon." With that, she rose from the side of his bed, turned towards the door and left.

TiME TO LEAVE (iF ONLY FOR A SHORT WHILE)

It was not long after this that Snowball had his first dalliance with absconding. It seemed to be the fashionable thing to do at the time and, in many ways, it was damned rude not to 'blood' yourself if you were to be a 'cared for' child of any credible merit in the system. Snowball had come to appreciate that there always comes a point where the systemised use of intimidation, and the pervasive underlying threat of violence in order to force compliance, becomes negated and no longer credible by the mere fact that you are inflicting that intimidation and violence regardless. It was a fact, young though he was, Snowball fully understood. Indeed, he had indulged in many a fist fight on the basis that the threats of attack were nothing more than a prelude to an attack. Victories were rare, but he was always in the game. He had seen and suffered too much in his brief life, and the beating from Mr Rivers had in many ways cemented the final nail in the coffin in which he was about to bury his fear. Brutality in Melbourne House was not only anticipated and expected, it was understood to be an unavoidable consequence of life, such was its prevalence. Within that prevailing climate, Snowball, like many others, had become increasingly numb to the threat, and some of the more errantly foolhardy actively sought to challenge it on occasion.

Absconding was a definite badge of honour in the system, and those who had done it were talked of in glowing terms amongst their peers. It was heroic, rebellious, "grown up", and a sign of personal strength and "fucking hardness". After all, what greater rite of passage was there than to venture out into the world on your own? However, it was not just a case of running away. Your very status amongst your peers could be enormously enhanced by the duration you were gone for. Gone and back in a day simply meant that you were a bit of a mug, and in all reality, the beating you got on your return simply was not worth it in any form of reckoning. No, you had to be gone overnight minimum, preferably more than one night, and the longer the better from a credibility and "hardness" point of view. Snowball knew that the more nights you were gone, the greater the kudos. Being away on school days was even better, though chances were it doubled any punishment that was meted out on your return, as Hughes was known to work in conjunction with the home to ensure that any punishments meted out were reflected in the school environment as well. Home and school were linked at the hip and working in synchronised harmony in the application of a catalogue of abuse.

Distance was also a great factor in how you came to be perceived by your peers after absconding. In fact, apart from a proven act of violence or the 'screwing' of a shop, distance was the primary factor upon which you would ultimately be judged. The further you claimed to have roamed (proven or otherwise in most instances), the more your status as a latter-day Christopher Columbus and potential member of the Kray Gang rose. The older boys would regale their peers with stories (true or not), of how when 'on the run', they had screwed a series of shops to sustain themselves, or 'turned someone over' for money, to fund their 'Ronnie Biggs' lifestyle. Few, if any, of the tales were likely to be true, but it all added a sense of glamour to the occasion, serving as valid justification for the beating they had received, and gave Snowball and the young ones alike, heroes to worship and respite from the daily drudge of abuse.

Snowball's first tentative steps into this murky world were, however, far less glamourous. He was basically a mug. A big mug. HUGE MUG. Far less Rio de Janeiro, and much more Garstang Road just around the corner. But to be fair, he had in point of fact actually run most of the way, not quite cognisant of the fact that running away was a description that did not necessarily have to be taken quite so literally. The brutality of Rivers had played on his mind. He had felt increasingly trapped and helpless, as did many of the other children. A victim of circumstances beyond his immediate control and not of his making, but a victim nonetheless. A dreadful past and an uncertain future, running was the only way he could manifestly exert some control over events in his life.

The big day had been planned for a short time. He was ready, he was willing, and he was adamant he was going to go far. He had it all worked out and in his own mind, he had reached the point of no return. He would screw countless numbers of shops and turn over an endless number of people in his heroic bid to circumnavigate the globe alone. He would aim to touch all four corners of the globe (if only the earth was flat), and they were not going to measure his absence in nights away. They would be talking months, if not years. In Snowball's mind, there was a good chance the Rivers would have retired by the time he returned, and there would be a new sheriff in town – hopefully Miss Bradwell – but he would wait that one out and see. Snowball was about to become a legend, or so he thought. He spent his first hour away, trying to find a way through the fields of wheat. Yes, those endless fields of wheat. They appeared to just go on and on forever, not helped by the fact that he could not see above the tops of the crops, so all sense of direction had been summarily lost and given up to chance upon entry. One field after another, separated only by horizontally pulled barbed wire rows strewn between randomly drilled fence posts. At one point, he strayed out onto a path and could see the tops of trees in the distance, along with a small plume of smoke that appeared to be coming from a farmhouse, of which the roof was all he could see.

More fields separated by more barbed wire fencing, and then the land flattened out into a cow-pat strewn minefield that required careful navigation if the adventure was not to end in an early bath, and a sore backside. The fear of what lay ahead was nullified by the fear of what lay behind. He knew he had passed the point of no return, as he had been absent long enough to be noticed or so he thought, and he wondered whether he would hear a siren or klaxon go off, once they realised he was actually missing. Perhaps there would be a search party, maybe the police and rescue services. They might even rustle up a search and rescue helicopter. Who knew where this was going to lead?

It was at about this point, and quite without rhyme or reason given the time of day, that hunger began to set in. He had been gone over an hour, and it had been tough going. He wondered if it was perhaps nearing the time where he would have to 'screw' his first shop, such was the surging instinct for survival. But first, there was the small necessity of finding a way out of the fields. The Smiths' farmhouse was roughly half a mile ahead, and from there he knew there was a road that led both in and out of town. It was a big ask, but he knew if he could make it there he would find a shop, and from that point onwards, this absconding lark would be plain sailing, so Snowball ploughed on. The terrain was now becoming too tough as leg fatigue set in, and he figured it would be much easier to walk through the cow pats than around them (Lesson 1). He soon learned that traversing around the fields was far easier than ploughing through the centre of them (Lesson 2).

As he neared the road, he could hear the ever-increasing sound of the background traffic. Car, pause. car, pause, lorry, pause, car. Familiar sounds that would herald lesson 3. He reached the end of the path, and between him and a lifetime of carefree abandon stood only a small stile. One last hurdle. He casually observed the handful of cars that passed as he stood atop of the stile, holding tightly to the uprights on either side. Left leg placed across, a small body swivel, and the right leg followed. 'Done, dusted, how easy was that?' he thought. The view was magnificent. Captivating. He was enthralled with his own success. So utterly enthralled, in fact, that he failed to notice the familiarly ageing Ford Cortina that had momentarily passed him by, stopped, reversed back across the grass verge, and pulled up alongside, before sounding the horn. Startled, he glanced over in the fading light. Lesson 3 had just arrived, in the form of Mrs Rivers returning from the nearby shops (the ones he now would not be screwing), and demanding to know exactly what he was doing. It was at this point, as she disembarked the car, took hold of his shoulder and pulled him forwards, that he came to understand that 'fuck all' was not an acceptable answer and so, physical rebuke administered, he immediately owned up and was placed in the back of the Cortina, and taken back to the home.

He was incredibly disappointed on his return. Not least because it had taken less than a few minutes to drive what seemed like hours for him to walk. Further disappointment swept over him when his return raised no eyebrows as he simply had not been gone long enough for the other kids to realise he was missing (Mug). Mrs Rivers, left hand grasping tightly at his right arm, marched him forlornly passed his football playing peers, through the back entrance, passed the stinking, recently used toilets and into the foyer. No time to pass pleasantries with Miss Bradwell, as his head passed her eminently recognisable thighs at eye level and down the corridor he went, images of the floor punctuated by the swing of the strap Mrs Rivers now held in her hand. He was first in bed that night, sleeping on his stomach and the only one hungry through lack of food. Nobody even mentioned his big adventure, not a word. He had a lot to learn, but for now, he would just let it go.

In hindsight, he came to appreciate that there was not much point to his second, nor third or fourth attempt at liberating himself from the realities and harshness of everyday life at Melbourne House and the attention of Mrs Rivers. It was not the case that Snowball was ever short of ideas, and he had in fact become known as something of a thinker, in the context of his ability to sit in a corner and dwell miserably on all manner of things. No, it was more the ongoing case that he simply did not appear to have any good ideas, in the sense of resolving something in the here and now, and more often than not, if he came up with a good one, a lack of intelligent planning would often render it as completely useless as his more disdainful efforts. In many ways, his primary problem (in regard to absconding), as it was for so many of his peers, was that he knew very little of how life and the world outside of the confines of Melbourne House actually worked. He had never used public transport without help, never caught a train, or traversed across town unaided. Nor was he particularly well endowed with any specific knowledge of the geographical topography that would confront him once out of the gates, as he headed out that afternoon, intent on reaching Rio de Janeiro by sunset. He was like a Belle-Vue greyhound. No matter how fast he ran, how much effort he put in, he would always end up back at the starting blocks, and feeling somewhat bemused by the lack of reward for the effort he had put in.

His fourth attempt at absconding had in fact been a more entertaining affair personally, in that he had solicited the unwilling assistance of Miss Greenhough in the process. Greenhough was an experienced social worker of some years standing, extremely confident in her abilities, strident in manner, ferocious in look, brutal in action, but with an occasional gentler side that would surface periodically, as if she had become momentarily overcome with guilt about her own actions, and sought to remedy her wrongdoings with random acts of kindness towards those she had victimised.

Mrs Rivers had been her usual sadistic self, and had singled a number of children out, Snowball included, for some particularly harsh treatment that day. It was not that they had done anything wrong of note, more that it was simply their turn for her attention, and as so many of them had become used to it, you simply tried to 'take your turn' with grace and an outward display of resilience. It was all psychological fuckery in the main, but Snowball had his limits, and today he was having none of it. Snowball had been beaten twice that day by Rivers, and the afternoon was still young. He had taken to playing in the front garden as it was the habit of Mrs Rivers to retire early afternoon into the back office, where she could both rest and keep a watchful eye over those playing out back, and any returnees from the school opposite.

Snowball had already decided that he was leaving that afternoon, he just had not decided where he was going, nor how he was going to get there. But the detail could wait. Chances were he was due another beating from Mrs Rivers that day, and so it may as well be for something he had actually done using his prevailing logic. It was all a matter of when he would go, but it was not that easy. The afternoon sun reflected against the windows at the front of Melbourne House, making it extremely difficult, if not impossible at times, to see who, if anybody, was watching his antics through the windows. He could take a chance and just saunter out of the gate, or over the fence, but he was all too aware that if he was being watched that would initiate an immediate response, and he would barely get to the end of the street. It was a problem, but not one that was insurmountable, as the gentle caress of fate feathered his brow and out walked Miss Greenhough, shift completed and heading wearily towards her blue MKI Escort in the staff parking area.

It all suddenly became very clear for Snowball, as he sauntered over to the downcast Greenhough and enquired as to whether or not she was finishing work for the day. Greenhough reluctantly confirmed that she was, albeit in such a tone as to make it perfectly clear to Snowball that it really was none of his fucking business, even though she had both flattered and dignified him with a response.

"Will you drop me at the end of the street in your car, and I will walk back?" he enquired. It was not an unusual request as many of the older children often did it, usually when a staff member had arrived in a new car they were interested in and wanted to check out. But it was unusual for Snowball, as one of the younger children, to ask and it immediately raised her suspicions. She eyed him up and down inquisitively and was clearly trying to mull over all possible outcomes that would ferment should she grant the request, but fatigue was getting the better of her at this stage, and she simply did not have the energy to be arguing with him.

"End of the street and straight back," she commanded, nodding her head towards the rear passenger door, and fumbling in her bag for the elusive set of car keys.

It was the break Snowball needed. The only break he needed. The sight of Greenhough shutting the car door behind him would allay any and all fears of the staff who may have been watching through one of the windows. Not only that, she was then going to drive him to the start of his journey, like the fool he had just taken her for. She duly fired up the car, slipped it into reverse, and gingerly pulled out of the parking space and into clear ground. Moments later, they were at the gates and within what seemed like seconds, they were heading down the street towards eternal freedom. Or so it appeared.

Greenhough pulled up at the end of the road, leaned over and flipped open the rear door, before pointing back towards Melbourne House and stating with an incisive authority, "Straight home". Snowball nodded in agreement and hit the pavement in a state of euphoria. All he had to do now was head back towards Melbourne House, until such time as Miss Greenhough had satisfied herself all was well and gone on her merry way home. He turned briefly, smiled, waved in her direction, and then broke into a light canter. He heard the grind of a gear stick as it painfully went from neutral and into first, before the still afternoon air was broken by the sound of her dropping the handbrake. He was seconds away from liberation, all that remained was for her to pull away and disappear. In a moment, he had stopped, turned and looked back up the street. She was gone, and he was free.

He walked gingerly back to the end of the street, looking right into the long cul-de-sac that was Princess Mews, before peering left and up Brookman Street into the distance. She was truly gone, and he was now free to roam, and the world was his oyster. All he had to do was head straight up the road to Long Meadow Gardens, and from there he could cross the park, make his way into town, heading in any direction he desired. So head for Long Meadow Gardens he did.

Long Meadow Gardens was full of a wide mosaic of shops, two restaurants, numerous bars, a post office, dry cleaners, many sweetshops, the police station, a newsagent and sadly the breaker of all hearts. It had taken him less than three minutes to reach the mouth of the dragon, before he turned confidently into the street, and surveyed all that was within eyeshot. The 247 bus was parked by the covered shelter and a police car had just left the station yard. There was a plethora of delivery vans, lorries and cars spread from top to bottom of the street. And then he heard it. Just the one sound of a horn as he glanced up the right-hand side of the road, casually taking in each and every car that was parked there. Again the horn sounded, and again, and again. He looked across to the left-hand side of the road, his eyes casually rolling over the parading vehicles, and completely failed to register the light blue MKI Ford Escort that was parked and facing him.

It took another loud and sustained toot of the horn, before his eyes eventually roamed back to where they needed to be and then suddenly glazed over in abject fear. It felt as if his heart had dropped out of his chest and hit the floor with a sickening thud, as though he had simultaneously been kicked in the stomach by a rodeo bull. He could see the offside door slowly opening, and then the top of Greenough's head, as she slowly manoeuvred her way out of her seat and rose to her feet.

Miss Greenhough, the Irma Grese of Melbourne House, was silently motioning him over, and she was not happy. Snowball knew there was no point in contesting her, in much the same way that he knew no words were required as he slipped under her arm, and through the open rear door she had propped in readiness for him. There was an expected slamming of the door shut, the grind of the gear as she pushed it into first, and the rattle of the handbrake, as once released, it slammed itself to the floor, and the car pulled away. Snowball was right about one thing that day, as her car pulled back into the grounds of Melbourne House. He was going to receive another beating, and it was for something he had done this time; he just had not guessed who the beating would come from.

FOOD FOR THOUGHT

Meal times at Melbourne House were never anything to write home about, which was a blessing really, as most of the children there weren't wanted at home, and any form of communication from them, would have been most unwelcome, and violently received. Meals generally served no other purpose, than that of filling a hole in the stomach, and Snowball soon learned that the taste of the inferior diet, was masked by most of the kids, with dollops of lumpy gravy, and ladles of foul tasting, thick density custard, on the rare occasions that a dessert was served. It was also the case that children were not only expected to be grateful for the inedible shit that was placed in front of them, but that they showed how grateful they were, by clearing every morsel from their plate, regardless of what it was.

Herein lay a problem for Snowball. His foster mother had always ensured that they ate well and that the availability of food was never an issue her children were ever aware of, with both meals and treats alike being welcomed by her often very hungry brood. There was also a great deal of flexibility in her willingness to pander to peculiarities, likes and dislikes, which she had come to find was the best way of ensuring that children ate healthily, if occasionally unwillingly. This methodology suited Snowball, who, while by no means a fussy eater, had a clearly defined set of likes and dislikes, in which he had been consistently indulged. They were, however, indulgences that Melbourne House felt they could ill-afford to pander to, regardless of their simplicity.

Thursday tea-time had arrived with the normal lack of fanfare, and Snowball had dutifully taken his place in the queue at the serving hatch to await his turn to be fed. There were no Olivers in this queue. No fucker ever asked for more, and each of them would have been delighted if there hadn't been enough food to go around, and they had been the 'unfortunate' one to miss out. It was, as usual, an unremarkable culinary experience that was placed before him, but as his outstretched hand reached the edge of the plate, and the contents suddenly became visible, he came to realise that every bit of the food had been covered in a thick swathe of unappealing, lumpy, brown cold gravy. It was everywhere, and he couldn't even see what the fuck was beneath it.

He peered up over the hatch, pausing as the face of Miss Bradwell appeared above the plate. "I don't want gravy," he muttered, as she held her face in quizzical quandary. She paused for a second, and was about to speak, when Mrs Rivers appeared to her side, and demanded Snowball take the plate he had been given to the table and sit down. He casually glanced back towards Miss Bradwell, who, moving her eyes sharply to the right, gave him a little knowing nod, that directed him away from the hatch. Snowball knew instantly what she was saying. He had seen that look and nod many times before, and she was telling him to avoid any trouble by moving along quickly. He took the hint, and was seated in seconds, though the unappealing meal remained untouched, as he then awaited permission to leave the table when the other children had finished eating.

Miss Bradwell ended up sat two tables away and directly facing him. Mrs Rivers seated herself to the rear of the room, in her familiar perch that afforded an unhindered view of the entire dining room, and everyone in it. Miss Bradwell could see the plate of uneaten food in front of Snowball, and on several occasions had cast him the same quizzical look she had thrown him at the serving hatch, before nodding her eyes downwards, in a carefully crafted silent instruction to eat. Snowball looked away on each occasion, and simply ignored her. The food was bad enough on its own, without having to plough through the unsightly gravy to get to it, and by this time he had quite frankly lost all will to eat, preferring to wait until the following morning for a cold breakfast if he had to. He could see the frustration building up in Miss Bradwell's face, but continued to ignore her silent pleas, as the thought of eating the unpalatable mess in front of him, emboldened his resilience. Yes, resilience. A great human trait when deployed appropriately in an enemy Prisoner of War camp, or under torture, but wholly misappropriated in the circumstance that Snowball currently found himself in.

In the course of time, Mrs Rivers duly gave her permission for everyone to leave the table if they had finished eating. Snowball, as with many of the others, was quick to his feet, plate in hand and heading to the serving hatch, where plates were wiped off into a nearby bin, before being stacked tidily on the servery, ready for washing. He had barely taken four or five steps, when he heard Mrs Rivers call out his name, and beckon him towards her with a finger. He took a momentary look across at Miss Bradwell, who threw him a knowing and somewhat disapproving 'I told you so' glance, before he headed over to Mrs Rivers, who was now calmly rising from her seat, with the fury of the devil's own in her eyes. "What is wrong with your tea?" She was curt and fiery faced. Snowball replied that it was covered in gravy, and that he didn't really like gravy. It wasn't strictly true, as it was an on/off romance, subject to the thickness, texture and general look of the offering, but on this occasion, contingent with the fact it was stone cold, it was a bang on appraisal of what he was looking at. Rivers took an open palmed swipe at his face, which narrowly missed, as her sudden movements caused Snowball to recoil backwards in anticipation. She reached out and grabbed his shoulder, before directing another blow that landed across the left side of his face and sent him sprawling to the floor.

He could see the rage in her face, as she demanded he scrape up the food that had fallen from the plate, and as he turned to do so, she landed a kick to his legs, that sent him spinning into the table opposite. He recomposed himself, before attempting for a second time to pick up the food, and place it on the plate, and again she directed a kick, that sent him sprawling. It was third time 'lucky' as he eventually got the food to the plate and rose to his feet to face Rivers. Her only word to him was "OFFICE", and Snowball knew exactly where to go, alongside having a pretty lucid idea what was to follow. He also knew there was no way out of the predicament, and he was aware from experience that, with Rivers, it was better to let her have her way, than it was to protest what was coming, and make it infinitely more unbearable than she was likely planning it to be.

Within seconds of arriving at the office, she was upon him. She had relieved him of the food as they had left the dining room, and brought it with her, along with a spoon from the cutlery tray, and a fucking bad attitude. Snowball was pulled into the office, and the door was slammed behind them. Rivers pulled a chair into the middle of the floor and sat him upon it. The plate of food, that had previously spent its time on the floor, was rammed into his hand, and while pulling a chair into position opposite him, she demanded that he eat. Snowball remained silent and motionless, neither looking at Rivers, nor motioning towards the food. Rivers raised her hand and struck him to the left side of his face. "EAT!" Snowball remained defiant, impassive, but afraid. In a further act of defiance, he deliberately dropped the spoon to the floor and attempted to stare her out. Again, she raised her hand, and struck the right side of his face, almost sending him crashing to the floor. "EAT!" He offered no response. Rivers struck him a third and fourth blow, again with no response. Her temper rising to boiling point, and about to lose control, blows five and six were landed with such force, that once again Snowball was sent crashing to the floor, where he remained, impassively staring at his abuser, but defiant in his refusal to eat. There was a method to the madness. He always knew he was going to get a beating – that was a cast in stone fact – but the eating was potentially optional if he held out long enough, and she boiled over sooner rather than later.

Rivers angrily brought him to his feet (this was becoming a habit). The grip around his arms, so tight that it left fingernail imprints in his fledgling bicep. She repositioned him on the chair and started again. "You are going to eat every bit of it, and we're not leaving this room until you do," she callously informed him, with an air of sadistic dominance he had become only too familiar with. If that was the case, and Snowball had his way, they would never be leaving. But Rivers was bigger, she was stronger, and she had all the time in the world. Snowball would never be able to match her, if for no other reason than the fact she also had sadism, brutality and a thick leather belt by her side, and she was willing to use it all. She pulled him across the floor, and in seating herself, wedged him in an upright position between her legs. She grabbed a handful of the food, and forced it into his mouth, as he struggled to free himself, and attempted to allay her attack. He was struggling to breathe, as the force of food being pushed into his mouth caused him to inhale deeply, and food to be ejected through his nose as she forcibly closed his mouth with her now open palm. As he momentarily found opportunity to open his mouth to take in air, she rammed in more food, forcing him to again swallow and choke. "EAT," she bellowed into his face, "EAT!" Her legs were tightening around his chest and stomach. Her face was etched in anger, and she was inadvertently forcing him to vomit everything that she had so subtly rammed into his mouth. She was on a roll, and nothing was going to stop her.

She reached down and took up a handful of the food he had just regurgitated onto the floor and forced it back into his mouth. Time and time again, he found himself gagging and choked, only for her to repeat herself, and force more of the slimy vomited stockpile back into his mouth. His eyes streamed and bulged, as she forcefully pummelled the food back into his mouth, and smeared it across his face, in an act designed to deliberately humiliate, as she overcame his defiance. She constantly repeated the word 'EAT' like it was some hippie mantra at a Manson Camp, as she first smeared him in the food, and then proceeded to slap his face wildly. She had lost control, completely lost control, and he was at her mercy, alone and in peril, as her onslaught continued, second after second, minute after minute. Time and time again he vomited, only for her to pick up the strewn liquified mess and force it back into his mouth. Prone on the floor and in a state of near exhaustion, he finally succumbed to her onslaught and ate.

It was moments later that Miss Bradwell appeared at the office door. Peering around the gap, she could see Snowball on the floor, arms lying forlornly by his side, face bloodied, and Rivers utilising a bent knee to pin him to the floor, as she force-fed him the remains of his own vomit from her hands. Bradwell, having seen all she needed to see, stepped forward, and in a sweeping motion that saw her cast aside Mrs Rivers like a ragdoll, picked up Snowball into her arms, and removed him to the safety of her sleeping quarters, before attempting to restore some calm and sanity to his troubled mind. It was a full fifteen minutes before his heart stopped pounding in his chest, and he returned to a semblance of physical normality. She popped him in the bath, and cleaned him up, before switching on the television, and telling him to remain in the room, until she came back for him. It wasn't an instruction she needed to repeat, nor one he would ignore on this occasion. He had made that mistake once already, and he wasn't about to have a re-run, so in the room he waited, before drifting off into a trauma induced sleep, only to find himself safely tucked up in his own bed later that night.

BLIND OF EYE AND
SHORT OF MEMORIES

Mr Rivers was as predatory sexually, as he was violent. His 'special trips' out for the girls were something that were often alluded to by the older kids, but nothing substantive ever seemed to be made of it. Shame and fear no doubt displaced notions towards justice and safety for many of the girls, alongside the threats of worse to come if they talked, and a constant air of intimidation. Who knows why they kept quiet, they just did. Quiet was what they all kept, and the cycle of child sexual exploitation continued unfettered by fear of unmasking or punishment. Maybe it was a fact of life at the times, but the care homes in which children were placed were rife with sexual predators, and they enjoyed unbridled access to their prey. Decades later, society would recoil in horror as the scale of historical sex abuse became known across the country, and its institutions, but it would be nothing more than surface level, cosmetic, faux disgust in the eyes of Snowball, and the many who either knew, witnessed or experienced it first-hand. Too little and too late. Many lives had been destroyed beyond repair, and there was no turning the clock back.

Society might express disgust, but what transpired in those homes, over decades, was known about and ignored. Inevitably, some girls would eventually break and report their abusers, only to be told they were promiscuous fantasists, tarts, slags, liars, deceitful and more, before being returned into the clutches of those whom they had reported and left to the vile attentions of what appeared to be an endless stream of state authorised abusers. Report after report ignored, and each time the victim returned to the hell from which they had tried to escape. Each time they were burdened with the guilt and shame, as a network of criminal co-conspirators conspired to hide the truth and propagate the continued abuse.

Across the country, there were thousands of lives ruined, shattered, destroyed, and lost, because society placed little or no value on the life of a child in care. The police, social services, government and judiciary, united in complicity with their blind eye approach to a national network of predatory males and females, who, without fear of reprisal, redress, or criminal accountability, sexually preyed on vulnerable and captive children, and Mr Rivers, by all known reckoning, was a prolific serial offender.

Girls were taken on 'trips' in his car, only to return hours later, tearful, distressed, bruised and hurt. They would be summoned to his family quarters, and be gone for hours, locked in a living hell that was also their home. He took and enjoyed full, unfettered access to his prey. His sexual deviancy was, in essence, officially sanctioned by the socio-cultural climate in which he expressed it. So many, and too many lives destroyed by a system that was supposedly set up to care for them. In many ways, it was the girls that had things tougher at Melbourne House. Exposure to sexual abuse was not a 'get out of jail free' card when it came to the physical punishments that were meted out daily. But they contended with both, as predatory males sought their presence for both pleasures and pains. There was also a great psychological pain for all to endure, upon seeing a solitary female child being taken from the group and marched away. The sense of pack being destroyed as one by one, the weakest amongst the group, were picked off by the predators that roamed their habitat. They all knew what was to transpire, and they were united in complete helplessness, or lack of understanding, and a pervasive sense of relief that today wasn't 'their turn'.

SELF-HARMERS
ONE AND ALL

There was a point at which Snowball came to understand that the harm done by others, could be, and was often matched and usurped by the harm done by oneself as a consequence. He had seen it too often not to know, and the only question in his mind was if or when the same fate would beset him.

Sharon was a seven-year-old from a broken home in the north of England. She shared a bedroom with three other girls directly opposite his and was known to regularly sit cross-legged on her bed at night, gently rocking herself to sleep, whilst she mumbled a strange chant, and slowly scratched weird shapes into her arms with pins she had collected throughout the course of the day.

Daniel was a prolific self-harmer, who would use razor blades to etch small slices into his skin. He would be found dripping in blood from the elbows down, and in a time where psychological help with a mental disorder failed to filter down to the unwanted and uncared for in society's children's homes, the solution to his problems was to beat him with a cane, until he swore blindly that he would stop, then await the penitent's relapse that would duly come with the passage of time.

Bobby was a serial arsonist in the making. Snowball was made aware that his penchant for self-harm was fire, masked as accidentally burning himself, whilst he set light to various objects, insects and small animals. Snowball had been duly advised to stay well clear of Bobby, but that was easier said than done, and in fact, by some weird quirk of fate, Bobby had become something of an occasional friend, when the requirement for alliances was in the air. He had been arrested on a number of occasions, taken from the home, and returned hours later, confession elicited by the police, and punishment by the staff outstanding for his return. Bobby disappeared one year just after bonfire night and was never really spoken about again. There was fevered talk of a spectacular fire being caused as a result of misuse of fireworks, and it was widely believed amongst the children that Bobby was responsible. Nobody really knew whether there was any veracity to the tale, but neither was there any evidence to refute the story, and so it pervaded.

Little Harold was an unfortunate boy, who had been given a crap name, before being beaten and shook so ruthlessly as a baby and toddler, that he had been left with a severe stammer, and a left eye that twitched constantly and seemed to wander around its socket at will, with scant regard for where Harold actually wanted it to be. Compounded by the presence of a mild southern accent, he was ripe for bullying, and often the butt end of jokes, from staff and children alike. He spent most of his time hidden away behind bushes in the garden, cupboards in the house, desks at school, and anywhere else that he felt he could domicile himself away from the constant torment and attention that he received. When he wasn't hidden away, Harold, like Bobby, was burning himself from head to toe with matches, and attempting to set various parts of the home alight, usually in the dead of night when most of the kids and staff were in bed, and as a result, having made it clear by his actions that they couldn't beat sanity and good behaviour into him, he would eventually be sent to a secure mental unit, and like his fiery counterpart Bobby, never seen again.

Andrea was a serial absconder. A troubled child who had befriended Snowball after his earlier arrival at Melbourne House. A street-wise kid, who had shown him the ropes, but not wise, or able enough to avoid the persistent physical and sexual abuse that came her way. She appeared to have no pretence to sexual shame, as she was older enough to know what was happening to her and others was wrong. Absconding was her response, closely followed by slicing symmetrical lines across her forearms and upper thighs with a razor blade, or more commonly a pen-knife. She had eventually graduated to scarring her face, after being overheard expressing the opinion that, as long as she remained ugly, they wouldn't want to touch her. She was wrong of course, but it was a belief that had given her momentary mental respite from the terrors of her daily life.

It was all a far cry from the safety and security Snowball had enjoyed with his foster mother. There was no way out of this veritable mess, and he quickly learned to adapt and survive. He lived without hope, without aspiration and without peace. Every day a fresh trial, a fresh abuse, and another day lost to the insidious creep of those who sought only to maximise his suffering and tear the heart out of him. Oh, for the long-lost days at home. Safe, secure and wanted. How times had changed.

STUPID LITTLE SAMBO

"Stupid little Sambo," she muttered as she slammed the door of the minibus shut and switched on the engine. The vitriol from Mrs Rivers was plain and spat from her lips with an enthused contempt for all to hear. They were running over five hours late, and she clearly wasn't happy. Her contempt was something that Snowball, like his peers, had over time learned to ignore, as the challenge, or dissent as she liked to call it, often brought with it a far harsher reality than the mere name calling in which she so readily chose to indulge. The latest verbal onslaught had been brought on by an incident on a nature walk that the Rivers had arranged in Alderley Edge. Mr and Mrs Rivers had loaded a few of the children into the minibus that morning, and with packed lunches in hand, and a small bag of sweets to share on the journey, they had set out on one of their day trips during the school summer holidays. Snowball was made aware that the trips had become increasingly unpopular over the years, as they were often an occasion that would set off from Melbourne House in the right spirit, but as the Rivers indulged in their widely known habit of drinking excessively when together, it was inevitable that things would turn sour later in the afternoon, and that some of the children would be routinely abused in one form or another, as a matter of course. The sight of the smiling faces of Mr and Mrs Rivers on departure was recognised solely as a prelude to something more sinister that would take place away from prying eyes.

The unwillingness of many of the girls on the trips, and the deathly silence that ensued as they were loaded into the minibus, and driven away by the Rivers, lent credence to the frequently aired rumours of sexually inappropriate behaviour by Mr Rivers, whilst the often, raw strap welts and raised marks across the back of many legs, served to highlight that Mrs Rivers had also indulged herself as a prelude to them arriving back at Melbourne House. It clearly wasn't always the case that such abuses took place, but the relative frequency with which children relayed the tales of their misery, only served to ensure that trips with Mrs and Mrs Rivers were something that you never dreamed of volunteering for, and tolerated only as a means of mitigating further punishment if you were chosen to go and were stupid enough to refuse the 'invitation'.

Snowball, still one of the youngest, had been chosen as one of the unfortunates on this occasion, and filled with as much apprehension as everyone else, had climbed into the aging green minibus and sat quietly in a window seat wondering what the day would eventually bring, and to what extent he would be involved. He knew Mrs Rivers hated him. He duly hated her. But she held all the power, and if she chose to make it so, his day away would quickly turn into a painful nightmare that he would wish was over quicker than it had started. Leachy had also been summoned to go along, which didn't bode well for him, as the hate and contempt Mr Rivers held for him was widely known, and routinely ended up in a beating of some sort. Barry Jones had also been brought along, which wasn't too unexpected as he was a firm favourite of Mrs Rivers, and if the talk was correct, used his athletic prowess to great effect in her bedroom, when Mr Rivers was away overnight, and she felt in need of some masculine company.

Mr Rivers hated him as much as he hated Leachy, if not more so. It was understood that their young son had once witnessed Barry coming out of their bedroom late one night, wearing nothing more than an erection, and subsequently passed some unwittingly infantile comment regarding the incident to his returning father, who had added two and two together, and for once, come up with exactly the right answer. But Mr Rivers had to sit out the marital deceit and humiliation, as Barry was effectively in a Witness Protection Programme, by virtue of his relationship with Mrs Rivers, and as such, was completely untouchable in her eyes. Jessica, Mary and Nadine silently occupied the remaining seats, as the bus of hate and misery trudged its way in a plume of ozone killing fumes across the North West, and headed for Alderley Edge.

They had arrived a short while later, and as lunchtime approached, and the nearby bars began to open, the Rivers had left Leachy and Barry in charge, and headed for the pub. The orders were clear. You don't leave the park, and you are back at the gates by three o'clock. It was in all likelihood a level of responsibility that neither Leachy nor Barry really anticipated, appreciated, nor wanted, but the reality was that they were all safe until at least three that afternoon, and as such, they should try and make the most of the brief period of pain-free liberty that had been granted to them, albeit burdened with accountability. They had all roamed and played freely for some time, when Leachy came across a football that appeared to all intents to be ownerless and abandoned. He organised an informal kick around by the woods, and they had all played happily, until Nadine, in a display of exuberant pique, had kicked out wildly at the ball, and sent it straight into the woods, and careering down the large unseen hill that lay across its upper boundary.

Snowball set about giving chase, and within seconds had found himself running completely out of control, down the large hill as he pursued the ball. The further he went, the faster his legs moved and the more out of control he became. Within seconds he came to realise the profound predicament that he was in, and it wasn't long before the outright speed of his upper torso, appeared to be moving at a considerably faster speed than his legs were capable of maintaining. It was only seconds after this, that the name Silver Birch Tree flashed through his mind, as he recalled a lesson Mr Hughes had conducted at school about the various types of tree that could be found in the British Isles. Yes, the name Silver Birch flashed through his mind seconds before the aforementioned tree made violent contact with his high-speed head, and his whole world began to spin. Snowball was down. Really down. Down down, and he wasn't getting up any time soon. Through a cloud of thick silent haze, he caught a fleeting glimpse of Barry arriving at his side, before his eyes closed, and his world descended into total darkness.

It was well over an hour before he finally opened his eyes again, only to find himself prone on a hospital bed, and surrounded by medical staff. He caught a passing glimpse of a furious looking Mrs Rivers in the background, before closing his eyes a second time, for a further two hours. When he finally awoke, and the haze had cleared, he could hear the nurses surprisingly arranging his discharge, and handing out instructions to Mrs Rivers, for his immediate care, once he got home. He would have preferred a stay in hospital, and they clearly didn't understand the regime from which he hailed, but Snowball was at least wise enough to feign continued drowsiness until he had arrived back at Melbourne House, and been put to bed, in order to avoid the beating that Mrs Rivers would gladly have administered, if she had the slightest inkling that he was well enough to take it. So, Sambo slept peacefully that night, Mr and Mrs Rivers drank away their miseries, and Barry had to make do with a quick wank under his blankets, instead of pleasuring his matronly conquest.

SO, I GUESS RACE
IS AN ISSUE

"**W**hat's a fucking Black Bastard, Miss?" Snowball asked inquisitively. There was a slight feign to ignorance about the word fucking, as it always brought a warm inner smile to him, when he managed to slip it into conversation, in such a manner as to avoid punitive rebuke. It didn't go unnoticed. The sharp tap to the back of the head in response wasn't designed to hurt, so much as it was to politely remind him that she had heard and dealt with it all before, and that it couldn't go completely unchecked. He was wise enough to both receive and acknowledge the sharp tingle around the back of his head without fuss and absorb the implicit message it conveyed accordingly.

"Who called you that?" came Miss Bradwell's calm, but guilt-edge razor sharp reply. "Nobody," he hastily retorted, finding himself in that oh too common position of having seriously dropped oneself in the proverbial 'it', or having to drop someone else in it, alone or alongside you. Sensing it was going pear-shaped, Plan B was to simply stroll away, and hope that in not calling him back, she had furtively decided to drop the matter. Miss Bradwell had an extremely sharp rasp when she wanted to make a point, and when she uttered the words, "You can stop RIGHT there", Plan B had just come to a grinding halt in the corridor. Snowball was out of options. She took him gently by the hand, and led him down the long corridor, and into the staff quarters that would be her home for the duration of her back-to-back night shifts throughout the upcoming week.

Visits here were usually the prelude to a whimsical beating by a member of staff, the severity of which was determined only by knowing who had in fact summoned you. The message would usually come from another child, who, after their own beating, would be told to 'send child X to me next' and they would tearfully convey the message, to the now equally distraught recipient, before seeking solace amongst the other children, who in equal measure shared their torment, as they had no idea if or when they too could receive a summons. It was later referred to as the Conveyor Belt Beatings where you hadn't seen a Cuddly Toy, Dishwasher, Children's Bike and a Holiday Voucher for your family, but instead you had seen the output of a twelve-stroke caning across the front and back of Susan Jones' legs, and Jonathon Perry's face slapped raw, Snowball's belt-bruised back, because the red wasn't showing up through the brown skin, and much more, if only you had the stomach to look.

However, in that respect Snowball was in a safer pair of hands, if not entirely safe. Miss Bradwell had limits that you couldn't breach, but they were so far over the horizon, nobody he knew of had ever travelled that far and met them. Bradwell was well known amongst staff and children alike, in regards to her reluctance to participate in, and her total abhorrence at the presence of, such institutionalised and ritualistic brutality. The remaining staff saw her as a clear and present threat. They could collectively defend against any allegation coming from a resident child, and ultimately, if required, they could beat a retraction from that child with relative ease. Mr Hughes at the school had undertaken such a task several times, and he had always survived any inquiry.

But another staff member was different. They needed her cooperation, complicity and participation desperately, in order to close the circle of abuse, and strengthen it from within, but she wasn't playing ball, and they couldn't change her. As a consequence, she was regarded as an outsider amongst the adults, picking up more of the disliked duties, including nightshifts, hospital appointments, school visiting and much more. They were dangerous times for all concerned. This staffroom Mexican Stand-Off however had a further detrimental consequence for Snowball and his peers. It wasn't uncommon for members of staff to brutally punish children in the absence of Miss Bradwell, on the pretence that Miss Bradwell had indeed herself, before leaving for home, forgotten to administer the punishment for some perceived transgression earlier in the day. It was an attempt to somehow manufacture a vicarious liability on her behalf, but the children knew Bradwell too well, and rarely, if ever, was the pretence believed.

She sat him on the end of the bed, and calmly asked again. He remained silent. He was fretful of the consequences he had encountered on previous visits to the staff quarters with other members of staff, although he was also well aware that Miss Bradwell was cut from a different cloth, and he desperately wanted to tell her. Miss Bradwell had never struck him, nor any other child to his knowledge, but he was in no position to extrapolate her passivity in regard to discipline. "You're not in any trouble, but I need to know," she whispered almost silently, as he gazed nervously at the floor. "Lots of people" came the response, as a solitary tear began to slowly trickle down his face. She retook his hand in hers and raised his chin upwards.

She was a woman who had an extraordinary calming effect on all the children. In tense times, when children were at their most vulnerable, she was the one who could be relied upon to bring balance to mental turmoil. To bring the calm they all desperately needed from time to time. Snowball succumbed to this hypnotic charm, and recanted all she needed to hear. Blackie, Nigger, Black Bastard, Sambo and Golliwog (remember this isn't racist according to white people who were never called it), Black Jack (after the sweets of course), he had been called them all, and he had been called them often. He was unsure of whether he should 'get back to Africa or wherever he came from', or 'get back on his jam jar', where by all accounts, golliwogs resided, such was the contradiction in the abuse that he suffered. It was frequently a generic retort to anything he said to some people. Tagged onto the end of whatever reply they had conjured up with their fledgling or stunted intellects. Hostile, intimidating and abusive. He would hear far worse during the course of time, face greater hostility, and rise above it. But these were troubling times for him, as he struggled to establish an identity in hostile, oppressive, abusive and very, very 'white' times.

Apart from the Smithers twins, he had never encountered the issue of race in any negative form prior to arriving at Melbourne House. Indeed, back at his parents' home, being different skinned had always been a positive advantage. Affectionately known as Grandad's Little Snowball, he had enjoyed being in the spotlight in such a warm and positive way. But this was different. This was hostile, oppressive and it was intimidating. He was ill-prepared to navigate his way around or through this issue, and on many occasions, had succumbed to the intent of the oppressive abuse. Miss Bradwell was at pains to explain that he was just the same as anyone else. An enlightened individual for the times, she reassured him that the colour of his skin was neither a point for the amusement or hate of others, nor was it a point of which he should be personally ashamed. But these were not enlightened times, and there wasn't an abundance of black skinned people around to share the concerns, or troubles with. Fact was, he knew he was different, but he hadn't realised that it could be used to his detriment.

Racism had reared its ugly head, and so began a lifetime of struggle on the frontlines of the battle of equality.

For many an antagonist, his colour was their own way out of oppression. He was small in comparison to most, fragile even, vulnerable and without the help of his protector Leachy, he was largely defenceless. He was easy prey for those more linguistically volatile, and physically gifted than he was. Miss Bradwell wouldn't always be there as she had often promised, and he was inevitably going to have to defend this one alone. Life became a very isolated endeavour. There was a fear of his carers on one side of the equation, and the fear of his peers on the other. There was nowhere to turn, nowhere to run. How he longed for the umbrella of sibling care back home with his mother, before their forced separation. Surviving was hard enough at Melbourne House, without attempting to exist alone and without friends. It boiled down to fight or flight, and flight hadn't worked out well on previous occasions. Easier to face up to a bully than visit Mrs Rivers in her quarters, he would muse. When you arrive at the junction on the Road to Damascus, you'll be surprised to find a very clear road sign. It was time to toughen up.

RACISM AND VIOLENCE
LET BATTLE COMMENCE

There is a subtle problem with isms (racism, sexism, no brain-ism) and violence, that perpetrators rarely seem to grasp. In their pursuant zeal to make someone else a victim, and deflect negative attention from themselves, they rarely recognise that, in principle, what they are actually, in fact, telegraphing to the immediate world that surrounds them, is that violence and intimidation is ok, making victims of people is ok, hate and prejudice is ok. Now if you are the biggest lion in the pride, that can be pretty cool for you and the immediate 'family and friends' you hold dear. In essence, your jive-arsery and generalised muther-fuckery will go unchallenged. But there can be only one (yeah, I watched Highlander as well), and this provides something of an intellectual conundrum, for those lacking the intellect to understand the dynamics at play. The normalisation of racism, and the associated violence that was so prevalently sidled up alongside, had a habit of back-playing to those very same people who had cosied up alongside it. As they made victims of others, so in turn did they become victims. Now it wasn't all racism, but they assisted in ushering in the principle, and thus, for them, their big nose, or red hair, became the black skin equivalent that Snowball had to bear.

Snowball was happily playing football on the basketball court. He was recovering from illness and had been kept away from school for a few days, which served the purpose of both protecting others from his germs, and the staff from any overly inquisitive enquiries as to why he was carrying so many bruises. Now well on the road to recovery, it was deemed that the fresh air would 'do him good' and so outside he went. He practised long and hard, running from one end of the court to the other, attempting to hit the central metal upright that constituted the net, and claim an imaginary goal that could potentially send him into raptures. Like most other boys his age, he aspired to be a footballer, but the fact was, he was awful, if you were being polite, fucking dreadful if you weren't. Often the last to be chosen, when it came to the arbitrary process of picking sides, he often found himself put into the 'nets' by the older boys, as a means of keeping his ill-coordinated feet and legs, which had been disconnected from his brain, as far away from the football as was physically possible, without actually just telling him to simply fuck off, and play somewhere else because he wasn't wanted. As a result, his footballing 'skills' stagnated at Melbourne House. Sure, he was a Wembley Legend in his own mind, but he just didn't cut the mustard with his peers and elders. He arrived with poor footballing skills, and he failed to maintain that standard most of the time. In the general scheme of things, he knew he was shit at football, and was upset about it. But as time passed by, he started to see being shit as a challenging aspiration in terms of the development of his skills, as he fell further and further behind the other kids on the pitch.

After scoring a prolific solo effort, from at least 'fifty' yards away, he glanced up in his celebrations, and in the distance caught sight of the older boys, crossing the fields on their return from school. Their return was often a mixed bag of blessings, misfortune and violence. One the one hand, he would be jokingly informed of the day's antics, and made to feel part of the group, as stories of who had done and said what to whom, who had been caned, and who had been given the slipper were relayed to all within earshot and willing to listen. There would be the obligatory tale of who had gotten a glimpse of Miss Bowes' knickers in PT, and whether or not Mr Hughes had gone apoplectic at anyone during assembly. But on the other hand, he knew that it signalled the complete end to his on-court domination of the ball, and that soon he would be domiciled, exactly where he belonged, and where his lack of skill-set demanded, in his 'beloved' nets, or worse still, watching from behind the dining room window, having been completely rejected as a potential team member, having been given short shrift with the back of someone's hand. It was all very routine, with half the fun of their daily return, finding out what had transpired, and of late, whether Mrs Keeney the school 'Matron', and a woman fond of fondling the penises of the older boys under the guise of a 'cough and drop' health check, had satisfied her almost daily predilection for meat and two veg. He always enjoyed that first hour after the older boys returned, as although he wasn't really part of their crowd, they were often in need of a willing audience, and for that purpose alone, he and many others would do nicely. The older boys rarely if ever had time to indulge him or the youngest of the group, but during that first hour, when tales of bravado and 'derring do' were in plentiful supply, they were all on an equal footing, all welcome, all avid listeners, who knew when to laugh and exactly how hard.

He could hear some of the jocularity as they neared home. There were sporadic outbursts of laughter. He could see some of them gesticulating as they described what they had done, or what they had witnessed. These times were few and far between. Times when everyone presented as happy, jovial, free from fear and anxiety. The air filled with childish mirth and humour. Carefree times, when they appeared to be 'normal' kids.

The boys were meant to walk round to the front of the house, and enter through the gate off the main driveway, but they rarely did, choosing instead the perils of being caught climbing over the rear fence, which was in a failing state of repair and would bring on the wrath of a housemother if ever they were caught. They had been warned often enough and ignored the warnings in equal measure. One by one, they climbed the fence, jumped from the top onto the grass below, and then made a dash to the concrete court, often seen as the place of safety and refuge, as once there they could claim to have arrived from a number of places, none of which included climbing over the dilapidated fencing. As usual, Leachy was always last to arrive on court. The coolest of characters by a country mile at Melbourne House, and in reality, probably the toughest. He was the one who would casually climb the fence, drop to the grass below, and then stroll in a defiant 'I don't give a fuck' fashion to the court, caring little for who might see him, or indeed the consequences. As such, he was a revered character. Not to be fooled with, though never to be emulated as the consequences could be dire. Regardless, Snowball was happy to call him his friend.

As was demanded and expected by his lack of status, Snowball relinquished control of the court and the tatty football he had been kicking around for the last hour or so, and adopted his familiar position on the side-lines, to await the draft. He had quickly come to understand that it was a game of numbers. Excluding himself, if the sum of the assembled group was an odd number, he was in the game (needed but unwanted). An even number meant he was surplus to requirements (a popular and often organised outcome), and unless someone was called away for a beating, or otherwise, he wasn't playing football that evening.

Seven, eight, nine, ten. The dejection was written all over his face. Then he heard Leachy boom. "Come on, darkie, you're on my side." He looked up and caught sight of Leachy rising from the floor. He had miscounted, as Leachy had been hidden by the rest of the boys, as they had circled and began the pick. His face lit up, as Leachy pointed towards the goals. He didn't need telling about the goals as it was the only position they would allow him to occupy most of the time, bar the few occasions he had been brave enough to moan about his lot in life and been given an outfield position to pacify him. However, on this occasion, the goals would do nicely, and without further ado, the game duly commenced. Snowball made some prolific saves that day. Well, not so much saves, as great shots hit him, and bounced back into the field of play, to the chagrin of the attackers. Time after time, he seemed to be living a charmed existence, with regards to placing his body in just the right place, to be punishingly hit by the stinging football. But then came that inevitable clang, as the ball hit the hollowed-out metal upright, signalling that the first goal had been scored. Here we go he thought to himself, retrieving the ball, and gingerly rolled it back into play. Within seconds there was another clang, followed by another, and another. His team had gone from actively competing in the game, to four-nil down in less than ten minutes, and strange though it appears, they weren't happy.

"You FUCKING USELESS NIGNOG." The words rolled casually out of the mouth of Smithy, as he retrieved the ball from the backfield, after yet another goal. Snowball ignored the slight. Not that he wanted to, but Smithy was a big lad in comparison, and there was no way he could challenge him on any level. Ball in hand, Smithy walked back to the court, and in passing Snowball suddenly jutted out his elbow, catching him painfully on the bridge of the nose. Again, Snowball ignored the slight, as his eyes watered up and the game recommenced. Another goal, another slight, then a kick and a punch. Smithy was pushing it.

"Get off the pitch, you fucking Golliwog" came the chant from Smithy, accompanied by laughter from his immediate circle of closest 'friends'. However, what Snowball heard was, 'you might not win the fight, but always let them know you were in it'. His 'brothers' were clearly with him. What followed next was an ill-fated and comical attempt to bring Smithy down. Snowball launched into a rugby style tackle around Smithy's knees, fully expecting him to fall to the ground, where he would be the unwilling recipient of the pummelling he deserved. Predictably, Smithy at fourteen years old to Snowball's seven, stayed upright and rigid, as Snowball slowly slid slowly down his right leg, and onto the concrete court by the penalty spot. Quite apt, as he was about to pay the penalty for his abject foolishness. It was about this moment, that Snowball had the mental image of his brothers leaving the arena in disgust flash before his eyes, and subsequently realised that he was, in fact, all on his own.

Smithy back-heeled him in the stomach, knelt across his upper chest and lower neck, and began to punch him around the head and face. The stinging rasps adding injury to insult, as Snowball rapidly succumbed to Smithy's dominant strength and aggression. He could feel a slight trickle of blood start to run from his nose, and down the side of his cheek as Smithy, first relented, then continued his assault, upon realising that his prey had not been fully subdued. Snowball tried to cover his face, but it was pointless. The greater strength invoked by Smithy, meant that his punches simply forced their way through his defences, and landed exactly where they were intended. This wasn't an earlier version of Muhammad Ali's famed 'rope a dope' strategy, this was a one-sided beating, and as plain and simple as it can get.

However, simultaneous to Smithy ceasing his attack, came the traumatised shrill of "Fucking Hell". Indeed, Snowball thought, as he gazed upwards from the floor. Leachy was now stood above him, right hand outstretched, and motioning for him to get up. While pre-occupied with the attack on the unfortunately brave Snowball, Smithy had failed to see Leachy circling in the background awaiting his moment. When that time came, Leachy had unleashed a ferocious kick into the face of the inattentive Smithy, who was now rolling across the floor, holding his face and screeching wildly, as blood poured from his nose. Smithy, meet Karma.

Leachy helped pull Snowball to his feet. "You alright, Sambo?" he beamed, ushering him back towards the goals. "You need to pick on someone your own size, Smithy" came the next retort, as Smithy, now on his feet, chest fluffed up, and looking to save face amongst the assembled horde, slowly re-took to the field of play, while attempting to stem the tide of claret running from his shattered nose and split lip. Stupid as it was, Snowball took another lunge at Smithy, but was held up in the air, legs flaying wildly, by the now bemused Leachy. "Save it for another time, Blackie, today is not the day," Leachy mumbled, with an air of superior indifference that typified his outwardly calm demeanour when things actually kicked off.

He placed Snowball in the nets, and gently slapped him across the back of the head. "Enough" being his only word, as he swept up the ball with his left hand and kicked it back into play. "Next goal wins," he commanded, and the punctuated game recommenced. It was inevitable that Snowball would let the next goal in and bring the game to a timely halt depending on which side you were on. But the goal went 'unpunished'. There were no histrionics from Smithy, no need for Snowball to demonstrate how well he could take a kicking, and they all gathered their belongings from the side-line, and headed into the house. Time for Snowball to reflect on another day, his peculiar friendship with Leachy, and the need to adopt a better strategy when it came to dealing with boys who were clearly much bigger, and more able, than he was. As much as he would enjoy the protection afforded him by Leachy, he knew that Leachy wouldn't be there all the time to look after him. Soon he would need to fend for himself, and the sooner he learned that lesson, the better.

At just under eight years old, Snowball was coming of age in care home terms. The wafer-thin blanket of protection afforded by age was becoming thinner and thinner. The wolves were trailing, and the vultures circled. He couldn't afford to stumble or fall. He had a lot to learn. He needed to grasp the fundamentals of identity, aligning himself to a group, the saliency of group dynamics, and the potency of hierarchy. The veneer of protection, rubbed over him by the likes of Miss Bradwell and Leachy, was giving way to the realisation that if he was to survive, alone and standing on his own two feet, he had to adapt and be able to establish and defend himself in the eyes of his peers, or he was clearly doomed.

Slight of build and of a fragile, weak disposition, he was clearly at a disadvantage, both physically, and ethnically. But, as he found with Leachy, ethnicity could be turned into an advantage. There was novelty value in having a 'black' mate. It was unusual for most people he came across, and if he could use it wisely, it could easily become his salvation. And so, his learning curve commenced. Under the constant threat of racial intimidation and daily assault, he became the politician he needed to become. An occasionally vocal diplomat, forging partnerships and alliances throughout Melbourne House. He started at the top and worked his way down. He formed friendships at every level of the perceived hierarchy that there was. He created bonds by occasionally fighting alongside others, always mindful that the bigger picture justified the short-term pains that were often inflicted. Even amongst the staff, he became known as an operator. Rueful respect being gained by the manner in which he would navigate the troublesome waters in which he lived. His sharp wit and acidic tongue afforded him many visits to the punishment room, with a caning becoming commonplace, but he was in the fight, and letting them know. Tony and Harry would have been proud, if not a little surprised, at the enthusiastic abandonment with which he undertook the task.

As time passed, he began to see race as less and less of an issue. He had turned certain corners, and established an identity, a place in the hierarchy, a sense of self and group that would serve to insulate and protect him against the harshest of encounters. He had allies. Mutual self-defence alliances had been formed. He was, in every essence, a gang member in all but name. Sure, he wasn't a signed up member of The Crips, but he had transitioned from having the world against him, to being part of it. Safer, less fretful, protected and happier. More friends, fewer enemies. Now all he had to do was get through childhood. What could possibly go wrong.

CHRISTMAS TIME, NO MISTLETOE OR WINE

There is always a point at which you realise that violence, abuse, intimidation, fear, is often an organised, systematic and deliberately destructive strategy. For Snowball, this always became apparent at Christmas time. In contrast to the joyous, fun filled Christmases he had experienced with his foster parents, yuletide at Melbourne House was always a sombre affair, generally lacking in goodwill to all men, let alone children, and with a marked absence of any Christmas spirit, bar that which Mrs Rivers guzzled. But there was one notable exception that was adhered to by most of the staff, which also lent itself very well to the idea that their violence and abuse was proactively organised, rather than situationally reactive.

Staff behaviour at Christmas mellowed. It was more an unwritten rule than enforceable policy, and not universally applied, but the abuse invariably seemed to stop, the intimidation disappeared, and the beatings would generally come to a sudden halt, with the canes, slippers, plimsolls and straps, the ever-present instruments of oppression, sent into a semi-retirement for the period of the festivities. Why, he would wonder, so much misery and hurt had been inflicted in the name of discipline, in the name of maintaining order, and yet, at the drop of a hat, or the whim of the Rivers, that could all disappear, because it suited them. Because it was Christmas. Maybe, he would wonder, just maybe it was nothing to do with discipline at all. Perhaps it was all simply to do with the pleasure of inflicting pain and misery upon a captive and defenceless prey. Yes, Christmas at Melbourne House was a decidedly sombre affair, but welcomed by most as a period when they could at least relax a little, drop their guard, and get through the course of a week, free from abuse, free from fear, free from the saliency of suffering.

THINK QUICKLY, TALK SLOWLY, SNOWBALL

When it came to stars shining through the darkness that was life, Miss Bradwell was a rare breed, in troublesome times. Snowball had never seen, or heard of her striking a child, nor was she the sort to raise her voice, believing that a quiet word in a secluded corner, was eminently more effective than ripping her own larynx from her throat by bellowing at someone, who in essence was probably going to ignore her. She was, however, by no tangible means, averse to waving her floppy plastic-soled slipper at you, as a warning to be heeded, that things could imminently change should you not cease and desist, from whatever misdeed she had interrupted. Most children took the occasional liberty, as the chances of Miss Bradwell resorting to beating a child was slim to zero in the eyes of most, and as Snowball had once overheard, 'she probably wouldn't hurt you anyway'.

However, confidence in check, the possibility that she might was often enough to deter both the foolhardy and the bravest alike, as she pointed a slender finger towards you with one hand, waved her slipper with the other, and verbalised a straight forward and direct warning loud and clear for all to hear. Snowball had been the recipient of this spectacle, on more than one occasion, smiled back, and wandered away, to conduct mischief out of sight, and therefore, in his eyes, out of mind. However, as with most liberties taken, there is an unquantifiable, and somewhat randomly applied force called karma, that usually has the final say, and generally at a time when it is least expected, and most unwanted.

With three previous warnings unheeded, having two friends holding your arms for stability, while you Kung-Fu kicked the fire doors at the rear of the house had seemed like a very reasonable pastime for a young Snowball, awaiting the regularity of the clockwork call to tea. Out of sight, out of mind. What could possibly go wrong? Well, numerous things in hindsight, the most palatable of which was Miss Bradwell leaning out of the upper floor window, and politely requesting that you attend the private chat she has just organised. Snowball looked around, uncertain as to whether or not she was talking to him, only to realise that his cohorts had scarpered upon hearing the window open, and Miss Bradwell following up on her request with a polite and dignified "yes you" and another finger pointing in his direction. Friends are not all they are cracked up to be, a lesson Snowball had just been taught, and the fun hadn't even started.

It was a long slow walk of penitence, but in Snowball's mind, it hadn't taken anywhere near enough time as he would have liked, and two flights of stairs later, he was confronted with the sight of Miss Bradwell, casually propping the door to the upstairs landing open for him. As he walked beneath her outstretched arm, he heard a calm, but clinical "Follow me", her words hitting home hard, as she strolled nonchalantly towards the staff quarters. Snowball's mind was racing. She had to be kidding, right? Right! RIGHT! Oh, for fucks sake! Holding open the remaining door between relative safety, and a probable painful embrace in the staff quarters, she tilted her head towards the open space, indicating that it might be within his best interests to enter, and see what was coming.

Snowball heard the door close behind them, and her footsteps slowly move towards him. He turned around, just in time to see her stretching out her hand, and taking hold of his upper arm, swiftly seating herself on the edge of the bed at the same time, and pulling him towards her, with a cold indifference that he had never witnessed in her before. It was getting decidedly frightening, and the tension was palpable. He could feel his chest becoming congested with the familiar tinge of fear, as the words from her mouth faded into deafening silence, though strangely as he would recall later, he remained perceptive enough to notice that this seemed to be the only room in the entire home that had wallpaper on the walls, comprising a pretty floral-mosaic of red and blue flowers, punctuated by what appeared to be golden stems and cascading green leaves. However, his focus wandered only slightly from the fear that was now welling up inside him, and which would imminently come flooding through his tear ducts, as the tension became overwhelming, and the gravity of his situation became oh too real. If there was a time to think quickly, this was the moment. The predicament was upon him. Think quickly, speak slowly, Snowball.

"How many times have I told you today, about kicking that door?" she asked, pausing only to slip the wooden sandal she was wearing from her foot, and casually place it on her lap. "Twice," replied Snowball, transfixed by the sight of the imminent painful misery that she had quite deliberately placed before him. "How many times have I told you today, about kicking that door?" she repeated. Snowball paused, and with great reluctance came the reply he knew she wanted to hear. "Three times," he mumbled. "So, what do you think we should do about it?" she queried, taking a visibly firmer grip on the sandal.

The mind game wasn't lost on Snowball. She was at least 3-0 nil up at this point, but he did consider it a pretty dumb question. He was hardly going to request that she take the much-feared wooden sandal and beat the crap out of him, but he knew that he needed an answer, and "I don't know" seemed as good as any, as the words tumbled uncontrollably from his mouth, and his eyes once again began to well up. It's now 4-0, and Miss Bradwell is on a roll. It was at this point that he was beginning to realise that Kung-Fu wasn't really his thing at all.

The tears were now free-flowing down his face, as he heard Miss Bradwell reply, "I have an idea – do you want to hear it?" He remained eyes cast down, one eye on the floor, the other on the painful menace held firmly in her lap, while he contemplated her second stupid question of the afternoon. It wasn't really going well at all, and emotionally he was now a wreck, not least because it was Miss Bradwell that he had upset and brought to this situation (5-0). Miss Bradwell, the only woman in the entire home who had brought him unconditional happiness, treated him properly, and cared for him as she should have. 'Of course, I don't want to hear it,' he thought, the nuance of her asking the question completely lost in the turmoil that rampaged through his mind. She countered his silence with an opening salvo of, "Well, I can put this sandal across your bare backside a few times...or–" (6-0). Snowball took a deep breath and resigned himself to a painful encounter, unable to control the tears that now streamed down his face. Bradwell was on a double hat-trick. "Or, I can give you one last chance, to do as you're told, and listen to what I am telling you," she told him, as she released her grip of the sandal, and with a casual indifference dropped it to the floor in front of him, before slipping it loosely onto her foot.

This was the point that Snowball first realised that tears of misery and tears of joy were exactly the same. They look the same, tasted the same, ran down your face the same, leaving the same damp patches on your t-shirt, the tell-tale sign of which was that you perhaps weren't as tough as you thought you were. Think Fast! "Yes, Yes, Yes" came the internal shout, bouncing around the inside of his skull, like a pinball. Talk Slow! "Soooooorrrrrrryyyyyyyyyyyy" was his long, slow, singular offering, as she took his hand, and pulled him closer. "You have to learn to do as you're told; you stand out, and people are looking for you, and wanting you to trip yourself up, that's why they hit you so much," she told him. There was a protective tone to her voice, that resonated within Snowball, transforming his tears of relief, into a focussed fixation on the words that were flowing from her mouth. "You might not be here long, you are a very clever boy, but you have to be careful. Do you understand what I am telling you?" He nodded, although he wasn't completely certain, but he had picked up on the key words, and added the contextual meaning himself. "I can't be here to watch out for you all the time – you have to smarten up." By now she was on her feet, and shuffling her foot firmly into the sandal that had threatened so much, and delivered so little, while still getting the job done. It had been a resounding victory. There was no extra time, no penalties, no refereeing controversy. Miss Bradwell had won (the fuckery of some women). "Wipe your eyes, then go and get your tea," she told him, holding the door ajar, as he slipped slowly under her arm, and headed for the stairs. At the head of the stairs, he paused briefly, turning towards her to see a wry smile sweep across her face, as she wagged her finger in the direction of the stairs, gesturing for him to be on his way. He smiled back, then disappeared into the stairwell. Lesson learned, experience gained, friend found. Live, learn, move on.

Snowball had learned a valuable lesson, and in the process, realised that he had a priceless friend. As time moved slowly on, and weeks passed to months, and months to years, he learned to confide in Miss Bradwell, to seek sanctuary with her, sheltering under the umbrella of protection that she afforded him. In troubled times, he would seek her out for comfort or knowledge, and in response she would find some isolated spot, where he could spend a few lonesome, unhindered and uninterrupted hours, drawing, reading, playing, or just buried deep his own thoughts. It was the ideal scenario for him. Protected space, relief from the torments and tribulations of everyday life. She found time and space for him to grow, to learn, to understand, and to be himself. There was time to smile, time to rest, time to feel and understand his feelings. She facilitated mental and physical growth, and best of all, there was no charge levied. He paid no penalty, his only commitment being to listen, learn from her, and move on as a better informed and more experienced child than he was. With his respect for her deepening, it soon became the case that explaining to Miss Bradwell the beating that had been inflicted upon him by another member of staff, was far more painful than the beating itself, whether he felt there had been any justification or not. Her words of rebuke and overt annoyance often cutting harder and deeper than any cane or strap ever could. Her upset, sense of being let-down, hurting more than any other had hurt, as his sense of commitment and responsibility towards her expectations grew daily. Though the daily ritual of physical and mental abuse continued at Melbourne House, Snowball, under guidance, began to learn to circumvent as much as was humanly possible, and stay aloof from the fray. Miss Bradwell provided a welcome cloak of protection, and much needed respite, but she wasn't there all the time, and he had to learn to make himself invisible, and remain relatively inobtrusive when he couldn't.

BOBBY AND KEVIN
BROTHERS IN ARMS

Bobby and Kevin were two firmly built, athletic looking brothers, who had arrived at Melbourne House just over a year before Snowball, Kevin being the older by two years, and both in their teens. They were closely bonded siblings, from a troubled background that had seen them brought into care at an early age. Kevin provided the umbrella of safety and security for Bobby, in much the same way that Miss Bradwell afforded it to Snowball, and would often be seen using his athletic prowess to defend his younger brother from harm or intimidation, as they seemingly cruised through life at Melbourne House together, relatively unhindered.

Though they were friends in the main part, Snowball always harboured a deep envy of Bobby, as having someone like Kevin looking after your interests, minute by minute, hour by hour, and day by day, and willing to step in and defend you, was something he could only ever dream of. For sure, he had Miss Bradwell, and there was always Leachy, but they weren't there all the time, like Kevin was for Bobby. They were never seen apart, and as a result, Bobby's life was much easier than that of most in Melbourne House. Kevin was envied by most. His physical prowess meant that he had no natural predators amongst the wildlife that preyed on the vulnerable in Melbourne House. All Kevin had to contend with was the abusive tendencies of the staff, and their systematic and ritualistic abuses, of which, like everybody else, he would have to take his turn at receiving.

Kevin was also a boy of immense mental strength, given the struggles that he and Bobby had overcome. He towered above people mentally, and stood out from the crowd, with his outwardly calm disposition that oozed confidence and experience, without appearing cocky, or conceited. There was no chip on his shoulder, and he was often the person that had the right soothing word, at the right moment, or would casually place a reassuring hand on the shoulder of some troubled child. Kevin was a short-term protector. Never in it for the long haul, but he would occasionally let it be known, that for a few hours at least you were under his wing, and as a consequence, relatively untouchable. He was a boy to be envied in every sense. Impervious to most of the strife that life was throwing at him, intelligent, popular, and respected, as far as respect amongst your peers goes. Kevin was the 'daddy' to most. It was as simple as that.

Bobby simply sauntered along under the protective glow that radiated his way from Kevin, his bright blonde hair always visible, close to his brother's side. Wherever you found Kevin, it was a certainty that Bobby would be in the immediate vicinity. Kevin had trained Bobby well. Unlike other sibling groups that Snowball had encountered, being the younger protected one had never gone to Bobby's head. He used his brother's counsel and protection wisely, and avoided actively seeking out or engaging in trouble, regardless of the fact that he had protection. Snowball and Bobby were very much alike. They were learners, observers, social navigators. An unusual eclectic mix of untypical characteristics, that made for a curious personality, which resulted in a certain degree of enigmatic charm. They were both young in years and in the process of developing a much wiser perspective on life, as they faced the daily challenge of survival amongst the pack. They were never to be seen at the front, nor the back, with both successfully striving to remain invisible to the stalking pack that viewed them as potential prey.

The only real issue with Kevin and Bobby was that they were both serial absconders, and arsonists, needing no excuse for their behaviour, which in fairness was entertaining to most, but nonetheless a blight on their characters as far as the law was concerned. It was their hobby, and they were good at it. When Snowball absconded, he was gone a few hours. When the brothers absconded, they were gone days and sometimes weeks, with their fire-raising skills ensuring that they never returned cold. It was this facet of their behaviour that provided many with the tales of daring escapades, which brought light and entertainment into what were otherwise drab, boring and oppressive lives. Kevin had a way of telling a tale that captivated all those who listened. Bobby was like a small but eager bit part player, always on the periphery, waiting on a pause from Kevin, so that he could interject with some tale of perceived bravery, which in most instances was either patently untrue, or treated with a level of contempt and indifference that would have deterred most from continuing in the same vein. But Kevin was his brother, and so, as the crowds were regaled, Bobby was patiently tolerated.

NEVER FORGET,
PATIENCE IS FINITE

As with most good acts, there comes a time when they have unfortunately been on far too long. Miss Bradwell had pulled Snowball to one side and warned him away from his continued and overt friendship with Bobby, and by vicarious default Kevin, as in her words, 'things were going to change, and soon', and she didn't want him 'wrapped up in it all'. She had taken him by the arm, turned him around and stared him straight in the eyes, before uttering the words "trust me". Snowball knew that was her way of ensuring that the importance of the message was not only heard, but that he had understood it, in its entirety. It was the point where she became serious, and the lesson had to be absorbed, and Snowball duly obliged. It was something of a hammer blow, as his friendship with Bobby was a mutually beneficial one, but he knew better than to ignore her words, and he had come to trust her implicitly. It seemed that Kevin and Bobby were due a fall from grace, and that fall was currently being instigated by forces unknown. The clever money was on keeping a distance, and Snowball wisely stepped back from his friendship with Bobby as instructed and waited for events to unfold.

It was over a month before events actually climaxed in a final day of reckoning. A week after the talk from Miss Bradwell, Kevin and Bobby had absconded again, stealing some petty cash from the office in the process, and had been gone for over two weeks. The police had caught up with them eventually, and Kevin had been charged with the theft, although the rumours circulating back to Snowball were that Bobby had actually taken the money without his prior knowledge, but it was Kevin who had stepped forward and taken the blame. In addition, there was a reported arson involving a shop that they had 'screwed' one night, and so it was fair to say that they had courted trouble, and found it in abundance. The police had brought them both back to the Melbourne House, and for a week or so, while the Rivers family were on holiday, all was calm, and there appeared to be no penalty or consequences to pay. Kevin had again regaled the impatient and waiting throng with tales of their adventure, while Bobby had chirped in during appropriate pauses, and Snowball waited for the information to find its way back to him, as he knew that he couldn't afford to be seen to be too close to the brothers, and had duly maintained an appropriate distance from them.

However, the return of the holidaying Rivers family signalled a dramatic change in events. They had arrived back at the home late in the night, with Mrs Rivers apparently settling their son into bed, while Mr Rivers woke both Kevin and Bobby, and informed them that he would deal with them first thing in the morning. Snowball noted that Bobby had struggled to get back to sleep that night, and in the still sanctuary of the darkness, he had dared to sit up, and chat throughout the night until, weary and fatigued, they both succumbed to a fretful sleep that only too quickly led them into the start of a new day.

As they all rose from their beds, and began heading for the bathrooms, it became apparent that Kevin hadn't really slept much either, after the late-night intrusion into his sleep. There was a tension in the air, and the older boys appeared to be providing Kevin with some clearly needed moral support and comfort. There were stifled conversations taking place in the bathrooms and corridors, and while reconciled to his fate, Kevin seemed to take comfort from the occasional friendly pat on the shoulders, and words of commiseration, that were offered by his friends. There was a palpable fear in the air, as well as an eagerness to be ready quickly that morning. It was a strange atmosphere to inhale. As had happened so many times before, everyone was eminently aware that there was trouble afoot. They knew there was invariably going to be a beating, but somehow, things were always so much more palatable in the knowledge that it wasn't them in the firing line, or the recipient of the wrath was deemed to somehow deserve it. Snowball had sought out the guidance of Miss Bradwell, but she hadn't been rostered that day, and so he sat, fearful and subdued, as events unfolded in front of the assembled throng at breakfast.

Kevin and Bobby were called forward, as the dishes from the solemn breakfast that preceded were being hastily swept away. Mr Rivers was by now incandescent with rage, having brooded all the way through breakfast, as he had been forced to bide his time, due to the absence of Mrs Rivers. Mr Rivers was furious not only with the absconding, but also the theft of money, the arson and the apparent indifference shown by Kevin and Bobby when they had been questioned at the police station, and brought back to the home. He was positively seething.

What followed was a long, painful to listen to lecture, on the shortcomings of stealing, and the consequences to be expected both now, and in later life. According to Rivers, it was likely that Kevin would be sent to Borstal after his court appearance, followed by the assumption that Bobby would be following shortly afterwards. It was all very Nostradamus as it rolled towards its predictably brutal climax. It all seemed like pointless information as far as Snowball and the rest were concerned. They had been told too often that they were no good, that they would end up on the streets, or worse, in jail, and that they had no future, so there seemed little point in repeating it over and over again, other than for the dramatic effect which Mr Rivers seemed to revel in.

Lecture concluded, Kevin and Bobby were both taken to the staff office by Mr Rivers. The sound of his strap meeting naked flesh could be heard resonating around the nearby rooms, as could the profusion of tears that Bobby cried, and the defiant abuse that Kevin had directed back towards Rivers. Mrs Rivers remained seated with the remaining children in the dining room, her snake-like squint perusing every face in the room, to ascertain whether or not the sound effects being emitted from the office were having the desired effect on each and every one of them. She was a smug heartless bitch at times, but they all knew not to cross her, as she enjoyed nothing more than beating a child to tears for the slightest of transgressions. Each slap of the strap sent a shudder down Snowball's spine, as the ability to count the strokes faded in correlation to the length of time it was taking to administer the punishment. It seemed like an eternity had passed before Kevin, closely followed by a remorseful and distressed Bobby, reappeared in the dining room, and indignantly retook their seats at the table. Rivers promptly returned and dismissed all those present, and another day at Melbourne House was underway. Within days Kevin had been moved out to another home. The brothers were now separated, and Bobby left alone to fend for himself. Gone was his safety net, his protection, his umbrella. He now had to learn the hard way, as Snowball and many others had done before him.

TOFFEES AND TABLETS

Miss Williams was a middle-aged woman, of tall and gangly stature, with a flash of ginger hair that shone as brightly as the teeth in her smile. She had worked in social work all her working life, having started out undertaking administration duties in an office, before 'graduating' into children's homes, where in her opinion she could do significantly more good than pushing a pen. She was a kindly woman at heart, though notably more willing to undertake the thrashing of a child (for its own good obviously) than Miss Bradwell ever was. Snowball was acutely aware that she was not of the same ilk as the remainder of the staff, and that there was a nurturing and caring streak to her personality, but still, she needed to be treated with caution, and as Miss Bradwell had warned when he had previously fallen into the trap of being coerced by the older boys into a few misdeeds, 'trust nobody' and you won't go too far wrong.

Miss Williams was the lady with the toffees. What Miss Bradwell sought to achieve by verbal coercion, clever psychological manipulation, and the occasional wag of a rigid finger and wave of a slipper, Miss Williams achieved through direct, overt, unashamed bribery, and sweets were her much appreciated chosen methodology. While she could turn her hand to discipline when she needed to, she clearly wasn't an advocate of the 'spare the rod, and spoil the child' brand of childcare, which many of her colleagues courted an over-zealous adherence to. Miss Williams was a lady who gave out warnings. Plenty of warnings in fact, and by the time you found yourself upended and over her knee staring at the Axminster, you were probably just about reaching the same conclusion as she was, that you were indeed a 'little fucker' who had gone too far, and actually deserved all you were about to receive. So, if you were smart enough to take the sweets, and avoid the lap, Miss Williams would be found to be a rare blessing in an unblessed life.

Snowball was an enthusiastic recipient of her bribery strategy, as was his close friend and roommate, Craig, who together would eagerly anticipate the shift changes that rid them of the casually brutal and somewhat less sophisticated members of staff, and installed the likes of Miss Bradwell and Miss Williams, for the much-needed respite and solace that they desperately needed. Craig was a wafer-thin boy, who had been at Melbourne House for around seven months. Like Snowball, he had arrived under the cover of darkness, an emergency placement who suddenly appeared one morning, tired, bewildered and amongst strangers, and Snowball had extended the courtesy of warning him not to rise before he had been told. A courtesy he himself had chosen to ignore some time before, and for which he had paid a painful price for. Craig had arrived undernourished, covered in bruises, an arm in plaster, and severe burns to both of his buttocks, the direct result of having been sat on an oven ring, as a punishment by his stepmother. They had immediately struck up a friendship, and between them they would often rig up small acts of mischief, in the knowledge that Miss Williams had arrived with a bag full of sweets to bribe them, and the most brutal of the staff had already left.

Months of systematic abuse had reduced Craig both physically and mentally to nothing more than a walking zombie, and he had fared quite poorly under the harsh regime of Melbourne House, which had done nothing to mitigate his physical and mental decline. His father was a long distance lorry driver and had by all accounts been oblivious to the carefully concealed abuse that had been inflicted upon his son. It had been a rare visit from his birth mother, now remarried and living in London, which had brought his condition to the attention of the authorities and had promptly led to the arrest of his stepmother. His birth mother had promised to take Craig into her custody, but as the months passed, Craig was coming to terms with the fact that she had abandoned him to a fate in care, and that his father was unlikely to be coming to his rescue any time soon. It was a familiar story to Snowball, and one which brought him closer to Craig than anyone else.

Craig had latched onto Snowball, and they had become good friends over the months they had been together. Their friendship strengthened when Craig was moved into the same bedroom, and they would idle the bright nights of summer away, chatting about anything that came to mind. It was telling that they both rarely spoke of their families, resigned to the fact they had been abandoned, they sought simply to develop a shared understanding of where they were, and how best to make the most of their shared predicament. There was strength in their small numbers, and when aligned with others in small numbers, they were able to begin the process of carving out a relatively safe environment, in which they managed to co-exist with an element of security from bullying and intimidation.

There was, however, a much deeper psychology to Craig, one which was beyond the comprehension and interpretation of Snowball and rooted in the profound abuse suffered and endured during his early years. Craig was both disturbed and disturbing on many levels, and desperately needed help, when there was no help to be offered. He was a prolific self-harmer, a disposition not at all helped by the 'status' that afforded him amongst the like-minded in the home, and he could often be found with blood dripping down his arms, from the wounds that he had re-opened with a razor blade. He had scar patterned arms from wrist to elbow, and had occasionally taken a blade to his face, with his forehead bearing the signature of his troubled mind. He would claim that his stepmother had once tried to 'bleed' the badness out of him, and it was thought that this was the root cause of his self-harming. Snowball would never know the real truth, he just knew that Craig was often to be found covered in blood, and staff attempts to beat the 'stupidity' out of him were failing.

For many (Snowball being an exception), Craig was a child to be avoided. He was known to occasionally carry a pen-knife, which was common enough, and largely innocuous, but he was reputedly unafraid to use it, or at least, as most likely was the case, brandish it with a posture of serious intent. A few had been deceived by his physically fragile appearance, and had subsequently been forced onto a back foot, as his uncontrollable rage erupted, threatening a consequence that seemed far outside his normally passive capabilities. It was also notable that the staff had a tendency to deal with Craig in pairs. Male pairs, as if they knew something that they simply weren't telling anyone else. And while it never afforded him protection from their brutality, and in truth most likely exacerbated it, the absence of available numbers to supervise his ongoing subjugation, could at least occasionally delay the inevitable as far as Craig was concerned.

Craig had become a progressively more volatile child after his arrival at Melbourne House. He suffered a lack of sleep caused by severe mood swings, and a fragile temperament, and he was constantly agitated by even the smallest of things. He had little focus, no attention span, and a psychological fragility that caused temper flashes which could erupt at the slightest perceived provocation, whether real or not. And, so it was, on that unusually arid summer's day, as the assembled great and good had gathered for the daily kick-about on the concrete court. Both Snowball and Craig had been amongst the last picks, and whilst

Snowball was always simply happy to be in the game, Craig had taken umbrage, given that in his eyes, he was a significantly better player than some of those who had been picked early in the draft. Snowball knew he was right, but he also knew that you had to account for the dynamics of the group, alliances, friendships, and all those other things that Miss Bradwell had patiently educated him in.

The game proceeded in its usual manner. Tackles were harsh dependent upon where in the hierarchy that you fell. Scoring goals was always down to the exceptional play, and the unbelievable skills of the scorer, and his team-mates, whilst conceding a goal was always attributed to the contribution of those who were considered fucking crap at football. This was unfortunately the category within which both Snowball and Craig had found themselves. Completely unjustified, of course, but that is where they were. Their side was now 2-0 down, and Craig had just let one of the opposition players ghost past him, with consummate ease, before scoring a goal that rattled the very framework of the nets, and consequently brought a torrent of abuse, which proved one step too far for Craig's fragile disposition, as chants of 3-0 rang through the air.

Players were still celebrating wildly at the point Craig slipped his pen-knife from his trouser pocket, and with dirty, cracked and broken fingernails, prised the blade from the housing. The abuse was still flying his way, and uncharacteristically, but buoyed by the presence of Leachy, Snowball had just told Smithy and a couple of others to 'fuck off', as they continued to mock their efforts. The boys were either enjoying themselves too much to be bothered retaliating, or they just couldn't be bothered, but either way, what they hadn't noticed was that Craig was now in full predator mode on the other side of the concrete, as his eyes narrowed to a pinpoint squint, and he identified the most vulnerable prey. Snowball caught a fleeting glimpse of the blade, as Craig brushed past him with a cold, harsh, steely determination in his eyes, that narrated and informed of the depth of his intent. Snowball, immediately conscious of his friend's intent, called out to Craig, but his words had barely fallen from his mouth before Craig had lunged forward, and rammed the knife straight into the left leg of Smithy, who immediately fixed him with the stare of disbelief that befalls unassuming prey in the immediate aftermath of an unexpected attack.

There was a stunned silence as Smithy went to ground and began screaming. Blood quickly saturated the light blue pants that he wore, and began to trickle through his fingers, as he frantically clutched at his thigh, while rolling from left to right, with both fear and pain etched across his face. He wasn't to know at the time, but the fanny was screaming like a banshee over what would turn out to be nothing greater than a flesh wound, albeit a large one. The rapid spread of claret across his lightly coloured pants more than adequately served the purpose of increasing the drama, and as Smithy tossed and turned around on the floor, the insidious creep of panic bedded itself in.

The panic spread quickly, and moments later, Snowball felt a hand grasp his right arm, and looked up to see a frantic Miss Williams, as she waved manically in an attempt to corral the younger children, while verbally imploring the older boys to head indoors to what she assumed would be relative safety. Mr Rivers flashed by, and quickly began to tend to the injured Smithy who still lay where he had fallen. A stunned but irate Mrs Rivers followed shortly afterwards, barking instructions at the remaining children, and imploring Miss Williams, whom by now was close to the door with a handful of children, to make sure that someone had called for an ambulance. Oh, how every adult panicked when the violence wasn't of their own instigation. It was a scene of chaos, and in the hazy midst of it all, stood an unrepentant Craig, hands bloodied, rage satiated and conscience completely untroubled.

As the afternoon unfolded, the ambulance arrived, and Smithy was promptly dispatched to the nearby hospital, where he would remain until the next day. Miss Williams implored the younger children, Snowball included, to remain in the upstairs living room, and had provided the appropriate bribe, in the form of a bag of sweets to be shared out evenly, while she hastily looked for the key, before locking them inside. Mr Rivers was busy interrogating the older boys, trying desperately to find out exactly what had happened, while Mrs Rivers had set about looking for Craig, who, amidst all the chaos that he had caused, had quietly slipped away, destination unknown. How the meek had inherited the earth that afternoon, before quietly slipping away to enjoy the spoils. The police dutifully arrived, and in turn had joined the search for Craig. A large, burly policeman had entered the upstairs living room, followed by a WPC, who subsequently assumed responsibility for ensuring the younger children were kept safe from harm. There was another siren heard in the distance, and as the noise grew louder and louder, it was apparent that it too was now in attendance at Melbourne House. If only there had been this type of police response to the remainder of the unchecked, randomly administered, staff instigated violence that was the ever present and over burdensome feature of life at Melbourne House.

The afternoon seemed endless. Miss Williams had replaced the WPC and brought a fresh bag of sweets and cold orange juice for them to enjoy (a stabbing a day was beginning to look like a favourable option). She had already interrogated them all about the events of that afternoon but had frustratingly come up blank with regards to useful information, as only Snowball had seen the events unfold, and he wasn't for talking at that point. Talking had often brought him nothing but trouble in the past, and there was no certainty that wouldn't be the case this time, so he had decided that silence was his favoured option while things unfolded. She tried again some thirty minutes later after the finger had been pointed in Snowball's direction a number of times, and under the threat of some 'quiet' time across her knee, he had duly sung like canary, and relayed the entire events of that afternoon into her attentive ear. In Snowball's eyes, there was a time and place for acts of bravery and cowardice, and through experience, he was smart enough to know the difference.

A few hours after it all started, they had their tea in the living room, and under the guidance of Miss Williams, they had each been ushered to their bedrooms and instructed to change into pyjamas, before returning to the living room, where they quietly watched TV for the remainder of the evening. Snowball enquired after Craig but had been told not to worry about him. As darkness fell, the night culminated with Snowball peering through the bedroom curtains, as the remaining blue lights from the attendant ambulance and police car flashed bright and clear as they departed the street, and disappeared into the night. Craig had been found by Mrs Rivers in a cleaning cupboard that he had locked from the inside. The last remaining ambulance had been for him. He was unconscious, with an empty bottle of pills by his side, and bloody fingerprints smeared across everything that he had touched. He was never seen at Melbourne House again. That was the day some took toffees, and Craig took tablets.

ANY QUESTIONS?

Witnessed though rarely understood, it would be years ahead before the full horrors of Melbourne House, and the multitude of other establishments, in which he was 'raised', were fully understood and reconciled in Snowball's mind. Ripped from a loving home, abandoned in fear, Snowball bounded fretfully from day to day, month to month, year to year, simply surviving. Navigating a path no child should have ever have to walk. Alone, endangered, and scared, this was his world, and he had to adapt. Each and every day, week or month bringing fresh turmoil, in the cycle of abuse that had become everyday normal life. He would learn to put names to the once almost anonymous abuse, as his childhood propensity to almost forget as soon as the tears dried, gave way to a determined developing belief that one day, as long as he could remember the details, he would take his revenge, and make his abusers pay. Tormentors and friends alike began to take on a greater significance, as he came more and more to understand and manipulate his environment.

Why, Miss, why? A question he and others would often ponder, as one seemingly mindless act of aggression followed another. What was being achieved by all this; why was it so, that nearly every day, every child, would be reduced to fear and tears, as the violence and abuse directed towards them, spiralled as if completely out of control? How they would often reflect on the pervasive and prolific misery that passed for 'care'. How they came to realise that some people only ever appeared happy, when all those around them were in fear and desperation. How the Rivers had wallowed in both the power and their self-proclaimed glory. How could it be that, a child from one abusive home was meant to thrive in another equally abusive home, to which they had been so randomly taken? And what of the complicity of those who knew of it all, every punch, every kick, every strike of a cane, and flash of a strap? What of their guilt, he would ponder.

They all knew what was happening, and they all chose to keep quiet. From staff at Melbourne House, to the social workers who dropped off their charges, and left both their responsibilities and consciences in the car park. The police, the school teachers, the congregation at the church, and the parents of friends. They all knew exactly what was going on in each and every home. They knew exactly what was happening, and they kept quiet. They simply didn't care enough, for the kids who needed their care the most. Tacit approval and encouragement for those who would seek to abuse, and condemnation and resignation to those who suffered.

Child abusing predators roamed the corridors of homes like Melbourne House. They relished and thrived in the free rein afforded them to do as they pleased, and they took full advantage of the blind eyes that were turned in their favour. There had been suicide attempts, self-harming, arson attacks, assaults, threats and all other manner of cries for help, as a result of the abuses that were inflicted. Each desperate cry for help, unheard, unheeded. In years to come, complicity would hardly seem a strong enough word. They may not have been present, but they held vicarious responsibility, and abused by proxy.

The entire system was biased and loaded against the very children it was allegedly there to protect. Society didn't care, their parents didn't care, the authorities didn't care. There was nobody. They were left exposed, vulnerable, damaged and alone, bar each other. Victims one and all. A tragic reflection upon society, and every one of its institutions. Snowball would come to witness and understand the enormity of psychological damage incurred in institutions like Melbourne House, as his life unfolded as a guardian of the courts, and their corrupt and brutal system of 'care'. He would see the spiralling depressions, suicide attempts, the violence and deviancy that would become ingrained in many of those who would follow his route, past, present or future. It would become so plainly obvious that many of them were never afforded a chance in life, many having lost them before they had even begun. It was never the case that they lost. They were simply never in the game.

For Snowball, the big unanswered question was, how could society allow this to happen? What were they thinking? Good people, who did nothing, allowing evil to prosper. The countless times he would see one absconder after another, himself included, returned by an uncaringly cold representative of authority, only to be beaten, abused and then abscond again. A never-ending downward cycle of misery and rejection, leading to countless nights spent sleeping in shop doorways, bins, skips and a multitude of other unholy places, that afforded better protections than that from which they ran. A revolving door that all those in authority chose to ignore, for reasons nothing more complex than a desire to protect the system at all and any cost. An unprecedented cycle of collusive child abuse that shattered thousands of lives, and damaged thousands of minds. Nowhere to run, and nowhere to hide. Unprecedented levels of abuse, conducted in the full glare of a 'civilised' society, and nobody stepped forward to stop it. If it can be said that, 'you can judge a society, by the way it treats it children', then for Snowball and many like him, it doesn't really leave much room for hope.

Melbourne House would prove to be the internal stain that Snowball could never remove from his soul. For sure, he would often sit quietly and relive the memory of the circumstances under which he had arrived. That was a horror that would never leave him, but Melbourne House was the point that life dramatically turned in a different, pitiful direction, and from which it would not recoil for decades to come. It was Melbourne House that cemented in his mind the horrific, evil and pervasive nature of child abuse. It was Melbourne House that taught him that, not only was physical and sexual abuse endemic, and occurring throughout society, but it was known about, and to be expected. It was as salient a part of growing up in child care, as the air he unconsciously breathed, and nobody cared.

In the years that would ensue, he would recover from the mental and physical pains that he suffered in Melbourne House, at the hands of those who were there to care for him. The fearful memories of the Rivers regime, the beatings, the brutality and futility of it all, though never forgotten, would begin to fade into irrelevance, as new challenges surfaced, and survival took on different forms mentally and physically, as he learned to embrace his life, and fulfil his dreams. The elusive kindness shown by Miss Bradwell would feature heavily in his thoughts, as he bounded from home to home, abuse to abuse, despair after despair. Pain and misery his constant companions. Why was she quite literally just one of a kind? He would miss his pal Leachy, ponder what eventually happened to Smithy, Craig and the others. His mind repeatedly cast backwards, in trying to understand his life looking forwards. How many more absconded after he had gone, been caught, returned, and suffered at the hands of the Rivers as a result? Whatever became of the self-harmers and suicidal chancers? And what became of the girls? Mr Rivers' little girls. Victims one and all. Used, abused and discarded like rubbish as the nefarious cycle continued unabated.

But the hard part for him came in the form of the helpless guilt he would succumb to during his darkest moments, as his recollection of the abuses he and others had been subjected to, began to haunt him. He recalled the nights he would lie awake in his bed, and hear the staff come for the girls, who were bedded further along the corridor. He could hear their cries in the still of the night, as the darkness closed in, and they were marched down the corridor, and into the staff quarters, where they became nightly prey to the sexual predators that staffed the home. He recalled with uncanny clarity the haunting footsteps that would come and go in the darkness, signalling the removal and return of yet another helpless victim, and how the number of steps, or weight of foot, clearly served to identify each abuser individually. Helpless to their plight, all he could do was lie there, listen, and be grateful it wasn't him.

He was far too young and under-developed for the attentions of Mrs Rivers, though the misery and fear she caused amongst the older boys was not beyond his comprehension. Used as her entertainment, they were beaten, fondled, abused and forced to masturbate for her pleasure. Her predatory sexual advances every bit as nauseous as those of her violent sexually depraved husband. There was the complicity and participation of the remaining staff. Why had they taken part, or stood aside, failing to act, in full knowledge of what was happening under their noses? Why were their lives deemed to be so worthless, that even the police and social services showed no interest in the plight of those who were suffering in their care? The horror of the open secret they all shared rendered them all victims. Cast into a recklessly abusive fight for survival, brutalised without remorse, a life without compassion, where only the strongest survived, and where nobody escaped untainted.

In the 1990s, they would demolish Melbourne House, and clear away not just the rubble, but also the memories and crimes that were committed there, over the decades of its existence. A cruel, heartless and cold place, landscaped out of visual history, with houses, bungalows and a play area for kids. Its dark satanic secrets scrubbed from prying eyes forever. Snowball would return many years later and ponder the pristine housing development occupying the site of his previous miseries. Gone was the playing court, the L-Shaped structure that had once been home, all a distant dusty memory in some council landfill site. Site cleared, guilt eradicated, memories distant.

GOODBYE MELBOURNE HOUSE, HELLO STOCKPORT COUNTY FC

The black Hillman Hunter came to a sudden, bone-jerking stop, outside number 33 Rectory Road in Stockport. It had been a long boring drive, and alongside it, Snowball's patience had withered considerably. Despite the sense of jubilation that had ignited his senses, as he had been driven from Melbourne House, there was an all-consuming sense of foreboding as the car that carried him turned into Rectory Road. Two days before, after being summoned to the office by Mr Rivers, for what he assumed would be another senseless beating, he had been informed that he had been fully assessed (whatever that meant), that his time at Melbourne House was up, and that he would be moving to a new 'Family Group Home' that week.

A Family Group Home. What the fuck was that, he thought to himself, as the excitement of leaving Mrs Rivers far behind was tempered with the knowledge that he better not let her see that excitement. After all, she could do a lot of damage in two days. The previous night had been a constant and protracted flurry of half-hearted goodbyes, and the ritual of packing his few worldly possessions into small plastic bags and leaving them in the office for collection in the morning. Yes, the anonymous plastic bag that signalled to the outside world that you as a child had no possessions, nothing of worth, and as a consequence, you had no personal value of note. The bag. The plastic bag. If abandonment could be symbolised, it was the plastic bag that did it. His social worker had dutifully arrived on time, and within minutes, the nightmare that had been

Melbourne House was fading into history, and he was heading southwards to a new home in Stockport.

"Are you ready?" his social worker had asked. He wasn't, but it didn't matter – the question was rhetorical, and she simply felt compelled to ask it. Snowball remained silent, and simply gazed at the large Victorian house that was stood in front of him, and which he was now expected to call home. He had been freed from the abuses and brutality to which he had somehow become casually accustomed, but in freeing him from that nightmare, he had been forced to enter an unknown other, where the price to pay was the sacrifice of all his friends, his alliances, and everything he had really known, good, bad and indifferent. He realised that Miss Bradwell was now gone forever and that, unfortunately, she hadn't even been there to say goodbye. He found himself deluged in a waterfall of conflicting emotions, elated on the one hand that he had been liberated from the Rivers family and the brutality of Melbourne House, and contrarily deflated about his friends and his secretive mentor, Miss Bradwell. Enthusiastic about his new start, but somehow altogether fearful of what it might all entail. As he had once overheard Miss Bradwell warn, 'Sometimes you are better off with the devil you know, than the one you don't.' But he was here now, and he knew whatever happened from that point forward, he was, by necessity, simply going to make the most of it. So was he ready? No. But nobody really gave a fuck anyway, so he just cracked on.

"You don't have to stay if you don't like it here." Right there and then he knew she was lying to him. He had never had a choice where he lived, and it was unlikely he would ever do so, but it was by all accounts a very nonchalant standard line, which he would eventually become used to, and it clearly made his social worker feel better about herself and the misery into which she would regularly drop him. It was a lie, the start of many.

Snowball knew he was there for however long it was decided, and he would have no participation in that decision. His social worker also knew it was a lie, but again, she felt compelled to say it, if for no other reason than the presumed soothing effect it might have over her temperamental charge, who was, by now, decidedly lacking in verbal charm and communication. Snowball simply nodded in her direction, told her to fuck off, explained that she was being a twat, before taking a firm grip of the door handle, and alighting from the car into the street. Why she had called him a charmer, as his feet hit the floor, he didn't know, but he ignored her nonetheless.

The surroundings were pleasant enough. Pleasing in fact, and there was a fresh autumnal smell that seemed to waft from every angle, in a coordinated attack of his nasal senses. Trees lined the street as far as he could see, and as he gazed across the well-tended gardens in closest proximity to him, he began to harbour a fledgling thought that maybe it could be the start of something different. Maybe this time he had landed on his well abused feet after all.

Plastic bags in one hand, and his social worker's hand in the other, they cautiously made their way across the road, and up the short gravel drive, before pressing firmly on the antique brass doorbell that aesthetically dominated the mock Tudor entrance. Snowball took a brief look back at the car, almost in silent recognition that once he had crossed this threshold, he would have reached a point from which he couldn't return. If there was ever a time to run, it was now, and despite the fact that every fibrous membrane in his body instructed him to do so, he remained, captivated more by the surroundings, than the fear of what lay behind the heavy wooden door in front of him.

He heard the door-latch springing open as he once again turned to face the door, and almost instantaneously, as the door swung open, he was confronted by an elderly looking lady, with a smile that exuded a warmth of welcome, the likes of which he hadn't experienced for a long time. She reminded him of the mother he had lost years before. How her warmth lit up the room, and conveyed to everyone in it, that while she was there, everything was going to be just fine. She looked down at the new arrival, and extended a pale, fragile looking hand in his direction. Snowball paused. 'What is this fuckery?' he thought. What on earth was she doing? What did she expect him to do? His social worker in an unusual moment of contextual awareness, spotted the confusion that the gesture had caused, and calmly interjected. "It's ok, this is your Aunty Beryl, you can shake her hand if you want to." He didn't want to, but that wasn't the point. What is all this handshaking malarkey? He knew it wasn't his Aunty Beryl and hated the fact that these people were imposed on him in such an overtly familiar manner, but that's how it was, and he reluctantly accepted it without grace, merely because he had no choice in the matter. It seemed that these fuckers had every angle covered in the forced compliance stakes, and so, with plastic bags in one hand, ill-fitting shoes on his feet, and a new aunty in the doorway, so it was.

He also wondered if shaking hands was a trick, and what the consequence would be if he fell for it. Smithy had once got him to shake hands, and then promptly punched him in the face, before pulling him to the floor in a vicious assault, and in his eyes, it wasn't too implausible that, as frail looking as she was, Aunty Beryl was probably about to try the same trick.

At this point, and without warning, 'Aunty Beryl' leaned forward and lowered herself to his eye level. She took his right hand and gave it a gentle shake, before enquiring what his name was. Mrs Rivers had adopted a similar strategy the first morning they had met on the landing, before promptly assaulting him, so his abuse alert-o-meter was reading high, as he slowly replied, "David", whilst hastily pulling his hand back, as she released her gentle grip. "Well, David, how would you like to come in, we're just about to have our dinner, and you can join us if you like." And with that strangely polite old lady leading the way, he was ushered into number 33, and life in Stockport had begun.

His arrival in Stockport signalled the start of a long, and psychologically uncomfortable transition, into the stability of what could only be described as a relatively normal life, for as long as it would last. His first few weeks were typified by well-founded suspicion and fear, but with a difference from the justified fears he had experienced at Melbourne House. In Stockport everything simply appeared to be normal, better than normal sometimes, almost perfect. He was treated well. He was spoken to politely. He was often asked what 'he wanted', in a manner that ensured he was aware that it was his needs they were trying to address. It was all very civil, all very polite, very caring, very safe, and so very fucking weird. He knew it had to be a trick, and as a result he remained in a constant state of readiness, for when it all went pear-shaped, and the fireworks were reignited. He couldn't help but believe that Mrs Rivers would somehow find a way to spoil all this newly found happiness, even though there wasn't a cane or strap in sight, and the people in the new home were killing him with kindness, such that he spent most days wanting to cry tears of joy, than those of the pained anguished life he had left behind.

Aunty Beryl had introduced him to Aunty Anne, her much younger deputy with whom she shared responsibility for the six children that lived under the roof. Aunty Anne was clearly of a different era to Beryl but seemed well versed in the methodologies that Aunty Beryl deployed in the home, and they both made all necessary efforts to integrate him smoothly into their operation, making him feel as comfortable as they possibly could within the confines of the structural regime that they had created.

For Snowball, the problem of people being kind was now the only hurdle to 'overcome'. For the first time in his life, he had his own bedroom. His own semi-private space that he could deploy to when he felt the need for solitude, quiet time, or to avoid giving some annoying little counterpart the kicking they deserved, but was unable to administer, for fear of the consequences. He started to sleep well; he was free from fear. Breakfast was always served hot when he arrived at the table, and he had choices about what he ate, the only compunction placed upon him being that he ate something first thing each morning, because as Aunty Beryl would repeatedly state, 'it was good for him'. Good for him, a concept he had previously had no knowledge of, but one which was now thrust upon him on a daily basis, as he ploughed through the mystery that was the kindness of Aunty Beryl and Aunty Anne.

He now had possessions that he could call his own. He was given books, toys, a bike, and clothes. The children were required to politely ask permission if they wanted to use the private possessions of another, and in the spirit of appreciation, they were each expected to look after their own possessions, and respect the possessions of everyone else. There was an expectation of general good manners, which, both Aunty Beryl and Aunty Anne constantly reminded him, actually cost nothing at all. Please and thank you taking on a new, somewhat cool and vibrant central role in everyday communication. It was a far cry from when Mrs Rivers had forced him to say thank you for every stroke of her belt that she delivered to his naked flesh. For Snowball, it was all very new, all very frightening, but oh so welcome in many respects, however difficult the transition was. He had become so accustomed to simply being 'told', that the transition to being 'asked' was a hard one to accept.

Beryl and Anne worked hard in facilitating the creation of six children, each with their own uniqueness and character. It was a difficult task that they stuck to. Each one from a troubled start in life, and yet each one now flourishing in an environment that appeared to care for, and value them, in a way Snowball had never really experienced since leaving his foster mother. There was a tangible effort to avoid the generic and develop the differences. Aunty Beryl had even introduced a system of age-related responsibilities in the home, and every child, Snowball included, had weekly tasks assigned to them on a rotation system, with the end of week reward for completion being a handful of pocket money, which they could proudly claim had been duly earned. They were all given savings accounts in their own names, and Aunty Anne would walk them to the nearby post office on Saturday mornings, with their plastic covered savings books, where they were expected to deposit some of their pocket money, before heading further down the street to the newsagent's, where the remainder was spent on sweets, Matchbox Cars, Top Trumps Cards, popular comics and children's books.

Yes, books. They were now mandatory, with every child expected to have at least one book 'on the go' for reading at all times, as it was how they spent the last fifteen minutes of the day, before being tucked up in bed, and the bedroom lights dimmed.

For Snowball, it was hard to understand, and quite overwhelming at times. For weeks he hadn't witnessed a violent act, nor been subject to a beating. He hadn't been verbally abused, or physically intimidated into a state of abject fear. Aunty Anne often threatened a spanking and could on extremely rare occasions be witnessed rapping the back of someone's legs, but in the main, it came to be understood that it was just that, a threat, and nothing more. He was becoming accustomed to sleeping peacefully through the night, never being woken by the sounds of tears from an adjoining room, or worse still, his own. There were girls in the home, and they appeared happy and safe. They weren't being used sexually and they were living a happy normal life. It was all a far cry from anything he had experienced at Melbourne House, and the transition was a painful one, as he came to realise the extent of the abuse he had suffered, the impact, and the fresh need to transition into a lifestyle that he could, previously, only ever have dreamed of. He finally had a home, and he had no idea what to do with it.

For Snowball, the only real downside once he got his head around his new situation, was the church. Yes, as was the case in many an abused life, the church raised its ugly head, albeit without the abuse and sexual manipulation of minors that would become synonymous with the institution as time moved through the decades. No, the problem for Snowball was that Aunty Beryl and Aunty Anne were avid churchgoers, devout Christians, and loyal members of the local congregation of god-fearing zealots. And there was no way out of it. These were times long before you could dish up an Amen on Facebook, and cure all known illnesses, and even death itself. It was so bad that weekends were truncated into Saturday, as with each and every week Sunday was totally devoted to worshipping the good Lord, and all of his godly virtues. Snowball, along with the other children, would be awoken early on Sunday mornings. They would all bathe and eat breakfast together, before returning to their bedrooms, where they would find that Aunty Beryl or Aunty Anne had laid out their Sunday best (black trousers, white shirt, black tie, and black shoes for the boys; Sunday dresses and smart shoes for the girls), and they would all dress for the day of 'happy clappy celebration'. No knocking on doors and converting people here, they were going straight to the boss man's house, and they would be going twice that day.

For Snowball, it was a slow, torturous and painful death every Sunday. Despite his young age, he was well aware that even if God existed, he had displayed such a level of inconsiderate fuckery towards him so far in his life, that he wasn't ready for any sudden conversion to the cause, which had seen him and so many of his unfortunate peers randomly brutalised at the whim of others, whom he clearly had no godly control over. It was, however, a burden that was tolerated for no other reason than Aunty Anne would make it clear that any objections or consequential bad behaviour in the big man's house, would be met instantly with a visit over her knee, where the punishment for 'showing her up' as she termed it, would be vigorously administered until she caught sight of tears. What a twat, but that's how it was.

It was a threat that Snowball took lightly for six days of the week, because discipline was nowhere near as brutal, nor as rigorously enforced as it had been at Melbourne House, but on Sunday mornings, Aunty Anne had the devil's own look about her at times, and any warnings that she had failed to administer during the week, were amplified on Sunday mornings, as she, with great religious fervour, detailed how the day WOULD go. Snowball knew oh too well that Anne was capable of bringing tears to his eyes, if she thought he needed it. It rarely happened, but Sunday was HER big day, and it just wasn't worth spoiling it. So, every Sunday, stomach full of a cooked breakfast, he would sit through the two and a half hour children's service, weekly confirmation study, and junior prayer class, before making the long walk home, only to return three to four hours later for the evening adult service, which he and the others were forced to attend, simply because they couldn't be left alone at home.

That's fucking child abuse right there, but who was going to complain? Needless to say, the weekly five-hour plus stints in the House of the Lord, did occasionally result in a visit to Anne's knee just as she had righteously promised, and a close-up inspection of the Axminster carpet would take place, while she thrashed the errant child, but in the main, Sundays would pass off without event for Snowball, and culminate in a much appreciated traditional Sunday dinner around the dining table, where each child was expected to inform on everything they had learned that day as they ate. The fuckery was never-ending on a Sunday.

IT'S ONLY STALKING, IF THEY KNOW YOU'RE THERE

Sundays complete, and safely tucked up in bed, Snowball could begin to dream about the upcoming day at school, and the delightful charms of Miss Gillian Tanner. School came in the form of Christchurch School. It was a large faith school, close to Stockport City Centre, that was both physically and ideologically connected to the church. A big negative in Snowball's eyes, but apparently some people thought it was a great idea. The mental tortures of Sundays with Anne always eventually came to an end, but in reality, school was simply a continuation of, and subtle indoctrination into, the ways of the Lord, whether he liked it or not. Church and school stood united on a large rectangular plot, entrapped by busy roads that were a constant hazard to the children who attended. The first day of each term was always spent indoctrinating the new schoolers into the correct use of the zebra crossings, situated at one end of the school, and the procedure for crossing safely at the remaining three corners, should they find themselves required to do so.

Mr Grimley, the headmaster (a kindly man for the era), took great pride in the fact that, by noon on the first day, everyone had been deemed competent to cross the road safely, and unsupervised, by their form teacher, despite the fact that several of the children had died of boredom, and most would be going home with blisters and sore feet. He hadn't lost a child to a road accident in his entire career, and as he casually sauntered his way towards retirement, he had no intentions of doing so. He had a system that was simple in design, and even simpler to effect. You walked in line to the crossing, and, one by one, implemented your 'Green Cross Code' training, before crossing the road to the teacher opposite. You then walked up the road to the next teacher and crossed back again. You continued to do this all morning, until the teachers had witnessed you cross safely enough times, as to deem you both safe and competent. Only then were you allowed back to your class to rest your weary feet. For some this took only minutes, others an hour or so, and for the less intellectually gifted, and those with an acute attention deficit to contend with, lunch could potentially arrive before they had mastered the basic skills associated with 'avoiding moving cars at all costs, because they hurt when they hit you'. But for Mr Grimley it didn't matter when you passed, it was simply about passing, and everyone would pass, eventually.

Mr Grimley was old school. Very old school, and these were the things that mattered to him. Children had a place in school, a place in society, a place in the home. They needed to be self-disciplined and obey the rules, but he also understood that they needed to be nurtured, and that it was easier to teach a well nurtured and self-controlling child, than it was a troubled and fretful one. It was a simple but effective ethos, that saw him implement many learning strategies, and after-school activities, which children not only found interesting, but also helped develop them into respectful, well-balanced members of society. He had even instigated a swimming programme in the school, which, once a week, saw a bright red double-decker bus pull up outside the school, and two or three classes were taken to the local swimming baths, where they were taught to swim over the course of a few months, before eventually being allowed to take a swimming certificate, for which, if successfully completed, he would award each child a small bag of sweets. Not really the sort of rewarding experience Snowball had imagined it would be, but in the absence of anything else, a small bag of sweets would suffice.

Grimley was a man who thrived on good order. He liked things to be just right, everything and everybody in, or knowing their place within the general scheme of things. He was always well presented, always dressed in a suit, always wearing highly polished black brogues, white shirt, a tie, hair well-trimmed, dirt free nails and well shaven. He believed society worked better that way. His way. Everyone with standards, and an expectation that they be implemented, and he was probably right. Though occasionally oppressive, it was a regime that turned out 'good kids', and he was immensely liked for it, by both children and parents alike. He also instigated the 'Lolly' system, which he applied on swim days. He always took a bag of hard-boiled lollies to the swimming pool. The exact number of lollies in the bag equalling the exact number of children on the bus. In the chaos that always ensued getting children dried, dressed and back out to the bus, Mr Grimley would simply position himself on the bus step, and as each child boarded, fearful that he might run out of lollies, and thus, hastily dried and dressed with the minimum of fuss, they were permitted to take a lolly from the bag. As long as there was a lolly remaining in his bag, he knew he was a child missing, and the bus was going nowhere. Happy days, but school wasn't always what it was cracked up to be in Snowball's eyes.

For example, for Snowball, it always seemed like an overly long walk to school. The reality, however, was very different. It was a few short streets, supplemented by a few long ones. But for small legs, and sore feet, the distance seemed to get longer and longer, the further he walked. As far as he could remember, it had always been that way. He would set off, carefree, bounding and happy, but within a short distance, pain would emerge in his damaged feet, and the distance to his destination would become a serious issue. His predicament was further exacerbated by many an unknowing adult who, ignorant of his physically impaired situation, would assume they had a lazy child on their hands, and act accordingly. It was a problem in school, as much as out of it. Sports days and PE were both traumatic experiences due to the widespread ignorance that surrounded him. Deciding what to do, when all he wanted to do was nothing at all, provided for many an upset, and confrontation with authority, and it soon became the case that accepting the punishment for refusing to play was easier than trying to explain to the ignorant and unhearing. Swimming lessons also proved to be an unblessed period, as the burns to his feet and legs drew the attention of children and teachers alike, who would often point, make fun and to some extent bully him, as he tried in vain, one foot placed across the other, to shield them from the unwelcome attention. As much as he liked the idea of swimming alongside the opportunity to dip his hand in the bag of lollies, it never quite compensated for the torment that preceded it, and simply bestowed upon him an undesirable level of the wrong type of attention, which occasionally resulted in a much heated outpouring of rage, closely followed by a shirt drenching flow of salty tears.

There was, however, one saving grace amongst the heartache and pain that constituted participating in sports and swimming. That came in the form of Gillian Tanner. The beautiful angel that was Gillian Tanner, was his first crush. Being two classes above him, it was a very rare occasion for them to be in the same place, and at the same time, for very long. But sports days, PE and swimming were the exception, and it was in these weekly gatherings, that Snowball's unreciprocated amour developed. It was always a race to be ready for sports or swimming. Feet almost always forgotten, as the thought of Gillian, resplendent in her green gym knickers, PT vest, white plimsolls and socks, and always managing to look as athletic as she was angelic, served to temporarily mask the discomfort that inevitably followed on from his participation.

Yes, Gillian was a goddess. Not his goddess unfortunately, but a most welcome distraction, in what was occasionally a rather mundane daily experience at the hands of Mr Grimley and his band of merry Christians. She had even spoken to him on one occasion, instructing him to 'hurry up and get on the bus', which he believed was clearly the start of a long-lasting and loving relationship, but as it transpired, she was simply eager to get her hands on a lolly from Mr Grimley's bag, and upon receipt, promptly disappeared onto the upper deck, licking furiously, and completely oblivious to the fact that Snowball couldn't follow her, as the upper deck was unsupervised, and only for the 'big pupils'. He wasn't too bothered, as he had his own lolly, and the seat by the luggage rack meant that he could at least hear her talking to her friends, and he would get to see her, as she disembarked, and was forced to wait on the pavement with her 'juniors', while Mr Grimley did the final headcount – which was always a mystery, as there were no stops on the way back to school, nor any reports of children climbing out of the windows – before everyone was dismissed into the arms of their waiting parents. Yes, Gillian Tanner. An unreciprocated love that never got to flourish.

FiRST REAL CHRiSTMAS

It came as quite a surprise to Snowball, when on a cold, late November night, his first in Stockport, Aunty Anne and Aunty Beryl, having just cleared the table from the boisterous tea they had enjoyed, suddenly produced sheets of white paper, small envelopes and pens, before placing them in front of the children, and boldly stating that it was time everyone wrote their list for Santa, then they could be posted in the morning. He had long passed the 'believe in Santa' stage, more as a consequence of having never received anything year on year at Melbourne House, than the passing of age, but it was a surprise nonetheless. Snowball sat and stared at the blank sheets of paper and pens, as the other children quickly grasped them, smiles beaming from ear to ear, and frantically started to write.

Oi You Fucker, is this 'just another trick' he wondered, as he watched the excited faces around him beam with a luminance that could have replaced a thousand candles, had they been hit with one of the all too common power cuts, which plagued the nation that would become known as the Sick Man of Europe. It had to be a trick, but why weren't the others realising that 'fact'? As far as Snowball was concerned, Santa was nothing but a big, fat, bearded judgemental twat, who had failed to visit on numerous occasions, and here they were falling for the oldest trick in the book. It was unseemly. He sat and stared a little more, his eyes starting to well, heart starting to pound, as the scene in front of him unfolded. Could it really be that this was actually happening, he wondered. Was he really expected to write a fucking letter to Santa, post it, and live through the manufactured expectation and anticipation that would then ensue in the following weeks, as the build up to Christmas Day became ever more fervent by the day?

He glanced across the table at Anne, who upon noticing the tears about to cascade from his eyes, beckoned him over, and asked 'what was the matter'. He looked her in the eye, rose to his feet, walked straight passed her, and headed to his bedroom, alone, confused and with tormented thoughts. It couldn't be true, he thought to himself. It just couldn't be true. His mind transported him backwards, to all the barren times he had experienced during the Christmases past. He recalled with an acute vividness, the excitement he had seen in others, but never really experienced himself. He could recall the feverish delight that children experienced on the final day of school, which generally signalled that Christmas had arrived, only for the reality of his own predicament to sweep brutally over him, with festive dulling monotony. He recalled all the conversations he had overheard between expectant 'normal' kids, and their teachers, families and friends. Oh how Christmas for some had been so much fun, and yet his had been nothing but a barren time of wasteful nothingness. Christmas had always been awkward. It was hard enough fending off questions about why you had no parents, or enquiries about whether it was only bad children who were in 'homes', but Christmas was always a particularly painful time, as it truly highlighted the disparity between what he was compelled to term his family and that of a real family for which he longed.

He felt isolated, vulnerable, ostracised, without value, and unwanted. He imagined every child in his situation felt exactly the same, and the pain of being unable to join in the festive build-up in any salient manner was equally as unbearable, as was the knowledge that upon his return to school the following year, he would have to listen to all the tales of, 'what I got for fucking Christmas' and the places kids had been, treats they had received, and the fun they had had. He always knew he would be the one with no tales to tell. Almost apologetic that he had received few if any presents, as if it was a testimony that he had somehow been bad, and Santa had found out. He had nothing to contribute to December, and it hurt. It hurt a lot.

His expectations of Christmas had always been nil, and they had always been fulfilled. Occasional sympathy gifts, church hand-outs and a miniscule allowance from social services, were rapidly sacrificed at the altar of the communal toy box or clothing cupboard, and life just continued as normal. His current life, however, had just been turned upside down, and spun around a few times for good measure. His own room, his own clothes, his own books, his own food and his own shoes, his own underwear, and even his own black plastic comb, which he couldn't pull through his hair, but it was nice to have it, because quite simply, it was his. He had his own dressing gown and pyjamas, his own bed, his own possessions, and now this. His troubled mind couldn't help but scream, WHAT THE FUCK IS GOING ON?

He'd been perched on the edge of his bed for only a few fleeting minutes, when there was a gentle tap on the door, and the soothing voice of Aunty Beryl could be heard asking, if it was alright if she came in. He remained silent, almost oblivious to the fact she needed an answer, and too confused to speak a word. She was going to come in anyway, but he appreciated the fact that she always asked first, and the fact that everyone was expected to knock at the door bolstered his sense of ownership of the room. The door slowly swung open, and Aunty Beryl hesitantly walked in and sat down beside him. Eyes cast down, he noticed that she had brought a pen, paper and an envelope, and had calmly placed them on the bed cover between them. It was her way of asking, but she knew it would take some time, and she understood the reasons behind it. It was all becoming far too much to handle, and he felt that he could implode at any moment. He couldn't assimilate the events that were being placed before him. It was all so unfamiliar, as if he had been dropped overnight in a strange town, in a strange country, amongst strange people, and with no knowledge of what to do, or where to go.

He was completely overwhelmed, and Aunty Beryl alongside Aunty Anne were killing him with kindness. There were times when he just wanted them to hit him, to abuse him, to call him names, or frustrate his life, just so he would wake up and realise it was all just a dream. But it wasn't a dream. He wasn't imagining it. It was real, very real, and he had absolutely no idea how, or even if he should respond at all. His chest felt like it was going to explode, his heart was racing, he could feel himself heating up, and the visible presence of beads of sweat were now forming on his forehead. On the verge of hyper-ventilating, he tried to calm himself. Deep breaths, followed by strained glances upwards at Aunty Beryl as she sat majestically beside him, and encouraged his fragile efforts to remain calm. And then it happened. As she gently placed a hand on his thigh, and told him it was ok, his eyes exploded into a raging torrent of tears that flooded down his face like a waterfall in the rainy season. 'You bitch, you knew exactly what you were doing,' he thought to himself, before sobbing uncontrollably, as she held him tightly in her arms, and reiterated that everything was ok, he was simply just to 'let it all out', and not to worry about a thing.

And she was right. It was going to be ok, because she was going to make it ok, as she had done for all the other kids before him and would do for all the kids that followed him. It was what she did, what she excelled at, it was who she was. But for Snowball, a short life spent amongst everything and anything that wasn't ok, it was a life changing moment that liberated him from the isolated silo mentality that he had been delivered into courtesy of a system that had been so abusive, so brutal, so demeaning, that he had been denied all sense of self-worth or value. He had almost come to depend on the daily ritual of violence and abuse that had been inflicted upon him, as the only means of being recognised as 'being there'. It was the only recognition from life that he existed, that at least someone recognised that existence, if only to fulfil their own need to hurt someone. But at least he was being recognised. And so it passed, that with the help of Aunty Beryl, it took over an hour to formulate his first ever Christmas list, before it was neatly folded and popped into the envelope that she had provided. "Let's take it downstairs and put it with the others," she politely instructed, and with that, tears dried up, wet shirt changed, and smiles across faces, they returned to the dining room, and joined the rest of the household with warm milk and biscuits. Snowball's first real Christmas that he could remember had just begun, and it was only fucking November.

Christmas that year came and went, in a blur of traditional events, and an explosion of happiness, that culminated in an excited household that barely slept a wink on Christmas Eve (despite the much-aired threat that Santa would pass them by, if they weren't asleep when he came calling). On Christmas Day, the children had raced down to the tree, to discover exactly what he had left them. Some greedy twat called Rudolph had eaten all the carrots, and there was a large bite out of the homemade mince pie that had been left on the table. But it didn't really matter that much, as the fat guy in the red suit had left a whole bunch of presents in the living room, and it seemed like a decent enough swap, for what they had left in return.

Aunty Beryl had ensured that Snowball's aspirations had been met in full, and for the first time in a long time, he felt that he had finally found somewhere that he could truly call home. There were carols and carol singing, church services, roasted chestnuts by the fire, Christmas plays, visits to a grotto, a real Christmas tree, which they had all helped to decorate. It was Aunty Anne who had left out the carrots for Rudolph, and a mince pie for Santa. She had also left him a glass of sherry, but Aunty Beryl had no idea where that had gone, just that Santa had been gracious enough to wash the glass and put it away in the cupboard, so there was no need for complaint on any front. There was a house full of decorations and Christmas cheer, topped off with an exhausted Beryl and Anne, who clearly needed a holiday after the events of December had passed them by. It was a monumental first real Christmas for Snowball, and one he wouldn't forget. It seemed as if the traumas of the past had finally passed him by, and at last he had a home where he was happy, safe and comfortable. Life had changed dramatically for the better, and as Christmas came to a happy close, he sat back and savoured the very moment. A moment that would be etched into his memory forever, not least because, finally, upon returning to school, he would have something to talk about, as they all wrote stories about their Christmases at home, before bragging about the presents they had received.

MORE PRESENTS, LESS TRAUMA

Valentine's Day. The only day of the year that Snowball was accustomed to remembering. It was his birthday, and for the first time ever, on this occasion, he was actually looking forward to it. He knew Aunty Beryl would be making a fuss of him, as she did all the children on their birthdays, and if it wasn't her, she would have left very clear instructions with Aunty Anne. He had seen her operate when the other birthdays had happened, and now it was his turn. He knew there would be at least one present awaiting him downstairs, as well as a cake, and a planned party later that afternoon. There was also a much revered, and well-practised tradition in the household, which would see all the other children enthusiastically sing happy birthday, before they left for school that morning. It was fuckery on a grand scale, but today was his turn for the fuckery, and that made all the difference.

It would be a day to remember, although there was a slight, but palatable, downside that he would need to cope with. Aunty Beryl ensured that any advancement in age came with the acceptance of added responsibilities around the home. It was all part of 'growing up' in her eyes, and appropriate responsibilities would come thick and fast, as she deemed fit. Snowball knew exactly what he was in for, as there was a clear methodology that Aunty Beryl deployed. Each child had a set of responsibilities, and as you gained a year, you were expected to take on the responsibilities of the child next oldest to you. They in turn would take on the responsibilities of the child in front of them, and Aunty Beryl would dream up new responsibilities for the eldest child, who would now be without portfolio to call their own. At the time it was largely unappreciated, and often seemed intrusive when in competition with football, the park, reading, or just lazing around in his bedroom doing nothing much at all, but it was all designed to ensure that they all appreciated that things needed to be done, and it was much easier if everyone helped out and contributed. It was about being together, being a family, taking responsibility, and growing up the 'right way' as Aunty Beryl would often tell them.

On this occasion, Snowball was quite pleased. Clare, the child in front of him, had previously been given the responsibility of organising the washing of the pots and pans, after Sunday lunch, and all the weekly suppers. She was, in point of fact, akin to a 'Little Hitler', dictating to all in attendance, exactly which pot or pan they were responsible for washing, drying and returning to its rightful place. The daily swathe of power clearly fulfilling something dark and sinister inside her, as she strode from one corner of the kitchen to the other, barking orders at her 'siblings' and ensuring that everything had been completed to her satisfaction. Snowball, whether imagined or real, had, in his opinion, been awarded the roast potato pan on far too many occasions for comfort, and had spent what seemed like countless hours trying to scrub the welded-on spud bases from the bottom of the pan, only to have his efforts rejected by Clare, who would return him to the sink, to 'try harder this time'. She was, quite frankly, a little fucker, who more than deserved a smack under the chin, but she had the power, and unless you could put up a compelling argument against her to Aunty Beryl, she was likely to retain that power.

At times it had seemed that no amount of soaking in hot water could remove the 'enemy of the people', from the bottom of the pan, and he had often thought of simply throwing the pan in the bin, or smacking Clare across the head with it. It was, however, the thought of going over Anne's lap in return for his aggressions that provided reason enough for him to tactfully refrain from doing so. But times had just changed, and revenge was about to be served up cold on a weekly basis. He could now quite smugly and with a stone-cold heart, assign that job to his nemesis Clare, subsequently freeing up vast chunks of his Sunday evening, and making the transition into Monday morning a much happier one. Oh, how the mighty occasionally fall, and how he would make her rue the day she first assigned him that hateful spud pan.

IGNORANCE ISN'T ALWAYS BLISS

It was an ominous knock on the door. Chilling for Snowball, and about to get a whole lot colder. Aunty Anne on one side, a shame-faced, downcast Snowball with a policeman on the other. As the cold night began to bite and close inwards, Snowball's world seemed to be getting smaller and smaller, and it was about to get worse if past experiences were anything to judge by. The door swung open, and Anne's welcoming Sunday smile dropped almost instantaneously from her face, as she was confronted with the sight of a grinning policeman to her left, and a repentant, head bowed and silent Snowball to her right. There was no point looking up at her. He knew he had just fucked up her day with the Lord, and there were most likely going to be repercussions.

"One of yours," mumbled the policeman, one foot in the door, as if he had been invited to a party. "Err, yes, he is," Anne replied, pivoting her body to the left, and conceding the entrance to the policeman, while finding just enough time to glare down at Snowball, with a rueful look that froze him dead in his tracks. "I didn't dooooo..." Snowball offered up, before Anne hastily placed a stiffened finger across her pursed lips beholding him to silence. "Come in," she called out to the policeman, and not without a hint of her trademark sarcasm, as he was already stood in the hall, and pondering the direction in which he might be ushered next. Snowball followed behind, collar grasped tightly by Anne, as she led them into the front lounge, and offered the constable a seat. You know the sort of front room. It's the room that's reserved for special occasions and adults only, always kept 'pointlessly' pristine, as there were never enough qualifying visitors to justify the exclusionary measures that were imposed for entry into its domain.

Anne's smile and tone were unnerving. Snowball had seen and heard it before. It was the tone that simply stated, she had you bang to rights, or that it was going to be extremely difficult to 'get out of this one'. It was that tone and look of confidence, when you know all your ducks are lined up properly, and all that is required is a suitable victim to impart your genius upon. "Would you like a cup of tea?" she enquired of the policeman, who by now was sitting comfortably in one of the large armchairs that Aunty Beryl normally occupied, during her quiet nights sleeping over at the home. "That would be lovely," he replied, perhaps not fully appreciative of the fact that it was a time gaining diversionary tactic, while Anne got her head around the situation, as much as it was a traditional common courtesy, and a sign of respect for his position in the local community. Anne's grip on Snowball's collar shifted to his hand, and then tightened, as she promptly swung around, and headed towards the kitchen, with a wincing errant child in tow. He wasn't so much 'up shit creek without a paddle' as he was 'up shit creek, swimming against the rapids, and about to go completely under'.

The large central Aga had often been the scene of many a quiet chat with Anne, but this was one Snowball wasn't looking forward to with any degree of relish, and he knew that the following minutes were going to be pivotal in determining whether, or not, his night concluded in the pain-free fashion that he had become so accustomed to, since his arrival in Stockport. For the next few minutes, important minutes in terms of his immediate life expectancy, Anne would be holding court, and he would be wise to listen to every word she had to say. "Biscuits," she commanded, pointing to the large metal tin on the pantry shelf. Snowball opened the tin and helped himself to a custard cream, before receiving a curt slap to the back of the head, as Anne informed him that they were for the policeman, not him. Point taken. It was always a long shot, but worth a try.

Anne grabbed the large metal kettle, filled it with water and attached the whistler, before placing it gently onto the front ring of the Aga. "Well?" she asked, as she spun round to face Snowball, the elevated inflection not completely lost on the fretful child in front of her. He had roughly four and a half minutes before the whistle on the kettle would begin to sound. Four and half minutes to convince her of his innocence and avert the almost inevitable upending that he would receive, if appropriate words failed him. If ever there was a time for an actor to take centre stage, it was clearly now, and seizing the moment, Snowball brushed the curtains aside, strode centre stage, and began to carefully relay the events of that late afternoon, early evening, which had culminated in his presence in the back of a police car, and an escorted trip back home with the weather beaten PC Smyth. Oh, how attending church suddenly seemed like the thing to be doing.

He had met up with some friends that afternoon in the nearby park, and after playing football for a few hours, they had decamped to the local newsagent's, as they had begun to make their way to their respective homes. It was a common enough occurrence, and there was nothing immediately untoward or premeditated, as they headed that way, jovial banter in full flow, and plans afoot for the time and place of the meeting the following afternoon, where they would resume the game. They had all entered the newsagent's, with most of the boys immediately heading for the penny trays at the front counter, where the best value for money could be gained, for the least amount of exchange. Snowball, however, bereft of any pocket money, had simply stood at the end of the newspaper rack, and closest to the door, while his friends had indulged themselves, by what transpired to be both fair means and foul.

All seemed perfectly normal, until the shopkeeper suddenly started to shout with an overt, if not overly exaggerated rage at the boys, and began to make his way around the counter, while waving his right arm aggressively in their direction. The boys began to spontaneously bolt towards the door, the eldest grabbing a bewildered Snowball by the arm as he passed, and imploring him to run, which in complete ignorance of the unfolding situation, he had done, if for no other reason than, the sight of the enraged shopkeeper struck a certain amount of fear into him, necessitating that both time and distance were best placed between them both.

They headed out of the shop, shopkeeper in pursuit, back towards the park, where they cut across the playing fields, and onto Smith Street. Smith Street led to Whitehall Road, which in turn poured the petrified group onto King Street, and beyond. Upon realising that they were no longer being chased, the pace had dropped, long enough for Snowball, amongst an abundance of descendent joviality, mirth, as well as a general disregard for the concepts of right and wrong, to be informed that two of his friends had been shoplifting sweets at the front of the store, while the others had provided for what they considered to be an appropriate diversion, to keep the shopkeeper occupied. Unfortunately, the newsagent had somehow spotted their nefarious endeavours, and thus the chase was on. Jonno had cheekily stuffed a handful of unwrapped sweets into his mouth, before smiling at the shopkeeper and running for the door, whilst his closest friend Parky had simply hurled a handful of sweets at the approaching shopkeeper as a distraction, in the hope of further facilitating their escape. It all seemed quite funny in the telling, but Snowball didn't know whether to laugh or cry. However, the answer wasn't that far behind them.

Beryl and Anne were devoutly religious. They ran the home on a very clearly defined and comprehensible set of rules, principles and values, which were drummed into every child that lived there. It wasn't a torrid regime, it was simply about right and wrong, the role of adults versus the role of children, respect, politeness, and all those good things that are never appreciated as a young child but insisted upon as an adult. It was fuckery at the time, but common sense as you age. Many of the rules had been hand-written on a sheet of paper, and they were hung in the living room at the back of the house. They were rules that provided for behavioural structure, and the overall comfort of everyone. Obey the rules and everything was fine. Stealing was high on the list of 'Do Nots', and there were many things that were considered to be stealing, even though they were far from criminal acts in any sense. Taking biscuits from the tin without asking, using the belongings of others, having your hands in the sweet jar that Aunty Beryl kept as treats in the front room. All acts of theft as far as Anne and Beryl were concerned, and the current situation that Snowball found himself in, was not sitting well with his conscience, and nor was the prospect of an imminent carpet inspection at the hands of Anne. He knew what they would say. 'You don't steal, you ask.' He had heard it from them many times before, even though he had had never actually stolen from them bar the odd cheeky biscuit from the tin, which in part was their fault for leaving it out in the first place. Nor had he stolen from anyone else for that matter. He had heard them repeat it to others, as often as they had to him, and he had heard it both at school and at church, which in his eyes seemed particularly strange, as abusing children appeared to be ok, but helping yourself to the abusers' sweets or biscuits was a definite no-no in the House of the Lord. But it was better not to go there with Anne, as she was holding all the cards, and she knew how to play them.

He relayed to Anne that, with a sense of impending doom and panic sweeping over him, he had swiftly turned on his heels, and began to head back towards the park, and home. "Where are you going?" he heard one of his friends call out, before he disappeared around the corner, and broke into a canter, that turned quickly into a frantic jog, and then a sweat dripping frenzied sprint towards home. It was in the park, that he came across PC Murray Smyth, a tall, robustly built and brooding Scot, who had moved south from his Edinburgh homeland to join the police in the absence of any available vacancies in his hometown. Smyth had quite literally taken hold of his collar as he darted past. Raising him from the ground, leaving him hanging like a rag doll in the firm grip afforded him by the shovel sized hands with which he had been endowed. Such was Snowball's fear, he hadn't even seen Smyth until he found himself swinging in the air, like a ragdoll pinned to a washing line. He heard a deep gravel-rich voice enquire as to where he thought he was going in such a hurry, as he suddenly realised that the reason they were no longer being chased, was that PC Smyth had driven around the corner closest to the shop, only fleeting moments after they had bolted.

The shopkeeper had stopped Smyth, and explained what had happened, and PC Smyth had duly taken on full responsibility for apprehending the suspects, who were now 'at large' in the vicinity, and clearly needed to be apprehended. It was all a little 'Dixon of Dock Green', but there you go. Snowball, dangling in the air, had caught sight of the large black boots that Smyth wore, closely followed by the silver looking buttons of his tunic, and finally his traditionally peaked helmet, as he swung in the wind. There was no clearer sign that the game was up, and all that was required was an ETA on the precise time that his feet would once again touch terra-firma. It seemed slightly trivial, almost amusing to PC Smyth, and there wasn't a lot to go on as he set about tracking down the culprits, but when the shopkeeper had mentioned to Smyth that there was a black boy with them, his recently acquired community knowledge kicked in, and Smyth was onto him in a flash.

For Snowball, it was one of the pitfalls of being the only black kid in an all-white community. There was a propensity to stand out, no matter how much he felt he was blending into the background when mischief ensued. If he hadn't been caught on his way home, PC Smyth would most certainly have called at the house, and so here he was, dangling in the air like a condemned man on the gallows, protesting his innocence, upon the deaf ears of a mountainous Scot, who seemed more interested in swinging him around like a kite, than he did about the missing sweets, or his partners in crime. Less than ten minutes later, repentant, in tears, but with feet now firmly attached to the ground, Snowball was stood in the newsagent's apologising profusely on the one hand for what had transpired, while strongly asserting his innocence of any wrongdoing on the other. It seemed to make little difference to the shopkeeper, who upon banning him for 'life' from the shop, instructed him to inform his 'mates' that they too were also banned. It all seemed a little harsh, but Snowball figured that it probably wasn't the time to protest the punishment, and upon instruction from PC Smyth, took his 'backside' to the pavement, to await the dreaded lift home that would culminate, in all likelihood, with the severest punishment he was likely to encounter for some time hence. Moments later, they were on their way to number 33, and a meeting with Anne!

By the time he had finished relaying his story to Anne, the kettle had started whistling, with the familiar plume of steam gushing from its peak, and she casually slipped it over to the warming ring on the Aga, which would keep it simmering in much the same fashion that she was. She gathered the small plate of biscuits together, and, passing them to Snowball, instructed him to take them into the lounge for PC Smyth, and wait for her there. The biscuits were still a bit of a disappointment, as his first assumption that the biscuits were for him had proven unfounded, and he clearly hadn't alleviated her annoyance enough to qualify for one. She had so far appeared unaccepting of his explanation, and his naive expectation that the truth would set him free, so to speak, was turning into an anticipated slapping in the quiet of her room.

It wasn't long before Anne promptly joined him in the living room, and seating herself opposite PC Smyth, queried him, with a slight feign to ignorance, as to why he was there. She was inwardly content that she knew the true story already, as she was experienced enough to look any child in the eye and know immediately if what she was hearing was true or not. Snowball was no different, and she knew that with even the smallest of intimations towards punishment, which she had dutifully and quite masterfully delivered, Snowball was just the sort who would definitely, and with heightened sense of haste, tell her the truth, the whole truth and nothing but the truth, in order to better mitigate what he thought were going to be exceptionally painful consequences if he failed to do so.

Smyth duly relayed a story very similar to that which she had already been told, confirming in essence that Snowball had merely been in unwitting attendance, and to the best of anyone's knowledge, hadn't stolen anything on that occasion, nor any other occasion as it happened. Snowball afforded himself a deep and silent sigh of relief, as PC Smyth concluded his summary of events. He wasn't out of the woods yet, but simply having the fact that he wasn't a thief confirmed, had just increased his chances of avoiding a thrashing exponentially, which for a boy in his position, was a clear win of some magnitude. Anne was no doubt still upset, but was admirably containing herself, and maintaining an outwardly calm composure, that weirdly enough was having something of a calming effect on a fretful Snowball, who had only just stopped perspiring, as she continued her discussions with PC Smyth.

Tea and biscuits consumed, PC Smyth rose to his size thirteen feet, and moved towards Anne, hand extended as if she had just offered him a new job, before turning towards the door and heading into the hallway. "I will leave it with you then," he said, turning briefly, before reaching for the front door. "Thank you," Anne had countered, as calm and composed as she had been throughout, but no doubt merely containing herself for the fireworks that were about to be ignited after she had successfully ushered him to the doorstep, and out of the house. "And I can assure you, he will be round there tomorrow to apologise," she added, before turning herself sideways to reveal a shame-faced Snowball nodding in agreement.

PC Smyth stopped on the driveway, delaying his departure with a handful of polite, and apparently customary pre-departure articulations, that had Snowball seething at the brim, as his anxiety levels escalated to Defcon One. 'Oh, will you please just fuck off, you 'Grade A' fucker,' Snowball's inner demons were screaming. Let me just get this over and done with, for Christ's sake. The tension was simply becoming too much, and as much as he wished he could avoid what seemed like the inevitable 'fucked up Sunday' thrashing from Anne, he was also of the mind that if it had to happen, he would rather just get it over and done with, so that things could return to normal, and the day's events could simply be drawn to a conclusion and forgotten. Snowball had risen to his feet upon the imminent departure of PC Smyth, but had been gestured by Anne to stay put, silently slumping back into his seat, only to rise again, as the adults had slipped from the room. He could hear Anne bidding the officer farewell at the door, and had quietly sidled up alongside her, before the familiar sound of the Yale latch engaging echoed through the porch, bounced off the stone tiled floor, and was duly followed by the sound of Anne flipping the locking mechanism, and heralding the start of his next nightmare.

Anne returned to the living room with him, clearly enraged, but exerting a surprising level of self-control, given the nature of what had just taken place, and the escalating embarrassment she had clearly felt. "Learned anything today?" she prompted as she retook her place in the armchair. It was almost an echo of his frequent chats with Miss Bradwell, whom he was dearly wishing he could deal with at that moment, instead of Anne. Oh, how he was beginning to appreciate the nuances of time, distance and place, as his current circumstances descended upon him, like a predatory feline seeking its next unfortunate meal. Anne had mastered the art of the sublime in every respect. Her delivery both pitch perfect and immaculately constructed, she played Snowball like a conductor played an orchestra. Each, finely tuned note, cued both in and out, on time and delivered with a consummate ease, that belied the expertise that had been honed through years of repeated practice.

Snowball, head cast downwards, slowly looked up and nodded. It was the only thing he could do, as the gravity of the situation hit home with an alarming force. "What have you learned?" she knowingly queried. She instinctively knew that he was playing the game, as he sat uncomfortably alongside her, and squirmed in his seat, like a worm on a hook. He hadn't realised it, but she was fishing, and he had to decide if he was taking the bait. He wasn't at all sure what he had learned, if indeed he had learned anything at all. He was just instinctively aware that he clearly should have learned something from the events of that afternoon and, given the nature of the question in the first instance, and the intonation she had used, any answer would have been preferable than, none at all. He remained silent, until Anne again interjected with a well delivered prompt. "Well?" she asked.

There was another pause. Shorter than the last, but it was without doubt a pause for sure, before Snowball replied by stating the blindingly obvious that "It's wrong to steal". Anne issued a barely audible sigh before adding, "I know that, and I know you know that, because you didn't steal anything, did you?" Snowball shook his head vigorously. Though completely factual, it was almost as if she was offering an imaginary lifeline to the guilty, and so he took a firm grip of her words, and absorbed them, sponge-like into his conscious awareness. If nothing else, he had offered her something with which she could agree, and it clearly demonstrated that he had absorbed all those lessons that she and Aunty Beryl had sought to instil in him, but he wasn't sure if it was enough.

"So, what did you learn?" she asked for a second time. 'Oh, for fuck's sake, do we have to play this game?' he thought, again remaining silent, uncommunicative, and at great personal risk of a thrashing. There was another more audible sigh from Anne, before she muttered with a quite deliberate and intentional calm, "Maybe a smack around the back of your legs might help you think", giving him a knowing look that clearly indicated it was better to say something, even if it was a case of saying something stupid, than it was to adopt his current strategy of remaining silent, and hoping for the best, every time she asked him for some input. It was another one of those stupid questions that adults ask. He was hardly likely to agree to her suggestion, but, as long as she felt happier having submitted the implication, and as it currently remained unexecuted, there was no need for immediate panic. "I don't know," came the reply. "You don't know what?" she countered, intent on ensuring that she didn't make this an easy ride for him. "I think you need to sit there, until you do know, and I will back shortly," she stated, rising to her feet, and disappearing out of the door.

Left alone with his thoughts, Snowball's mind began to meander through the events of the afternoon that had just passed. The need to avoid the threatened and imminent smack spurring him into a deeper analysis of the what and when, in order to fathom out an answer that might appear remotely plausible, and that she might actually be interested in hearing. He needed time to think, plenty of time to think, but time was something that was in short supply, and by definition, not a commodity that was entirely on his side. As if by feat of magic, Anne conjured up her reappearance, remaining stern faced, but with a hint of compassion, that leant itself to the idea that, if he could only come up with some of the right answers, things might just turn out to be ok, and they could put the entire thing down to experience. She sat beside him and remained silent. She had clearly made herself aware of the old interrogation adage, that a timely silence was often the easiest way to open a suspect up, more so than direct intensive questioning was. She wanted him to express himself, explain his thinking and his calculations, how he had arrived at his conclusions and what he intended to do about them, and unfortunately for Snowball, she was quite happy to wait for that to happen, regardless of how long it took.

He could sense her presence, hear her breathing, almost feel her heart beating rhythmically with his. There was a unity of purpose that was simply being approached from different directions. They were both cognisant of the end goal, both had it in sight, but for her there was a clarity of mind, and for him a lemonade cloudiness in thinking. It was either now or never and a visit to the knee in Snowball's eyes, and so began the tale of enlightened learning that had been visited upon him, along the road that led from Stockport to Damascus.

He had learned that friends are not always what they might appear to be, and he recalled forgotten lessons that had been both enthusiastically taught and carefully crafted by Miss Bradwell, about trusting nobody. He had learned that he needed to be more aware of his surroundings, and what was taking place both in and out of eyesight, and he had learned that there were consequences to be paid, if he failed to distance himself from that which he knew to be clearly wrong and had wilfully or otherwise failed to acknowledge. In his own words, he had somehow managed to get that message over to the avid listener opposite, and Anne appeared genuinely impressed with his efforts, despite the considerable amount of time it had taken for him to draw his own conclusions and articulate them clearly. She found that often annoying adult need to elaborate and clarify the position on a few of the points he had raised, if only to ensure they were both on the same page in respect of future behaviours, which was fair enough, as they had previously failed to occupy the same library, let alone the same page of a book.

He had avoided the smack by his own efforts, and she made an effort to let him know that was the reason why. "Not that difficult, was it?" she asked. "What?" he sheepishly replied, as a feeling of self-conscious sickness swept through his stomach. "Thinking for yourself – you should do it more often," she replied, rising to her feet, and ushering him out of the lounge with a pat across the back of the head, and into the adjacent hallway. "Go and get your pyjamas on, and then come down for some supper," she instructed, before he shot up the stairs and out of sight.

Now in the immediate aftermath of avoiding the consequences of trouble that you've either caused yourself, or found yourself in, as a direct result of your own naivety, the actions of others, or plain and simple stupidity, there is a golden rule that must be adhered to if you are to remain intact, and viable. That rule simply states that you should remain out of trouble (and preferably out of sight) for a reasonable amount of time (let us say twenty-four hours), so that the proverbial dust can be allowed to settle, and the lay of the land can be re-assessed. This is a strategy that is best suited to everybody involved, not least the miscreant, or those on the periphery, but whom have the possibility of being sucked into the vacuous whirlwind of retribution, if it all kicks off again. For Snowball this was a lesson he had learned long ago, but one that he had allowed to slip from immediate memory, in the newly found safety and comforts he was enjoying in the home he now found himself living in. It was a lesson he was about to wish he had allowed to remain a little more prominent in his developing mind, for a little longer than he had allowed it to.

The remainder of the night had passed away in relatively uneventful fashion. One of the other children had succumbed to a bout of intolerance, and struck out with fists and feet at Clare, who to be honest had deserved everything she had reaped, having had it coming all day, but it was a clear infraction of Anne's rules, and she had accordingly meted out an appropriate retribution, resulting in both tears and tantrums, which had disturbed the weekly viewing of Stars on Sunday, before the miscreant, isolated and alone, had been bedded down for the night. There were a few knowing looks from Anne cast in Snowball's direction, and a few remorseful looking endeavours returned in kind by Snowball, but nothing more than that ensued. Snowball had arisen the next day as usual, and got himself washed, ready for school, eaten breakfast, and bid both Aunty Anne and Aunty Beryl, who had just arrived for her dayshift goodbye, before heading off to school.

School that day, and in the main had been a mundane affair, until the mid-afternoon break, when the playground football had recommenced. There was always a heightened anxiety during the afternoon football, as it was the last opportunity that either team had to recover any goal deficit, before the goal tally for the day was done, and one team had the misery of going home losers, amidst an onslaught of childish ridicule, which grew more hostile as the afternoon drew to its close. One of the boys from the previous afternoon's mischief had grounded Snowball with a crunching tackle, the likes of which by any measure could have been a career ending tackle, had he had himself a career in the first place. But nevertheless, Snowball felt that it couldn't go without reprisal, and minutes later, in the finest tradition of letting them know that you're in the fight, had put in a rather reckless sliding tackle, which had brought his adversary to the ground in an outburst of screams, and left Snowball prone on the ground, with blood gushing from his grazed legs, sustained as the concrete had ripped the skin from the top of his thighs, to his knees. Revenge had been served up cold, and that might normally have been the end of the matter, but for the fact that the afternoon break was a supervised one, and the malice he had inflicted upon the other boy, had been witnessed by the playground monitor, who had promptly sought out the attention of his form teacher, as a direct consequence of being told to fuck off, when she had challenged him about his conduct, and advised that the cuts to his legs were nothing less than he deserved.

As push developed into shove, and the matter could not be resolved in the school yard with an appropriate apology, he had found himself stood outside the Mr Grimley's office, a hidden plimsoll mark across each bottom cheek, and waiting for someone to arrive from home and pick him up. That someone unfortunately turned out to be Anne, and it became immediately apparent that the plimsoll marks on his backside were to be the least of his immediate problems. Anne in attendance was a fifty-fifty call that didn't go his way, and it continued to be everyone else's day but his, when she angrily bundled him into the back of her Morris Minor, threw his satchel to the floor, and upon arriving home, patience exceeded by some considerable measure, had dragged her innocence-protesting charge upstairs, where she had in a fit of pique delivered what she considered him due, put him to bed, and left him there until the following morning to 'reflect on his ways' as she had termed it. Though the apparent injustice of it all was nauseating, Snowball chose to accept his fate with grace, and remained silent and bedded throughout the long night that ensued. A silent breakfast had been eaten the following morning, and he sheepishly headed out to school, for the start of another day, with the previously aired words of his old mentor Miss Bradwell ringing in his inner ear. 'Sometimes you just have to take the rough with the smooth' – because apparently, and according to Aunty Beryl who was the most intellectually sage of adults he would come across, 'that's how it works, my boy'.

Though Christchurch school could be something of a trauma, the good more often than not outshone the bad. It was the type of school that, though rigid in its instruction on right and wrong, and equally as stringent in its application of corporal punishment for transgressors when required, it was, nevertheless, a place where children were not only encouraged to thrive intellectually, but they actually did thrive. Snowball was no exception. It was an intellectually stimulating environment, in which his innate curiosity about most of the unknowns that he encountered were satiated by the fountains of knowledge that taught him daily, and encouraged his search for answers, at the local library, and bookshops that littered the town.

Christchurch was a school that encouraged the search for knowledge. As was the continued case at home, every child was expected to have book that they were currently in the process of reading. There were approved educational texts to be ploughed through, and there would be reading afternoons, where each child was expected to bring a favourite book from home, and explain the plot, why they liked it, and take a much-feared turn at reading aloud from the text, to a 'mesmerised' though captive audience. They were the sort of occasions where you either ended up looking much brighter than you probably were, or you wound up looking a complete twat. There was always a good smattering in each camp by the end of the day, so you were never alone, which clearly helped the less gifted as the twattery unfolded.

Snowball was also found to be something of a budding thespian and had found an accepted home amongst the dramatically inclined drama queens and general misfits at Christchurch, all of whom seemed to excel on stage when the school plays finally came around at the end of the term, or Christmas breaks. At Christchurch, it was also the year of the grand production of Joseph and his Technicolour Dreamcoat, which saw Snowball take centre stage, having been cast as an understudy to Joseph, only to see the principal 'actor' drop by the wayside, having found himself unable to either memorise or read his lines accurately from the script that had been provided. Not only did Snowball know the lines, he could recite them without the script, and was equally comfortable reciting the lines of all the other principal characters as well. And so it was, 'his people' talked to 'their people', the deal was done, and with 'equity card' in hand, the Christchurch Christmas production of Joseph and his Technicolour was launched, and a potential 'star' of the stage and screen was born, in a run that comprised 10 performances over five days and evenings, culminating in the grand finale, attended by Mr Grimley, parents, the local priest and the Mayor of Stockport himself.

CORONA, GYPSIES AND AN OLD FORD ESCORT

Snowball also found that with attendance at a normal school came the very much utilised ability to freely roam. There was a half mile walk to and from home to Christchurch School, and there were a variety of ways that Snowball could go subject to weather conditions, time constraints, and instructions issued by either Beryl or Anne, had he been so shoddy that morning as to catch their attention before he had slipped through the door, lunch pack in satchel, and satchel slung over his shoulder. He could do the clean route, but where was the fun in that was the common thought. Straight, neat and tidy roads, direct, hazard-free. No. Or he could take the clearly more 'obvious' route, which perhaps wouldn't appeal to most people, being indirect, time-consuming, through the filth laden fields, dirty and riddled with dangers ranging from untamed and vicious freely-roaming dogs, to most contractible diseases should you be unfortunate enough to go from your hand to your mouth after touching something, before you had been afforded opportunity to clean up. It was a simple choice, and one that didn't take much thinking about in Snowball's eyes, though his lack of wise choices was a much discussed feature of after school life, as he returned home, accordingly covered in the detritus of his escapades.

The fields provided for adventure. It was a landscape that changed constantly, whether that was through the old washing machines, fridges and cars that were regularly dumped there, and provided in themselves something to be explored and played with, or the annual inward migration of gypsies, who arrived every August, and had generally left by November, under a cloud of common prejudice and malignant hate. The route was often either covered in a thin, clingy dust, or a muddy quagmire of rain soiled filth, and was as undulating as it was fraught with hidden dangers that awaited the unsuspecting, the uncaring and the unknowing. Snowball would meander through the uncropped grasses, and abandoned junk, which would one day in the not too distant future, be the focus of a very professionally orchestrated, and concerted clean-up campaign. The council would eventually clean up, fence off and level the land for the very much needed construction of council housing, which in turn would bring with it a whole new era of adventure and trouble to Snowball's life, but for now it was a magnet of misadventure that was far too irresistible, and he frequented it often.

However, what appealed to Snowball most, was the pairing of the gypsies and the old Ford Escort. The gypsies would cleverly arrive overnight and largely unannounced, at a time when they knew the local council would be closed for the day, and the chances of them being impeded in their endeavours to illicitly occupy the land was slim to non-existent. They would immediately set up a semi-fortified camp, complete with ferocious looking German Shepherds anchored to a restrictive circle of movement by large chains that had been secured in place by rigid looking iron poles driven into the ground for security. By mid-afternoon the following day, their presence was always widely known of, routinely disparaged in street corner chatter, and being felt as an imagined nefarious presence throughout the local community.

They were largely disliked amongst the adult community for a variety of reasons, mainly based on nothing more than indifference and taught prejudice, but they had a knack of both welcoming and entertaining young children, as if it was a passion of theirs, though in reality it was most likely a hearts and minds game, in which they attempted to appeal vicariously to the parents through their children. Whatever the concerns that were widespread in the community, it mattered little to Snowball, and the reality was simply that those who cared little for the gypsies were likely to be the same people who cared little for the black face of the little sambo, who lived around the corner.

The gypsies were also a rowdy bunch, which also had the inalienable effect of disenfranchising the local community, and they could often be seen in the dark of night, sat around their fires, drinking heavily, and squaring up to each other for the occasional alcohol-inspired bout of bare-knuckle fighting. Snowball had been told about them by Anne, and warned more than once, with the familiar threat of a visit over her knee, that he was not to go near them, speak to them, or play with their kids. It was another case of dislike for the sake of dislike, and an uncharacteristic display of blatant intolerance, but in the main, threats from Anne still carried some weight, purely because she was the one most likely to carry them out, and so by and large he kept away. However, 'keeping away' can be a pretty subjective term of reference to a young mind, and without the added clarity so often provided by an adult interjection, who was to know what might happen.

From the rear bedroom window in a friend's house, the encamped Snowball could see the occasional fight break out in the gypsy camp, which was usually followed shortly after, by the blue flashing lights of the local constabulary glowing as they encroached on the closed-in skyline. They made heavy work of crossing from one side of town to the other, in order to attend the melee. The aim was always to be in attendance before things got too out of hand, and the gypsies started to make their way up 'the hill', and into 'civilised' society, where their very presence would cause hostilities to boil over into something that nobody wanted to witness.

It had happened on previous occasions, and resulted in numerous arrests, after one man had been struck with a broken bottle, and another an iron bar. It wasn't so much that the fighting was annoying, as it was infrequent enough to be tolerable, but according to local whispers in the wind, it was the fact that the gypsies always won, and the local testosterone filled youths and men alike were then forced into a humiliating retreat, which would rankle for weeks to come. However, with the police in attendance and maintaining a watchful eye, things would always eventually calm down again; the gypsies would fall into an alcohol induced sleep that would last until late morning the following day, before waking to find the smouldering embers of their fires, about to pass into the dull flicker of luminous history, which told no tales of, nor lent itself to, the previous night of hostilities.

Stone was roughly thirteen years old. A 'Romany' as he liked to be called, and a very popular one at that. He was unusually bright, addictively hyperactive, fun to be around, a whirling dervish of activity, as well as a tough boy to boot. He had been taught to fight by his father, who was reputed to be a leading bare-knuckle fighter amongst his so-called clan, which was spread across all four nations of the United Kingdom, and according to Stone, out into the distant wilds of Europe. It all meant absolutely nothing in general to Snowball or his friends, whose collective worldly knowledge barely extended no further than the borders of Stockport, with occasional skirmishes into the heady districts of Manchester, if they had relatives or friends who resided that far afield. He was, and widely known to be, as 'hard as nails' within the Romany community, and had very much become an attraction that arrived annually, and disappeared just as quickly as he had appeared, and with the same degree of pre-warning.

Snowball had first been introduced the year before, when as tradition demanded, the camp had been established, and again had proved to be a mesmerising attraction to the local children. Stone was something of a cocky braggart, but a very likeable braggart, friendly, approachable to most of the kids, and above all, worldly wise in comparison, for his overtly obvious lack of years. He had turned up this year as the proud 'owner' of an old MKI Ford Escort. It was debateable as to whether or not the car had been purchased, or 'acquired' on his travels, but neither Snowball nor the other kids really cared. He had a car of his 'own', and that essentially made him a god. It was a much sought after car of the day, and that pretty much cemented his status as a modern day hero in the eyes of his young impressionable sycophants. He had no licence that anyone was aware of, presumably no tax or insurance either, but he did possess a keen eye for the road, and a willingness to run kids around town at high speeds, just for the thrill it gave him and them. There were rumours that he had occasionally been spotted by the police, who had subsequently given chase, but been unsuccessful in apprehending him at the wheel, and he had remained at large to drive another day. The rumours were probably untrue, but they all added to the exalted status and sense of hubris that was conferred upon him by his young admirers, Snowball included. Stone and his Escort were extremely popular that year, for a variety of reasons, but there was one particular reason that had all the local children flocking in both admiration and expectation to his camp, and ensured that when he finally departed that year, he would be sorely missed by everyone.

Further up the fields from the gypsy encampment, was a pop warehouse that distributed most of the popular brands of the time, to the local houses throughout Stockport. The Pop Man was a regular weekly feature of life, driving a large open-backed truck, stacked high with six or twelve bottle crates of everyone's favourite drinks, and delivering direct to the door, where he would drop off freshly filled bottles of fizzy pop, before removing the empties and returning them to the warehouse for cleaning and a refill. Snowball's favourite was Corona, and he could drink it by the gallon if he had the opportunity to. It was the one thing that he couldn't get enough of, and in Stone he found a 'friend' who could and would satiate his voracious appetite for the fizzy nectar. You see, Stone was an observant young lad if nothing else, and it hadn't taken him long to notice in the first instance that the crated pop was largely stored outside, ten to twelve crates high, in a mesh fenced compound that was unguarded bar the owner's two German Shepherds, which were left to freely roam the compound during the night, as a deterrent to anyone compelled to trespass in order to alleviate the factory of a few bottles.

But Stone didn't need to trespass in order to acquire a few bottles at the factory owner's expense, as he had coolly worked out that, by parking his escort alongside the fence, and utilising the camber of the land to tilt the car inwards, he could stand on top of the car, where the upper front door sills met the inner rim of the roof, and he was just about tall enough, to help himself to bottles from the top row of crates. This simple, and yet ingenious act, theft though it was, made Stone the most popular of the transient kids in the district, and by a large margin, with a steady stream of 'thirsty' youngsters, Snowball included, making a nightly pilgrimage to his encampment, where they would sit swigging 'free' pop, and listening to stories of derring do from Stone and his extended family, before either the closing of daylight, or the local police sought to move them on, and out of 'harm's way'.

But as they say, 'there's no such thing as a free lunch' and everyone pays eventually. For Snowball, payment was unexpectedly and quite quickly invoiced. His hero Stone had graduated from taking the odd few bottles that had largely gone unnoticed, to lifting full crates out of the compound, and the irregularities had been pounced upon by the warehouse manager, who upon seeing the gypsy camp strewn with his clearly identifiable empty crates, had called the police and asked them to summarily investigate. The police had kept watch over the course of a few nights, from a house on the hill opposite, and had witnessed not only Stone taking the crates, but the gang of children that had sat happily swigging the ill-gotten gains, while clearly enjoying the banter that Stone provided, as he enthralled his congregation. The 'Only Black Child' in the district curse had struck again, as the 'lesser spotted black boy' twitchers had reported him on several occasions to the police, who had subsequently confirmed the veracity of their claims, and brought them to the attention of Aunty Beryl. Thus, with a tension filled visit from the police concluded, Aunty Beryl had grounded him indefinitely, until his behaviour improved.

It all seemed a little unfair to Snowball who, unable to contest his complicity given the raft of eye witness evidence against him, had opted to vigorously protest the outcomes meted out by Aunty Beryl, only to find himself with early bedtimes thrown in for 'good measure' as she called it, and a requirement to be the solitary post tea-time dish washer, dryer and 'putter-awayer' until further notice. How he sometimes craved the simplicity of a carpet inspection over Anne's knee, in preference to the protracted punishments that Aunty Beryl chose to administer to her errant charges. As Miss Bradwell had once told him, 'sometimes life isn't fair'.

Aunty Beryl had, through the process of worldly experience, her long years in managing the home, and also its children, come to learn that there were clearly more ways to skin a rabbit, and the ingenuity of her punishments reflected that fact that, in her opinion, some punishments, such as those preferred by Anne, were clearly over too fast, and did not afford the errant child enough time to reflect on the inappropriateness of their behaviour before they moved on to their next misdemeanour, having failed to assimilate the lessons of their last. Without time to reflect, there clearly wasn't the opportunity to learn, in her view, and so the protracted punishments that she chose to administer would in the first instance act as the deterrent she preferred, whilst at the same time they brought with them the 'benefits' of a daily period of reflection, as they were rigidly imposed, and the reason for their imposition reinforced.

Snowball soon came to appreciate that her punishments hurt far more than Anne's ever did, as they had the lasting impact she wanted, and were an assault on the mind, rather than the body. Aunty Beryl was also rigid in their application. Once an award had been made, it was always implemented in full. She never wavered, and as he had found out to his cost on several occasions, with the price of dissent being a heavy one. The complete twattery of it all wasn't lost on Snowball. He came to understand and appreciate that there was no way out, and eventually came to the wisdom that he would simply knuckle under and accept the unpalatable reality that he had unwittingly brought upon himself.

WHO ARE YOU AGAIN?

"**H**i, my name is Patricia Wilson-Hall, and I would like to fuck up your life, if that's ok," she said, with a large canyon sized smile thrown in for good measure. They weren't the actual words that she had used, but they were the exact words that Snowball heard loud and clear. He had arrived home from school that day, buoyant, upbeat, happy, with homework in satchel, knees grazed, and shoes scuffed at the toes, and completely unaware of the drama that was about to unfold, in the front living room, of number 33. He had been kept in the dark, about a problem that had been closing in quickly on Beryl and Anne. A problem not of his making, but one that would have a profound impact on his life from that moment onward.

Unbeknown to him, there was an upper age limit for the children that stayed at number 33, and his last birthday had seen him quietly slip past that limit and left him unknowingly wandering in unfamiliar and dangerous territories. Beryl and Anne had been happy to keep him, but in the background, plans were being made for his next move. On two previous occasions, he had been due to leave, but the plans had fallen through, and he had been quietly allowed to stay where he was. All that changed, however, when Patricia arrived on the doorstep, fresh paperwork in hand, and announcing that a placement had been found, and that she was here to take him away.

Aunty Beryl had greeted him on arrival home. It was immediately clear to him that something was wrong, because when Aunty Beryl greeted you from school, it was with a smile, followed by the standard question of "How has school been?". It was as much a question of interest as it was interrogative. It was her way of letting you know that she was interested, but also, that if there had been any trouble that day, she was most likely already aware of it, and it would be considered a smart move to simply come clean at that point, and own up. But today there was no smile, there were no questions, she just opened the door and allowed him to wander in, which, both wary and mindful, he had done so. He had started towards the large oak antique coat rack, which stood beside the stained-glass windows that protected the porch from the extremes of the outside elements, but Aunty Beryl had tapped him on the shoulder, and simply uttered the words "this way". He could hear his mind chattering, as he desperately tried to figure out what he had done to deserve this cold, sullen welcome from his much-loved aunty. He had only ever seen her like this on one previous occasion, and that had heralded in the biggest dressing down he had ever experienced, and he was eager to avoid a repeat. It was a much deserved 'taking to the cleaners' upon reflection, but one that was so severe, he had been happy just to survive, irrespective of the week-long cleaning duty that she had awarded him for his troubles.

Aunty Beryl motioned him into the living room, where, fearful of what was to follow, but both mindful and adamant that for once his conscience was clear, he casually strolled in, hoping that his confident gait wouldn't betray the manic anxieties that lay beneath the surface. "I have someone I want you to meet," she said, as his step faltered, almost in direct tandem with her own. "This is Patricia Wilson-Hall from the Social Services," she said, in a subdued, almost tearful tone, as she broke past the visual blockade that the open door had formed. Snowball moved slowly into the open space between the edge of the doorway, and the beginning of the large Victorian-style armchair that blocked any further advance.

By now Patricia had risen to her feet, and was grinning like a Cheshire Cat in heat. She had already begun to move in his direction, with hand extended, and a visage of sincerity now sweeping across what was, essentially, one of the ugliest mugs he had ever seen. "Hi, I am Patricia, nice to meet you." Snowball's hands remained firmly pressed against his sides, wandering only to fidget with the buckles of the satchel that swung from his shoulder. There was a gentle tap on the back of the head from Aunty Beryl, which was her way of reinforcing the message that 'manners were everything' in her eyes, and that she expected her standards to be maintained. It was enough of a prompt for Snowball to slowly accept Patricia's hand into his and shake it gently. As he loosened his grip, Aunty Beryl took hold of his other hand, and brought him to the side of the seat into which she was positioning herself. She cut a matronly dash as she perched herself serenely into the upholstered throne. It was a dash that was as scary as it was awe-inspiring, and whilst it was capable of striking abject fear into his soul at times, it somehow provided a much needed, albeit temporary degree of reassurance for Snowball, in his, as yet, unknown dilemma.

It was at this moment that he first caught sight of his belongs on the living room floor. His clothes in several bags, his toys, a small stack of books, everything just sitting there in full view on the living room floor. It was all there. Aunty Beryl caught sight of this, almost at exactly the same time that he turned to her for an explanation, face and spirit numbed, eyes dimming, heart pounding. She could see the fear sweeping across his face, as he quietly murmured "no" and took a firm grip of her hand. The next 'no' came out loud and clear, as did the next and the next, while Aunty Beryl tried to explain the circumstances in which they both now found themselves.

All he could muster was the word 'no' time and time again, as the words she spoke began to fade like distant drums on a faraway horizon. His mind was in complete turmoil. How could she do this to him, how could she let this happen? He was happy, he was safe, he was content, and she was sacrificing everything at the altar of some pathetically inhumane policy that clearly hadn't taken his needs, thoughts, aspirations or feelings into account. In total disbelief at Aunty Beryl and her betrayal, he called out for Aunty Anne. There was no response. He called out again and again, but all in vain. Anne wasn't even there, and if she had been, it would have changed absolutely nothing. He was about to be ripped from another loving home, and there was nothing he could do about, as a familiar picture of betrayal and hurt began to form in his mind.

Aunty Beryl assured him everything was going to be alright, but he knew it wouldn't be. They had told him that at Melbourne House and then left him in the hands of people who had systematically set about trying to destroy him both mentally and physically. The memories were still fresh in his mind, and it was those memories that had helped him understand just how much both Aunty Beryl and Aunty Anne had done for him, and how they had helped him to gradually start burying past nightmares and consign them to the darkness from which they had arisen.

He looked her directly in the eye and wondered how and why she thought it would be alright. How could losing all his friends, his school mates, his teachers, without even having the opportunity to say goodbye, be alright? How was being thrown out of his loving home going to be alright? How would never seeing the rest of the children, or Aunty Anne be alright, or the fact that they were proposing to take him miles away to a new home, where he knew nobody, with a new school, new 'Aunties and Uncles', new rules, new regimes, new diet, no bedroom of his own, or clothes he could say were his, 'how the fuck was that going to be alright, Aunty Beryl?' he wondered. It was clearly a case of not being able to polish a turd but you can sprinkle it with glitter. He mentally confronted the ugly spectre of the potential abuses he might once again have to suffer, the adversities which he thought were behind him, the solitude and loneliness. How was that going to be alright? He had only just made the mental breakthroughs from the last round of abuse, and was finally beginning to openly trust again, and then this. Oh, the fuckery of it. Miss Bradwell had been right all along. DON'T TRUST ANYBODY! 'Why the fuck didn't I listen?' he thought. The betrayal as he saw it ran deep, too deep. He now considered himself on his own, and that is how it would remain for as long as he deemed it necessary.

WELCOME TO THE MANORS OF MANCHESTER

It had been a quiet and fraught drive from the leafy suburbs of Stockport, into the sprawling mass that was known as Manchester. For Snowball, there was little if any need for discussion. They had just ripped him from a second 'family', and he felt no compunction to talk about it. If he had got things his own way, he would have ripped the scalp from Aunty Beryl's head, but history had taught him that wasn't always the most successful of strategies he had ever deployed, and the chances of it reaping benefit was slim. So, he just remained seated, quiet and in deep thought. He still couldn't understand why Aunty Beryl had done what she had done. Why Anne had not been there to help. He pondered the thoughts of the other children, who would be told that evening that he had been taken away and that he wouldn't be returning. And what of his friends, all just taken in the blink of an eye, and not one person had asked him what he wanted. It was all just so unfair, so brutal, so cold, so cruel.

He remained relatively oblivious to the short journey that was being undertaken. Patricia had entered into a one-way conversation, which involved her using every trick in the book to placate him, but the damage had already been done, and he simply wasn't interested in anything that she had to say. She had by all accounts been his social worker for some time now, but he had never seen or heard of her before that day, and all she had brought with her was bad news and an unwelcome change of habitat. As far as he was concerned, there was a place she could stick her strained conversation, and she was sat on it. His thoughts were now in distant pastures, his heart and soul still firmly lodged at number 33.

His mind wandered back to Farm Wood, to his early years, and the only family that had really been his. He could see his 'mother's' face, tears still

160

streaming as he had been placed into the back of the car that had eventually taken him away. He could vividly see the girls screaming as they had been ripped from the only home they had ever known, and the defeated image of his father as the gravity of what was transpiring in the family home, began to sink in. It was easy to envision himself, happily skirting the streets that separated him from the welcoming arms and sweet filled hands of Mrs Swarecki. How he longed to see her smiling face, just one more time, just once more, and today. How he longed to be back there at this moment in time, safe, secure and loved.

In less than an hour, he would have an entirely new and alien environment to contend with, to assimilate into, and to call his home. This nomadic existence wasn't for him, not for him at all. He needed the stability and warmth of a family, the smiles, the care, the attention; and yet still, all they could do, was deny him. How was it that these moves were supposed to be good for him, he paused to ponder. It was never going to be alright. Who was making these decisions and why? He had been happy in Farm Wood, and he had grown to be happy at number 33, and yet they felt an illogical need to disrupt that. There was no rhyme nor reason to it, and he soon came to believe that he was better on his own, than exposing himself to the constant disruption and upset, which they seemed intent on inflicting.

The long road from Stockport to Manchester, with its intermittent street lighting, plethora of shops, and short bursts of private housing, provided Snowball with an opportunist moment that Patricia would live to regret. A set of traffic lights can be a godsend or a nightmare, depending on which side of a story you find yourself, and Patricia was about to find out just how significant they could be. As she made her way through the traffic, she was completely oblivious to the freshly emerging travel itinerary that was being formulated in the passenger seat. She was clearly on safe ground as long as the car kept moving, and every set of trafficlights remained on green as she approached. But as the old saying begins, 'it's odds on that... and the odds eventually turned against the comfortable shoe wearing, lentil chewer, as the car approached the junction of William Street and Kings Road, and it came to a controlled halt. In the true spirit of carpe diem, and fuelled by an internal rage that he needed to release, Snowball pushed open the car door, and hit the pavement running, pausing only briefly, to flip an unwarranted 'V' sign at the startled and hapless Patricia, who by now was struggling to release the seatbelt that she had fastened around herself, whilst watching her charge disappear in front of her very eyes.

A momentary splash of hope was added to the mix, as Snowball, in colliding with a lamp-post, fell unceremoniously to the ground, and momentarily appeared to be hurt. He had remained motionless prey for a split second, as the force of the impact rocked his core, but as Patricia's car door flung open, the opportunity still begging to be taken advantage of, Snowball, wind now back in his sails, simultaneously rose to his feet, began running, and it was game on all over again. He had already crossed one road, by the time Patricia had reached the pavement, and glancing back momentarily he could see the advantage he had gained, and was intent on improving it. Patricia was now kerbside as her American cousins would have said, and checking for oncoming traffic, before she bolted into the road in pursuit. She had the advantage of determination, stamina and speed, but Snowball had the advantage of flat shoes and a willingness to go anywhere irrespective of consequences, which served him well, as he headed first through the front and rear gardens of number forty-two Manchester Lane, before exiting into the rear garden of number 11 Bolton Street opposite.

Five streets, four garden gates, two fences, a barking poodle, a leg full of nettle stings, and a near miss with a Hillman Hunter later (as he had dashed between two parked cars), and he was roaming free, with neither sight nor sound of Patricia in pursuit. It was time for a rest, and he needed a moment to gather his thoughts, and in crossing into the park opposite, he determined that a seat by the duck pond was the ideal place to coordinate his 'master plan', which in all honesty comprised nothing more than running for sweet life. Now all he needed to do was decide which country he would like to emigrate to, and of course get there.

It was seven hours later, when Aunty Beryl had peered through the kitchen window of number 33, and noticed the pinpoint flashlight that was shining and bobbing around in the tent at the bottom of the garden. Upon further investigation, and in the knowledge that 'all hers' were accounted for, she had found Snowball crouched under his coat, shivering wildly, and staring right back at her, with the big brown eyes that he had used to great effect on her, so many times in the past. He smiled, only briefly, as his chattering teeth were threatening to disintegrate in the coldness of the night, and she had begrudgingly smiled back, before extending her warm hands and pulling him from his not so secret hideaway. "Just tonight, do you understand?" she muttered, as they headed back to the kitchen, the softness in her tone, telling him that for the next few hours at least, he had won the day, and was comfortably back under her protective wing, and that, with the traumas of the day subsiding, everything might just turn out to be alright. Just as she had said.

OH FUCK IT, AND FUCK IT SOME MORE

The following day, Snowball was dropped off at The Manors in Manchester, by his bespectacled, and none too happy social worker, alongside a policeman who had been drafted in to ensure that the journey from Stockport to Manchester went as planned at the second time of asking. It was late in the afternoon as they turned into the large sprawling grounds, located a few miles north from the city centre. It was a large detached house, and a home that housed many children, from a vast array of backgrounds, all sharing one common strand that ran like a golden thread through all of their lives, that being deprivation and abuse.

Like Snowball, most had been physically abused and mistreated. Some horrifically. Many sexually abused, and if there was a sliding scale, some unfortunates had been subjected to a combination of the two. Each, and every one of them a victim with a story to tell. Each, and every one of them, plunged into a fresh hell that was not of their making, nor of their guiding, and certainly beyond their control and influence. They were like farmed salmon in a large tank. Boundaries well defined but hidden, but a tank nonetheless, where they could be prodded and poked at the owner's whim, and where the illusion of swimming free was exactly that, an illusion, and bar some unlikely miracle, their future was as pre-ordained as the salmon, from the moment they had arrived.

Where others may have seen a suburban beauty, Snowball only saw an austere facade, that he knew would contain and expose many horrors, much the same as Melbourne House had. It was by now easy to predict. It was an extremely large house, which signified a high number of children would be living there. There was a direct correlation between the numbers 'cared for', and the level of 'care' received. Big numbers were bad, small numbers were good. It was that simple. Likewise, he knew that the greater the number of children, the greater were the dangers of day-to-day living amongst them. It was a million miles away from the comforts he had grown to know, enjoy and appreciate at number 33. Even with the infrequent but painful carpet inspections at the hands of Aunty Anne, and the protracted personally tailored consequences initiated by Aunty Beryl, he knew he was far better off in their hands than he ever would be at The Manors. And so, as the car swung into the vast expanse of open drive, he couldn't help but fear what this next stage in life's peculiar little adventure was about to bring.

The Manors was very similar to Melbourne House both in design, and management as it transpired. A large multi-roomed and sprawling house, carelessly dropped at an obscure angle, into the centre of a huge urban footprint. It was surrounded by horizontally slatted, an equally irregular white painted wooden fencing, the offset angle of which was compensated for by the long open drive, that led from treelined streets to the front, whilst also shielding it from the public scrutiny that it so richly deserved, on all other sides of the house.

There was a smattering of established trees, dotted around the garden, and a large deep green hedge that ran the width of the front garden, and marked out the frontal boundary, separating it from the footpath that ran alongside the adjacent road, and down into the distance towards the city centre. The third boundary marker was a fragile looking wooden fence, that ran from the roadside, up to the rear of the property, where it was haphazardly butted into the rear wall that ran the entire width of the property at the back, and seemed designed simply to support and prevent the next property along from sliding into the grounds of the home at any given moment. There was an abundance of grassless areas, which had been covered in either tarmac or what appeared to all intents and purpose like deliberately cracked flags, and there was an over-bearing and pervasive perception of decay and neglect about the entire building and its surroundings, with the lack of care seemingly reflected from the outside inwards. If first impressions were important, it painted a very poor picture.

The home contained a small school within the confines of its walls, staffed and managed by a solitary teacher called Mr Young, who had assumed responsibility for the education of the entire age range of children resident in the home, and subject to its care. It was almost as if they were afraid to let the children out of the grounds, and for all intents and purposes, the integral 'home schooling' concept had turned The Manors into a prison, where only the staff came and went. There were social workers, referred to as Aunty and Uncle, who were responsible for the day-to-day care of the children, alongside housekeepers who worked in shifts to maintain cleanliness. There was a gardener who doubled as a handyman, with the remit of maintaining the general fabric of the building, a duty which was clearly in excess of either his abilities or his patience. It was all so fucking Local Authority.

"Are you ok?" Oh, fuck off, Patricia. It was her fourth time of asking, and he was fast losing patience.

They disembarked the car, and headed to the main door, which strangely was positioned on the side of the house, hiding both name and number from the prying eyes of public gaze, if anybody cared enough to pry that was. The first thing Snowball encountered upon entry was a cane carrying member of staff, who appeared unerringly comfortable with the idea of welcoming a new arrival, while brandishing both a cane and a smile. The fleetingly held belief that life might suddenly become a lot brighter, if only he gave it a chance, after his departure from number 33, had been instantly shattered, and he was ushered through to the office, for the polite, albeit generic welcome, that always took place in front of 'must impress' social workers, if and when they found the time to stay around long enough to receive it. The welcome was designed to serve no other purpose than to facilitate their unquestioned complicity, and future deniability to the abuses that would surely follow, once they had departed. It was the way they sucked people in, by ensuring that they had an equal stake in the maintenance of silence. Old School, but effective.

It always seemed rather ironic that a social worker, charged with the care of a minor, was quite content to deposit them into the hands of someone who carried a cane and an insincere smile, as a means of maintaining order. They wouldn't have left a family pet in the position, and yet here they were, dropping off human beings, and turning a blind eye to all that subsequently followed. It never seemed to resonate that they were supposed to be protecting children like Snowball from abuse, and yet, here they were, delivering them into the hands of a brutal regime that often far exceeded the trials and torments from which they had originally been lifted with a Care Order. The brutality of a domestic regime, simply replaced with the brutality of an unregulated, though officially sanctioned one, with the only key difference being that, people were now being paid for the systematic abuses that they inflicted, whereas their own parents had done it as unpaid volunteers.

Shortly afterwards, there would be the strange ritual of a brief familiarisation tour of the home, as if he was a patron arriving at a luxurious, well-equipped Spa Hotel in the heart of the Lake District. It was the point at which all the key locations, features, expectations and rules were explained in some detail, in the expectation that he would remember them all in the first instance and abide by them in the second. It was an amusing insight, in so much as it was all explained in the manner of it being optional to stay or leave, when in fact options were something he clearly didn't have. In his mind he knew that he could check out anytime, but simply never leave.

THAT WAS THE MANORS

Like most homes he would eventually land in, Snowball was completely underwhelmed with the environment that The Manors provided. There were white-washed walls everywhere, with the occasional splash of graffiti, which clearly denoted for all who had come to care, that somebody 'Woz ere' apparently, or that some unknown, and long departed twat had fallen so much in love with Elaine from the greengrocer's, that he'd felt the urgent need to engrave it into the furniture, so that all who came after him would appreciate exactly how strong the emotion was, reciprocated or otherwise. There were whitened skirting boards and linoleum floors downstairs, which added an unwelcoming clinical air to the place, with even more white walls, and carpeted floors on the upper landings, which then seamlessly seeped into every bedroom with insidious creep.

It was all very sterile, all very characterless, and totally lacking in the homeliness that he had just been wrenched from. The entrance hall fared better (when ignoring the drive in – first impressions are everything when conning people), with a dark, tiled and varnished mahogany floor, and unmarked brightly painted walls. Peanut-eating Patricia must have felt so at home. There was a three-stranded chandelier of sorts, albeit made of cheap reflective plastic discs that lacked any real chintz, as well as the essentials of operable bulbs. A green plastic telephone had been fixed to one wall, with the noticeable peculiarity, of a wooden shelf that was home to a telephone directory and Yellow Pages, affixed to the wall opposite, and clearly out of reach to anyone requiring the use of both items at the same time. Anything of value seemed to be bolted down in one fashion or another, and anything not bolted down was either undesirable or broken. Most wooden surfaces had, at some point, had the initials of one occupant or another engraved into them, alongside a variety of expletives, and bold statements regarding the sexual favours that certain female members of staff might have to offer, upon payment or simply in kind. If nothing else, it appeared to Snowball that one could survive quite happily, if only his prowess as a sexual gladiator could become widely known and appreciated.

Bathrooms and toilets were plentiful though barren. Basic amenities, for the basic existence that they serviced and supported. The bottom-shredding Izal toilet paper was in abundance everywhere, as was carbolic soap, which invariably would double as a body scrub and mouth wash, for those less gifted, with regards to containing the outpouring of colloquial expletives, and sexual innuendos, that constantly peppered their everyday speech. Plain white baths were moulded into plastic surrounds on the walls, with one end housing the customary set of cheap looking plastic taps and a shower head, while the other end was home to a small white tile-coated shelf space, upon which was perched a bar of soap, shampoo, shared blue flannels, and small white rubber plugs, alongside the remnants of the copperlook chains that once secured them to the bath. Frosted windows, and self-closing wood panel doors, completed the 'institutional' chic, with a moulded black rubber footplate, denoting where corridor ended, and bathroom began.

The bedrooms were in much of a similar vein, being both cold and bland. There were the same white splashed walls, familiar from the tour of the lower floors, interspersed with the occasional poster of some presumed heartthrob, which had been carelessly torn from a magazine, and seemingly trimmed around the edges with a blunt spade. Four beds to a room, identical sheets and covers on each. One bedside locker per person, slippers tucked under the bed, but close to hand when required, and pyjamas folded and tucked beneath the pillow, with a lack of pyjamas indicating either a bed wetter, or someone who was kept naked at night to prevent them from absconding. It was all very cold, all very clinical, all very institutionalised in every sense.

The prized possession of a window bed was distributed solely on either the whim of the staff, or the unregulated mandate of who had the hardest punch, or was prepared to use the most violence, with an occasional concession made to a weaker resident, who, whilst not the strongest or more useful in battle, was however widely deemed to be a fucking nutter, and best left alone. It was a useful strategy if you could get away with it, but carried the added danger that you one day might be expected to live up to the said reputation, and the penalty for coming up short in front of all present, could be a high price to pay. The bed closest to the door was largely unwanted and uncontested, and without variance always reserved for either the latest arrival, or the weakest in the room (resident psycho being the exception), as that was the bed that the staff saw first upon entry in the dead of night, and thus afforded the occupant minimal opportunity for mischief or wanderings through fear of being easily caught.

So, this was now home for Snowball. A home for the unwanted and the wretched. Long whitewashed corridors filled with equally long, unprotected fluorescent light strips, which ran the length of the ceilings. Fractured red 'break glass' fire alarms on every corner, with their small metal hammers detached and discarded in places unknown, alongside bland, speckled linoleum floors, carefully crafted and snug to the wall's joints, as if it were a direct measure to prevent its theft. Austere communal bathrooms and equally austere looking toilets, shared clothes, transient bed, decanted shampoo and no soap of his own. He didn't even have his own fucking flannel. 'What the hell is this place?' he thought to himself. Aunty Beryl would not have approved.

Toys came in the form of fire extinguishers that were randomly removed from their wall mountings, and discharged after being left pointing at imaginary targets in bedrooms and corridors. Snowball would soon learn that 'toys', unlike the parlance of which he was familiar, comprised just about anything that you were in the first instance forbidden from touching, and in the second, could be readily removed, relocated, abused or wilfully damaged. There was a pervasive, permanent smell of bleach and toilet paper that delivered more paper cuts to the body, than any Japanese torturer could ever imagine doing.

Pentagon shaped tables, and small grey plastic chairs filled the dining hall at meal times, and were summarily stacked in corners after eating, creating a wide versatile open space that became an imaginary battleground for some, with their 'Lucky Bag' toy soldiers, tanks and action men, and a real battleground for many, as it proved to be a most viable place to organise a fight club. If you were inclined to hit people with chairs, and other robust items of furniture during the course of a melee, with the occasional bloodstain bearing testament to the fact that the Battle of Hastings had regularly been re-enacted in that very space, the dining room was an ideal location to reside in. In The Manors, everything and anything was either controlled, abused or simply broken. Property and children alike. Nothing was spared the destruction, and as time shuffled on by, you simply had to learn to live with it. There were no exceptions made, there was no mending of anything or anybody. Objects, inanimate or otherwise, were simply left to decay where they fell. It was a far cry from the place they had dragged Snowball's unwilling soul from. How could they ever seek to justify this as being in his 'best interests'? If only Aunty Beryl could bear witness to this mess, she would surely take him back in an instant.

Mr London was a tall, skinny built, moustached Irishman hailing from the County of Cork, and around whose whim the home appeared to completely revolve. Deep in tone, and short in temper, he ruled with an iron fist, and a ferocious bellow, supplemented by facial expressions that were known to curdle custard. Snowball's introduction to Mr London was about as cordial as it gets, when addressing a child of his age, and the Irish charm that London exuded worked wonders on his female social worker on their very first meeting. She had rarely been seen again after that first encounter, and that was just how London liked it. The other children had been released from the daily torment of Mr Young and his homeschooling endeavours, and upon closer inspection, it became apparent to Snowball that yet again his was the only black face amongst a plethora of white. He'd have been forgiven for thinking 'here we go again' on all counts, as it became apparent that his departure from number 33 was not a salvation, in terms of his ability to blend into a crowd, but more a case of 'out of the frying pan, and into the fire'.

The daily routine at The Manors was simple enough to understand and even simpler to conform with for those who were lucky enough to have their brains intact, after the beatings they had suffered. On school days, there was what was considered by most, an early rise at around 7.00am, at which time there was a bed check, and a head count. Beds were checked for wetting, while heads were counted for the singular purpose of identifying absconders. Absconding was a regular and eternally present feature of life at The Manors, as was the brutality of the regime that prompted it, and so it was nothing new or exciting to hear a member of staff declare that one or two were missing each morning at the culmination of the count. By 07.30, everybody would be washed and dressed. The bed wetting fraternity were bathed and taunted accordingly by both staff and children alike, while those with control of their bladders would wash in the row of sinks housed in the walls of the upper bathrooms.

Breakfast would commence around 07.45am and be cleared away by 08.15am. It was often a case of, first up being best dressed and equally well fed, with stragglers often going hungry until lunchtime, and being dressed in ill-fitting clothes that had been issued from the communal clothes cupboard, from which everyone dressed. Mr Young would be in attendance by 08.45am, and schooling would commence at 09.00am. Lunchtime would come and go between noon and one o'clock, as would the afternoon schooling session, punctuated only by a mid-afternoon play break of around twenty minutes, which was supervised by the staff, in order to give Mr Young some desperately needed respite.

There was the occasional spectacle of him chasing an errant pupil through the corridors of the home, cane raised in one hand, while with the other he fended off a variety of objects that were being thrown at him with the most malicious of intent. Tea would be dished up at around four-thirty in the afternoon, with supper in the form of cold toast, cake or biscuits, alongside a glass of milk being placed on the tables at seven-thirty. Most of the younger children would be tucked up in bed by no later than eight o'clock, with the last of the elder children gone by nine. It was straight forward, efficient and ruthlessly executed with a brutal callousness for those who chose to transgress.

Boys generally shared a room with boys, and girls with girls, unless necessity dictated otherwise. Saturday was a short-staffed, school-free day, and Sunday was the weekly bath day for those who had avoided the humiliation of having their bed wetting exploits publicly exposed, and been shamed with a brutal mid-week bath brushing at the hands of a merciless 'Aunty', intent on demonstrating to anyone interested that you can scrub skin from the back of a child, if you only try hard enough. The Sunday bath was followed by an early night, in preparation for school the next day. And thus, the cycle would begin again on Monday morning sharp.

MEET KENNY

"**Y**ou're a nigger" were the words that spurted from the mouth of young Kenny Davidson. A fat faced, podgy looking, Billy Bunter of a child, but with a reputation for being one of the tough ones around the home. It wasn't that he completely disliked Snowball per se for any particular reason, or the fact that he was black. No, Davidson was a serial bed wetter, and anything that could detract attention from himself, and place the burden upon someone else, was something he grabbed eagerly at. Snowball's colour was an easy target, and Davidson knew oh too well that he could easily deflect attention from himself, by drawing Snowball into the discussion.

Dodgy Davidson as he was known amongst the boys, had adopted an outwardly overt and visible dislike for Snowball, though in reality, as Snowball knew only too well, it was more bravado than hate; but nonetheless, trouble would inevitably come from it in one form or another. Snowball simply smiled, as he had learned to do. The word 'nigger' offensive and unnecessary as it was, had been used too many times in his short life to have any serious connotations for his immediate sense of self, and the value and skill utilised in diffusing a situation with a smile and agreement far outweighed any gains from engaging physically with an oxygen thief like Davidson. He found it worked wonders in the main, as the last thing that most other children seemed to expect was agreement and a smile. It pretty much left them nowhere to go, other than to confront him with another desperate insult, or to skulk away defeated in objective, and frustrated by the non-confrontational golliwog they had attempted to engage. Snowball was developing intellectual prowess, alongside his burgeoning physicality.

Davidson would return time and time again to torment him. He was a child with a desperate need for acceptance and status amongst his peers, and bullying those he saw as weaker links was his chosen methodology. Davidson had lived his life amongst and been the recipient of much violence. He had found at his own expense that the fat kid is rarely the popular kid, and had suffered the consequences of his aversion to controlled eating and salads, by succumbing to bullying and violence, in a manner that was directly reflective of his own need to bully and intimidate others.

He had arrived at The Manors, battered, bruised and brutalised some years earlier. A waif like figure at the time, with bones protruding through his taught skin, bandy legs and an angular gaunt face. He had clearly fared well on the stodgy food regimen that was served up daily, not least because of his propensity to take food from the plates of those less greed-prone than himself, and all things being equal, he clearly didn't appear to be suffering any detriment in the care system. Stories would have it that his father had once beaten him quite mercilessly, before leaving him locked in a cellar for weeks, barely fed and close to death, so it was hardly surprising that he considered violence to be the resolution of all issues, nor that he found solace in over-eating and gorging himself. Whilst he clearly appeared to prosper from the culinary arrangements at The Manors, very little else had gone right for Davidson since his arrival, and he had constantly found himself to be a fringe player, seeking but never quite receiving, the respect and acceptance that he so lustfully craved.

It was into this climate that Snowball had arrived at The Manors. His arrival, in the eyes of Davidson, clearly signalling a monumental opportunity to move himself smoothly up the peer rankings, and out of the open 'victim pool' in which he had festered for so long. Snowball was his opportunity, and all he had to do was execute it. But therein lay the problem for Davidson. Snowball wasn't a team player, never had been, and the plan simply didn't appeal. Put simply, from Snowball's perspective, the cost-benefit analysis didn't stack up.

Davidson was always pushing. Physically and mentally. Always there, always in the face of Snowball. Always wanting to go one step further than he knew he should. He was as much a victim, as he was a bully. He was always desperately trying to prove himself worthy of acceptance, but too stupid to realise that it would never happen. He was as much an outsider as Snowball, and in the general scheme of things, he may as well have been fat, dodgy and black, rather than just fat and dodgy when push came to shove. Davidson simply didn't understand or appreciate the relevance of group dynamics. He didn't appreciate the need to develop alliances, as Snowball had learned. He couldn't make himself useful to the right people, nor insulate himself from the extremes of life on 'the outside' looking in. There were 'in' groups and 'out' groups, and you needed to understand which group you were in and why.

Understanding your place within your own group was essential, as was understanding where your group was placed amongst other groups, and where you, as a consequence, were placed within the broader sphere of all things people and groups. You needed to understand why others were in a different group, and for those who had aspirations to travel between groups, there was a pressing need to understand the dynamics of acceptance. Davidson never understood that, and as a consequence, often cut a lonely figure, unaccepted by the hierarchy he looked up to, and rejected by those he looked down upon. He was akin to a concentration camp Capo. Always seeking to ingratiate and please his boss, without ever fully realising that he was still considered to be just another Jew.

But as the summer night closed in, Davidson, aspirations intact, decided to act. Snowball was easy to find. As the only black kid in the home, there was nowhere to hide, other than in plain sight, and his habit of playing alone with a football, same place, same time, with religious monotony, made it so much simpler for him to be located. Davidson could cut an intimidating swathe when he needed to. He had a scowl that could curdle cream, and his sheer size in comparison to most around him, made for an intimidating combination when he found himself on a mission. It wasn't the case that he was particularly hard as far as kids go. In most instances he was just too heavy to fight against.

The punch to the back was more a surprise than painful. Snowball had been unaware of Davidson's looming presence and as a result was caught flat-footed by the surprise attack that Davidson had initiated. Snowball spun around to see Davidson stood there in his cheap hob-nailed boots. He wore tatty long trousers that failed to reach his ankles and exposed for all to see, his inability to tie a shoe lace properly. Snowball noted that he was wearing the very same t-shirt, that he himself had actually worn the day before, and inwardly smiled at the thought that Dodgy Davidson, cleanliness not being his thing, was inadvertently living up to both his nickname and reputation, by trawling through the dirty washing at night, and recovering the items he wanted to wear the next day. Not the smartest of children, but according to where the staff believed Davidson would end up in life, he didn't need to be.

Snowball backed away, ignoring the bounce of the ball as it passed from the wall, and almost to Davidson's feet. Davidson loomed large and smiled with sinister intent and menace. "Pick your ball up, Sambo," he barked. "Go on, pick it up." Snowball knew better than to accept Davidson's offer. He knew that the moment he moved towards the ball, Davidson was likely to aim a kick in his direction, and most probably towards his head. For a moment they just stood staring intensely at each other. A Mexican stand-off in the urban sprawl of Manchester. Davidson in dismay that his kind and generous offer had been rudely rejected, Snowball dismayed and affronted that Davidson clearly thought he was that stupid. The stand-off continued, with Davidson repeatedly beckoning Snowball forward, in a futile attempt to bring him within kicking distance, in order that his onslaught, muted as it now was, could continue afoot.

Snowball turned slightly to his right, in an attempt to walk away, Davidson in the corner of one eye, and the doorway to the kitchen and sanctuary in the other. Davidson seized the moment, and lunged forward, in expectant anticipation of catching Snowball off-guard and vulnerable. His boot catching a glancing blow to Snowball's leg, he stumbled, limbs flaying widely in the air, as his own bodyweight had countermanded his forceful intentions and sent him crashing to the ground. It was an error that he would soon live to regret as, with Davidson flaying and wobbling around like a jelly-fish out of water, and prone at his feet, Snowball found it to be too good an opportunity to pass up. Instinct can be a wonderful tool, and within seconds Snowball had landed a series of kicks to the body, head and face of Davidson, from which he was not to recover in this confrontation.

Davidson, pain and fear visibly etched across his face, rolled from side to side, vainly attempting to rise to his feet, as the onslaught continued. Snowball was as ruthless as he was relentless, following Davidson across the floor, and maintaining his advantage throughout. By now, the distraught Davidson was half way to his feet, only for Snowball to land another series of blows, which sent him crashing back to the floor. Snowball pounced upon his stunned prey, sitting astride Davidson's chest, and pinning him to the floor, as the hapless Davidson now became the recipient of a flurry of punches to his unprotected head and face. It had proved to be a regretfully brief encounter that eventually saw blood dripping from his nose, and on to the floor, from which he had still failed to arise.

A sudden sharp rasp of knuckles against glass brought Snowball out of his frenzied attack. He peered up to see Mrs Jones banging furiously on the kitchen window with one hand, while waving the strap she religiously carried as an instrument of torture in the other. No interpretation was needed. It was time to stop, or face her wrath, but there was always time for one more punch, and duly delivered, Snowball rolled away from Davidson, and rose to his feet victorious. Stunned and subdued, Davidson rolled firstly out of reach and then to his feet, before sloping off to the sanctuary of the locker room, one eye on Mrs Jones, and the other firmly placed on Snowball, in anticipation of a further onslaught.

Mrs Jones returned to her baking, and with a beating averted, Snowball returned to the football.

EMILY DEAR, SWEET EMILY

Emily was a beautiful young girl. Early teens, bright eyed, smart and street-wise. She had been around the block in more ways than one and had been dropped at The Manors by a social worker, only a few days before Snowball had arrived. They had homed in on each other, as they, the newbies, were the only two kids who appeared to be operating out-with groups, without friends and in total isolation. She had told him a few stories about herself. And asked the standard child care entry question of 'Why are you here?'. Everyone asked it of the new person, and Snowball and Emily were no different. "My mother doesn't want me," Snowball had replied. He didn't know whether this was true or not, but he had come to realise that it seemed to cover all bases for the inquisitive, and usually ended the conversation there and then, so for now, the generic nature of his reply would do. "My dad has been shagging me," was Emily's offering. Snowball didn't quite grasp the full significance of what she had said, or its implications, but he guessed that she only reveals what she wants you to see or know, and he was almost content to leave it at that.

The word 'right' probably wasn't the correct response that Emily had sought, but for Snowball, given that he wasn't exactly sure what this shagging thing was, only that it seemed to be a bad thing in the context of the discussion, it was the best he could muster in the immediacy of the moment. He had heard of this shagging thing of course, as most of the boys in Melbourne House and The Manors had, at one time or another, apparently indulged in it. Weirdly enough, always with the most beautiful girl you can imagine, and all of whom were endowed with what were generically described as massive fucking tits. But the pleasure had so far eluded him, and so he just took it that it was perhaps best not to comment or ask.

Emily had come from a well-heeled family. She was well spoken, and intellectually superior to the rest of them by a very wide margin. Her smart words and quick wit appealed to him, but also attracted unwelcome attention, as, by nature, she stood out from the rest, very much like he did, but for different reasons. Mr Young in the school loved her, and fortunately for Emily, for all the right reasons. She was his star pupil. The shining example of his system of education, even though her intellect had been nurtured, fertilised and stimulated elsewhere, and well before she had encountered his authoritarian strictures.

As time passed, their friendship developed, drawn together primarily by the intrusion of their difference to others. Emily was headstrong, and sharp tongued. She knew she could overcome most of the other kids, just with the use of some well-chosen words, witty phrases, and the occasional expletive, and she used her linguistic skills to great effect. But Emily was also extremely unhappy. Unhappy that she couldn't go home. Unhappy that she was in care. Unhappy because she missed her mother who, unknown to her, had chosen her predatory husband above the maternal instinct for her child. She missed her old friends and was struggling to make new ones. Everything was going against her, and Snowball knew exactly how she felt. Life was tough, and it never got any easier.

Snowball's friendship with Emily was a rewarding one. She was much brighter than he was, but happily shared her sharp intellect with her eager understudy. She also had a sense of humour that appealed to him, and she was fun to be around. She shared her intellect, taught him things, explained how things worked, helped him understand, and she had patience. She was big enough at times to hold her own, and would often be seen, sitting with him as he read, ensuring that nobody would come and take the books from him, as she had witnessed so many times in the past. She was in many respects a guardian angel, who seemed to have a strong desire to care for someone other than herself, and had found her needs satiated in her well-grounded mutually beneficial friendship with Snowball. The traumas of her not so distant past had clearly opened her eyes in a very adult way to the pains and the suffering that others endured, and it had ignited something deep inside her.

Emily was a girl who put her needs second. She clearly suffered like the rest of the children, had been beaten, used and abused. But somehow at times, she seemed to recoil from her own personal nightmares and family dysfunction, transforming herself into a small guiding light, a beacon of hope, that others found easy to follow, and naturally gravitated towards. Snowball had become a significant beneficiary of her benevolence. She protected him. She kept a watchful eye, observed the comings and goings, and where physically possible and practicable, stepped in, to ensure his path remained clear from the contents of the cesspit that was life at The Manors.

She would take him on his weekly walk to the sweet shop, where he would spend his pocket money. She would hide his sweets in the corner of her shoe locker, so that nobody else would steal them from him, returning on demand to the locker, as and when Snowball required a sugar fix. She started to ensure that he got to play in the games of football and wasn't excluded from the other activities that the boys of his age were undertaking. It wasn't long before they were constantly to be seen in each other's company. Emily leading, Snowball in toe under her protective radiance. They were a pairing. If Emily played, Snowball played. If you offered Emily sweets, you had to offer them to Snowball; if Emily was allowed, Snowball was allowed; and so, the friendship developed, matured and endured.

Snowball had nothing to offer Emily, and Emily wanted nothing from him other than his friendship. He probably wasn't even great company for her, but he was loyal, and helpful whenever and wherever he could be. There just seemed to be a mutual understanding that his aim was to learn, and her primary instinct was to teach. There was a reciprocity to it all, in that she chose the lessons, and he unquestioningly aspired to learn them. Emily would occasionally send him away with a casual "see you", when her need for 'grown up' time or 'girl talk' arose, with those nearer and within her own age group, but she always seemed to consciously seek him out once she had finished, invariably finding him cutting a solitary dash while he kicked a ball against the wall, and awaited her attentions. But in the main, they were relatively inseparable, sustained by the fulfilment of their mutual needs. Though both young in years, she clearly had a lot to offer his developing intellect. She appeared to know how to operate, at the levels they needed to, and the lessons that she had previously come to learn in her own development were naturally and instinctively passed down to the up and coming Snowball.

Emily was also a girl who had a hidden but well-developed adult streak to her. On a number of occasions, she had pulled Snowball to one side after he had received a beating from a member of staff, and casually rebuked and informed him that, (a) he deserved that, and (b) exactly why he had deserved it.

In her eyes, it was seemed to be part of his learning curve, and coming from her, it was far more palatable to Snowball, than if it had come from any other source. He would even occasionally apologise to her, only to be told "you don't have to say that". She had imparted her wisdom and was both happy and secure in the knowledge that it had been heard and understood. Snowball would always indulge in a period of self-imposed silence after such a 'telling', whilst Emily, wise to the fact that this signified his need for some attention, would calmly ignore the silence, and pretend he didn't even exist. She knew he would have to grow up quickly, and learn to take his medicine, and she wasn't about to make that easy for him. She would, on occasion, jokingly threaten to slap him herself, though always at pains afterwards to ensure that he understood she never meant a word of it. For a long time, Emily was a bright star in a dark divisive universe for Snowball. Always well lit, strong, resilient, almost averse to the passage and pains of time, and the transient flow of the micro-universes that circled around her. Though outwardly she appeared to have few friends, it was clear to those who observed, that many of the children looked upon Emily as an example. It was the intelligence, the manner in which she formulated her words, the outwardly calm demeanour, and the sense of presence that she brought to bear. Qualities and attributes most of them lacked, and many subconsciously aspired to, and perhaps it was this wholesome, catch all, everything to everyone character, that would ultimately become her downfall, as time passed on.

Rumours of sexual activity between staff and children was nothing new, but as time passed by, for the young girls in The Manors, as with other homes they had all lived in or heard of, it was something that was simply to be expected. In the main they appeared to understand and accept that there was a simple, unwritten rule that was adhered to, at all times. Boys were beaten, and girls were to be used. That's how it was. It was that simplistic. Occasionally the boys were also used, but in the main, rarely did the sexual proclivities of the male staff bound into the arena of homosexuality, and as luck or otherwise would have it, sexual liaisons with the older boys was the domain solely of the female staff entourage, and for some unfathomable reason, was never quite seen as abuse. It was, however, inflicted by adults and borne by children.

It always had been as far as Snowball knew, and nothing could stop that. Girls had tried. They had absconded and reported the abuse, but nothing had happened. The police had simply returned them, into the clutches of their abusers. He had seen them suffer the indignity of being returned, stripped, bathed and left standing naked, hands on head, in the corner of the corridor, as everyday life continued on around them. A punishment, a humiliation and a deterrent all rolled into one huge act of casually administered cruelty. He had heard their tears, their pleas, and he had witnessed their suffering. It was endless, and unstoppable, and there was nothing he or anyone else could do, as a conspiracy of silence colluded to ensure that whatever happened, it remained hidden from prying eyes and the authorities alike.

Emily was no different to the rest in that respect, and Snowball was helpless to act as, over the course of time, her star began to dim as a direct result of the abuse she was suffering. The glow that once radiated warmth from her eyes began to fade, and the waterfall of self-confidence, that had typified her demeanour upon arrival at The Manors, had shrivelled to a mere trickle, which only occasionally presented itself, upon an intellectual stimulation. She was tangibly agitated most of the time, often abusive to staff and her peers alike, and she had begun self-harming and absconding. She looked increasingly anorexic, and was clearly in a spiral of decline, that in any other environment known to humankind, would have begged the question, WHY? But this was child care. This was The Manors, and it was a place where nobody cared, or could afford to be seen to be caring. Like every other girl there, Emily was on her own, and she knew it.

The Emily he knew had gone. Been gone for a long time and was possibly gone forever. Emily was being abused, and on a regular basis. Her beautiful young looks acting like a magnet to the paedophile abusers that operated within the walls in which they lived. Idle talk held it that the Irishman was the primary offender, but nobody really knew for sure, and Emily wasn't for telling. She had alluded on occasion to Snowball that the Irishman had touched her, but always fell short of describing her torment in any detail. There was an age gap between them. Not huge in number, but enormous in terms of developmental awareness of the issues she faced on an almost daily basis. It was the unguarded moments that told the tale. The moments when the fear subsided, and the need to share her burden consumed her. It was then that she would momentarily open up, before slamming the door shut again, and withdrawing into her own private hell.

It was a warm night in July, when Emily finally succumbed to the unbearable torments that she had endured. Emily and Snowball had played together for a few hours after tea, and had been summoned individually within their peer groups, to get prepared for bed. Emily had seemed much more upbeat, more relaxed, more open and at home. She was relaxed, care-free and seemed content, almost happy with her lot in life. It was as if the burdens of the world had been lifted from her shoulders, and was a stark contrast to recent times, during which Snowball had barely been able to elicit any form of conversation from her. It was strange to behold, but Snowball was only too happy to have his friend back, that the underlying drama which was about to unfold, remained hidden. He had welcomed their interactions. It was a pleasant distraction, as neither of them had really made many friends, and they had inadvertently become dependent upon each other for company and friendship. He was largely led by Emily, but was happy to follow. Her older years meant she could teach him things, and all he had to do was listen, understand, and follow her lead, so having her back was a win for him. He just never understood that she was losing.

Snowball had bathed, washed his hair and was sat eating a supper of cold toast and warm milk, alongside Davidson and a few others, when the first panic-stricken member of staff dashed past him. Closely followed by another, all attention was now being focussed on the far side of the house, where the girl's bedrooms were located. Some of the girls were streaming down the stairs in tears, heading fearfully towards the dining room in which he sat. Staff ushered others and some of the boys in the same direction, and all manner of panic and fear was spreading throughout the house. But there was no Emily. No sight nor sound of her. The panic and fear were further heightened when what seemed like only minutes later an ambulance, blue lights flashing, and horns sounding, turned into the drive of The Manors, closely followed by a police car. The ambulance staff entered the house by the main front foyer, and promptly dashed through the dining room, and up the far stairs in the direction of Emily's bedroom.

Shortly afterwards, London, the Irishman whom they all hated, was ushered down the stairs, arms and hands lightly bandaged, and was escorted into the back of the ambulance. A stretcher was brought in, and quickly taken upstairs, shortly after which a member of staff had entered the dining room, and commanded they all go to their bedrooms, and not to come out unless instructed. The fear of penalty enforced an immediate compliance amongst the now information-hungry group that had assembled on the strength of previous instruction in the dining room. Before long, and with numerous eyes peering through semi-closed curtains, the ambulance left into the still of the night, and the home returned to a semblance of calm, not experienced for a long time.

Snowball would never see Emily again. He would later learn that she had attempted to take her own life, presumably as a means of freeing herself from the sexual abuse that had become her personal burden. She, just as he had done, had bathed herself that dreadful night, she had washed her hair, and dried herself, before putting on the night clothes that had been left on her bed. She had then calmly lay down in the covers, taken out a match, and set fire to her bed and presumably herself on top of it. By all accounts, informed or otherwise, she had survived, but she would never return to The Manors. London was also gone a painfully long time, but eventually returned and resumed his brutal dominance over the lives of all who were unfortunate enough to come within his predatory contact.

Emily undoubtedly caressed the unwanted attentions of self-blame and shame. She had been abused, degraded, used and humiliated most of her short life, and throughout all the trials that had been thrown at her, each and every abuser had made it plain that it was her own fault. Even her own mother had asked what it was that Emily had done, in order for her husband, Emily's father (who she claimed was a good man), to find her sexually attractive. It seemed that anyone with a responsibility towards her, had either failed in that responsibility or abused it. Emily's misplaced shame was as powerful as it was toxic. Though her outward demeanour betrayed nothing of the poisonous hurt that flowed through her veins, she was nonetheless being consumed from the inside out, by powerful and conflicting emotions that she was unable to contain.

Her shame was not of her making, and forcefully unhealthy. She was a strong, bright light that was gradually being diminished by the unbridled and criminally perverse abuse that was being inflicted upon her. She had been taken into local authority care for her own protection, and been horribly failed, as she landed in the clutches of one pervert after another, who had taken her sexually, and used her at will. She had come to silently fear many things. The staff changeovers that brought her abusers to their duty. She feared the coming of darkness, as her abusers' minds turned to the pleasures they would seek. She feared the cold distinctive clang of the isolation room drop lock, where she was frequently taken to service her abusers' illicit desires, and she feared the passing of time, as it was time itself that ferried in each new horror that she would be forced to endure. As she had once said to Snowball, 'if only time stood still, we would all be just fine'. It would be a long time before he fully understood exactly what she meant.

Like many others, Snowball witnessed Emily's decline, and like so many he was powerless to help. The system conspired against the weak and emboldened the strong. There were no consequences for the abusers. The violators had free rein and the system was complicit in protecting them as they rampaged through home after home, destroying the lives of children as they passed through. Emily knew only too well that if she complained about her own treatment, it would only escalate above and beyond what she had experienced already. There was no system to formally highlight the abuses she suffered, no means to pursue the abusers that sullied her life, raping her of her childhood and dignity, whilst maintaining the outward pretence of love, care and respect.

The loss of Emily was a blow to Snowball, compounded by the complete lack of salient information about her well-being and whereabouts upon which he could depend. She was one of the few he really considered a friend, and she had just gone in an instant. It was a troublesome time for everyone concerned. Children wondered who might be next, the girls wondered who would replace Emily in the 'affections' of the staff who preyed on her. Many of the staff no doubt reflected on the traumas that had driven her to such an act, and, perhaps, one or two reflected upon their own complicit behaviours that had and continued to facilitate the abuses in all their putrid vileness.

The childcare system had completely failed Emily. She had been taken from her home, and to a place of presumed safety, and then abandoned. Everyone knew what went on in those homes, but nobody cared. Emily wasn't the first victim of institutionalised abuse, and she wouldn't be the last. But the facts remained. She had been left, alone and abandoned in a hostile environment, stalked by predatory paedophiles, and with nowhere to turn. On reflection, Emily overtly displayed every possible sign of a child in distress to the people qualified to recognise those signs. She was a child being abused, a child being sexually tormented, and every signal that she sent went unnoticed by some, or was callously ignored by others. The simple reality was that while in Emily's terms, her father had been 'shagging' her, she would have been far better placed in remaining at home with her family, than she could ever have been, being placed into the predatory environment into which she had been 'rescued'.

The Manors was an institution, operated on the core principle of institutionalised abuse. Whether it was mental, physical or sexual, the entire operation was predicated on the belief that control could be maintained by violating children. Violating their rights, their freedoms, their bodies and their very existence. Snowball, like most of the others, had been abandoned into this systematic, abusive and intolerable nightmare, through which they were expected to navigate their way, in isolation, and egress at the far end, balanced, well-educated, socially aware and contributing adults, in a society that for decades would deny them even the most basic of care, consideration and acknowledgement of existence. Generations of children lost in a system of organised and complicit brutality. They were blind-eyed by the authorities, society, family and friends, with cursory value attached to them, as they wandered through the quagmire of infancy to adolescence, troubled, pained, brutalised, desperate and alone.

For Snowball, life went on, but it was never quite the same. His loss became quite profound, and he became consumed with hate, and a volatile anger. Hate for those who had preyed upon them all. Hate for a system that callously turned its back on them, and not just allowed it to happen, but was complicit in its facilitation. He hated his birth mother for the crimes that led him into care, his foster parents for the abandonment that he felt. He hated Beryl and Anne for allowing him to be removed from the only place he had felt safe in recent years. He hated the Rivers, Melbourne House, The Manors, the Irishman, and everyone who had anything to do with him, Emily and the countless other children that had suffered at their hands. He hated everyone and everything, and most of all, he hated Patricia and all she stood for in bringing him to this place of horror. Snowball underwent an awakening, and people were going to suffer because of it.

THE DAWNING OF CHANGE

Snowball cut a solitary figure that autumnal morning. Alone as he usually was with his thoughts, as he kicked a small blue football repeatedly against the wall of the garage that stood between the main entrance of The Manors and the garden wall of the house adjacent. Wearing a yellow t-shirt, and blue pants, he pondered how the grubby blue and black training shoes were the only thing he wore that didn't come from the communal clothing cupboard. He really did have nothing much that he could call his own, and it troubled him. Everything was shared: clothing, toys, bedrooms, baths, breathing spaces and most of all, punishments. Whether good, bad or indifferent, it seemed to always be shared. How he longed for something that he could just call 'his'.

The only reason he had his own trainers was because, having borne witness to the burns on his feet, the other children would play up at the prospect of sharing his footwear, through fear of catching something. He would dream of the days when he could have his own stuff. Call things his own and treasure his own belongings. He knew there was always a chance this could happen. He was aware that some of the children had been placed in foster care, others had been adopted, and they now had all these things. Some even had their own bedrooms, something of which was now just an historical fantasy carried over from number 33. But nobody ever seemed to want the black kid. How could they possibly pass him off as their own? What would the neighbours think? Would they lose their friends, and what if he wasn't like 'normal' kids? After all, he was black, and they just didn't know an awful lot about those black people.

Wilson approached him from behind, by enviable stealth. He didn't even hear him coming, and the first he knew of his presence was when the soon to be hapless Wilson slammed his foot into the back of his right thigh. The force of the blow sent him straight to the ground, crumpled and grasping at his thigh, as the pain flashed like lightning throughout his lower body. He glanced up to see a smiling Wilson, about to make away with the football he had been playing with, while in the process of mustering up a mouth full of spit that would soon be coming his way. And that was when the red mist descended. The final insult, the straw that broke the camel's back.

Wrapped in a veil of demonic possession, he rose swiftly to his feet. Wilson, wrapped in a veil of his own conceit and arrogance, was now strolling casually in the opposite direction. The first blow struck, landed square on the back of Wilson's head, landing just in the crevice formed at the top of the neck, and the base of the skull. Wilson paused momentarily, before stumbling forwards and collapsing to the ground. Snowball one, Medulla Oblongata nil. Eyes glazed, he had enough time to turn his despairing face towards the oncoming Snowball, before the full force of his trainer clad foot landed right between his eyes. His head violently jolted back and struck the concrete floor on which he was prone. By now Snowball had advanced again and was towering above the helpless Wilson. Kick after kick rained down on Wilson's head and body. Time and again his head slammed violently into the concrete floor, and the relentless onslaught continued. Snowball had reached the point where, through sheer anger and frustration his actions had become uncontrollably automated. The attack was as relentless as it was ferocious, and it wasn't going to stop, unless some divine intervention took place, or Wilson collapsed motionless, defeated and most likely dead.

Wilson let out a pitiful plea for mercy. Pleas turned into tears, and tears turned into outright begging. But it all went unheard, because this wasn't about Wilson. It was about the betrayal by his mother and the perceived betrayal by foster parents. It was about his Aunty Beryl and the brutality of being ripped from the only homes he had ever known and been secure in. It was about Melbourne House, Mr and Mrs Rivers and the brutality they had administered. There was also the loss of Miss Bradwell and it was about Smithy beating him on the floor of the basketball court, and most of all, it was about the long-standing brutality of the child care regime in general, in which Wilson had found himself feeling emboldened enough to come and attack him at will. It was about every police officer who had returned those poor girls onto the hands of their abusers. It was about the social workers who didn't care when they should have, the cooks, cleaners, and assistants, who by their very silence, had become complicit in the brutality and horrors he faced every day. It was about every single caning he had ever had, every strap that had flayed his naked skin, every corner he had stood in, traumatised by the brutal beating that had preceded it. It was about Emily. No, this wasn't about Wilson at all, but in that moment of time, that isolated piece of his transient history, Wilson would most certainly do.

Snowball stepped back, briefly pausing only to glance down at his blood-spattered conquest, before scooping up the football, and returning to the garage wall. He had awoken something dark, something deep, something troubling inside of himself, and in that moment in time, he quite liked it. It felt good. It felt liberating. For the first time that he could ever recall, he felt vibrant and alive. Things had just changed forever.

Wilson scrambled to his feet. Wobbling in the wind, he silently made haste towards the front door, mouth dripping blood, and wandered aimlessly along the corridor, until he had been stopped by Miss Halpin close to the kitchen door. He was only semi-coherent, barely able to stand unaided, and she immediately directed him to the safe hands of the housekeeper, who tended his bloodied face, while Halpin came looking for Snowball, who was still floating like a butterfly and stinging like a bee at the front of the house. He heard her coming. The distinctive sound of the foyer door slamming shut on its self-closing mechanism was a familiar one, and he knew it was either a pumped-up Wilson seeking redress or revenge, or he was in trouble of a very different kind. He cared little about either consequence. He knew he had gotten the better of Wilson, and that Wilson wouldn't ever forget that, and what was another beating from a 'carer' in the general scheme of things. At least this time, the beating would be for something he had actually done, rather than some perceived sleight, or transgression of some obscure unintelligible regulation.

Halpin was upon him swiftly. The Oi You Fucker moment had arrived. She executed a stealth reminiscent of the Wilson approach, and there were few words exchanged, as she grabbed hold of his left shoulder, while swiping the football from his hands. Snowball had often been told that his feet wouldn't touch the ground, as a consequence of one thing or another, and this prophesy was actually coming true. Halpin had lifted him quite literally as she pivoted from left foot to right, and headed back towards the front door, his feet only fleetingly contacting terra firma as she paused to grasp the grey aluminium door handle before her. Even then, it wasn't so much that his feet touched the floor, more that it was a passing glance from an old acquaintance in a crowded bar, as his feet flayed lifelessly in the air.

It was the same as she traversed the full length of the corridor, heading to what was commonly referred to in the movies as a 'place where nobody could hear you scream'. His legs flayed, and his feet had another brief dalliance with the floor, before being catapulted airborne again, collar creaking, as she added verbal chastisement to her physical onslaught. 'Hope we're not going far,' he thought, as they neared the stairs, and moments later found themselves on the first floor, before bounding towards the staff living quarters, and the private solitude where his beating would take place. Flung to the floor, he watched as she calmly closed the door behind her, before he rose with a wry smile sweeping across his face. Interesting times were ahead.

Halpin sensed the amusement in his vainly restrained facial contortions, and instantaneously delivered a swinging open palm to his face, which struck home with a vicious numbing sting. Another landed on the other side of his face, as his head and neck recoiled from the first blow. Barely had he recovered from that, when he felt her hands pulling viciously at the waist band of his trousers, and the sharp claw of her nails, grazing the skin on his upper thigh, as she yanked his clothing downwards, and pulled him across her outstretched knees and into position. There was just enough time to admire the weave of the Axminster before the first of many blows landed, in a monotonous synchronicity with the breath stealing gasps he emitted after each blow. Blow after blow, gasp after gasp. Gasps turning to squeals, squeals to screams, screams to tears, and tears into pleas. It was painful, relentless, almost endless, but all strangely rewarding, because he had in fact gotten the better of Wilson, and that was all that counted, and nobody, not even Halpin, could take that away from him

ZERO TO HERO

ood quality 'family' time spent with Halpin at an end, Snowball stood in the bathroom, washing away the tears from his face as instructed, and 'sorting himself out'. She would often threaten children with 'something to cry about', and from her perspective it was 'JOB DONE', though in her zeal for delivering the painful, she had tacitly forgotten to explain what the actual lesson to be learned was. Snowball kind of worked it out, but loose ends and all that. If you're going to do a job, do it properly. But why let the point of the exercise get in the way of a good beating? Eyes reddened, tail stinging, he headed to the landing when beckoned, fearful that he would get 'something more to cry about' if he dawdled any longer, and promptly headed to the rear garden, where some of the other children had congregated. He couldn't help but think that she had done enough for one day, let alone give him 'something more to cry about', but he figured, and wisely, that some things are best left unspoken. So, the garden it was, and would remain for the time being.

Griffiths, a small boy of fragile stature, pencil thin limbs, protruding rib cage, deathly in pallor, and with a strange looping gait, came bounding over like a three-legged camel on LSD. Snowball had never seen such a camel, but stick with it. "You twatted Wilson, you fucker," he bellowed. "Ha, you twatted Wilson." Snowball beamed a broad smile, and with Griffiths firmly attached to his shoulder, headed into the assembled congregation, to regale them with the afternoon's events. Tears now dispersed as fast as they had arrived, Snowball approached the amassed throng. "Halpin has just fucking leathered me," he offered up. "We fucking heard it," came the reply from an amused Janet. "Fuck that, what about Wilson, where the fuck is he, what happened?" came the chant from Philip. Centre stage, he began to unfold the events of that afternoon, to his enthralled and captive audience, who lapped up every syllable, word, sentence and paragraph of the tale. Poetic licence ensued, and for obvious reasons he omitted the bit about crying during his beating (despite the fact they had all heard him), but it all made for good listening, and kept them amused for a few minutes. Story time complete, Sonya strolled over with the blue ball in hand. "Guess this is yours then," she roared as she threw it into his outstretched hands. Snowball smiled. "Unless someone else wants to take it from you," she added with a wry smile that broke out into a throaty laugh. The group broke into laughter, and began to disperse around the play area, partly in recognition that the tale was now over, and partly because Halpin had appeared at the upper window, bellowing to Snowball that, "There is more where that came from, if you think it's funny". Snowball thought better of telling her where to go, and with a somewhat regal waft of the hand, promptly assisted in dispersing the group.

The Wilson attack signalled the start of a strange relationship between Snowball and Halpin. It wasn't that it was quality time together, or anything that remotely indicated a sense of parental concern for him on her part. It was simply that she liked to beat him, and he had a habit of telling her exactly where to go and when. It was a battle neither of them was ever going to win, but unfortunately neither of them realised. Halpin figured she was going to tame him, while he had worked out that the sting from her beatings was worth the kudos he reaped from the other kids afterwards, and so they engaged in a two sided competition of 'let's see who breaks first'.

The frequency of their 'cuddle time' together increased dramatically, as she sought to reign in his increased sense of self, burgeoning self-confidence, and heightened sense of status that the other children afforded him. It often appeared that the slightest of excuses would result in a visit to the staff quarters, where the routine of lowering his pants and positioning himself for 'justice' would be enacted. A demon had been awoken, and over time it would turn into a vicious game of love-hate, of which they were both victim and victor.

Her predilection towards summary, unwarranted punishments, served to contradict her apparent aim of instilling some form of mystical discipline in him. It was often the case that, in the belief that punishment was unavoidable, and an inevitable consequence of getting up in the morning, Snowball countered by simply doing as he pleased most of the time, and when it suited. This antagonistic behaviour further enraged Halpin, who would intensify the brutalisation, and so the cycle would begin again.

Halpin often arrived at work in her clapped out Mini, windows steamed, and exhaust bellowing out its own contribution to global warming, on a scale normally the domain of coal fired power stations. She was a single woman, who outwardly appeared to have few friends that anyone had noted, and she seemed slightly alienated from the rest of the staff. Tolerated rather than liked, she existed for her job, and her job alone. Snowball had seen her arrive that day. A Sunday afternoon, after a long week in which they had shared time together on two separate occasions, and without justification in his eyes, but such was life. She had parked her car in front of the garage, taking care to turn the car around, so that it faced the gate at the bottom of the drive, in preparation for when she left in the morning. It was her private winter ritual, undertaken in the knowledge that, when she came to depart each morning, the condensation on the inside rear window of the car, meant that she wouldn't be able to reverse it anywhere without running the risk of hitting something or someone. She had dashed across the drive, and into the house, closely watched from an upper floor window by Snowball and Griffiths. It was time to get the party started.

"Right, watch this," Snowball whispered to Griffiths. "Watch what?" Sonya had interjected, after yet again demonstrating that there was fuck all wrong with her ears, as the saying went. "You'll see," Snowball replied, heading down the corridor, and towards the stairs. Griffiths and Sonya hot-footed it behind him, the lure of the attraction mitigating the fear that had their minds half wondering what was going on, and half fearful that they were about to be landed in some serious trouble if they followed. Sonya had recognised the look in Snowball's eyes. She knew trouble was afoot, she just didn't know what, and how much.

Together they headed down the stairs, and calmly along the corridor that led to the kitchen, Snowball leading, not by any sense of knowing or direction, but honed by the tones of Halpin's voice, which he could hear as they approached. As they arrived at the kitchen, they could see Halpin sat, with her back to them, at the large wooden dining table that acted as an old-time centre kitchen island for Mrs Williams, who was the chief cook and bottle washer (well, slop Jockey was a more apt description than cook, but she was in comparison to most of the other staff a good person, so it does no harm to be nice). Stopping briefly at the door, Snowball kicked Griffiths on the foot, and pointed directly at the back of Halpin. He raised a finger of silence to his lips and glared psychotically into Griffiths' eyes.

The words "oh fuck" had barely and almost imperceivably departed Griffiths' mouth, before Snowball, spinning around on his right heel, had walked calmly over to Halpin, who had, by now, raised the cup of tea she was holding to her mouth. Tapping her on the right shoulder, while cheekily moving around her left-hand side, he simply asked, "You going to punish me?" By now he was looking her straight in the eyes, with the devil's own glare. "What?" she replied, somewhat taken by surprise with the question, and a look of bemusement sweeping across her face. "Have you done something that deserves it?" she added. "Yes, this," replied Snowball, before launching into a 'Green Avenger' moment of a few years back, grabbing Halpin by the hair, and swinging himself violently forward and to the ground, while holding on to the dear life she would surely be trying to take from him, any second hence.

Halpin let out a shrill cry that could be heard clearly throughout the home. The burn of the tea in her lap, and banshee attack to her hair, providing for a double centre of pain, the likes of which she clearly hadn't experienced before. The likelihood of his strategy succeeding was slim, not least because he didn't have an end game consisting of anything more than causing as much pain to Halpin as he could, before she got the better of him. Halpin met him at ground level. Her head bowed towards his chest, as his grip on her hair tightened, and he shook it violently from left to right. He was stronger and more determined than the first time he had executed this move on the hapless social worker, who had ripped him from his foster home, and much better placed to cause some damage, before the inevitable defeat came to pass, and the painful consequences administered.

Halpin gripped both his hands, in an attempt to stop the violent shaking, and pressed her head firmly into his chest, in order to keep him pinned to the floor. By now, he had partly succeeded in wrapping his legs around her waist, and was using her own body weight as leverage in his endeavours. Griffiths had bolted, and Sonya was stood, open mouthed, with a look of total disbelief on her face. The struggle was almost over, as the superior strength of Halpin began to show. Snowball's grip weakened, and as she rose into the ascendancy, the game was up. It would soon be a case of to the victor the spoils, but for now, and with her knee firmly planted across his chest, Halpin was content with nothing more than regaining her composure and straightening her hair.

Had he been with his foster parents, this was the very moment that Snowball would have deployed Plan B (cry loudly, give her a huge hug, while at the same time proclaiming remorse), but he knew this wasn't an option, and was resigned to the painful retribution that would shortly follow. By the time he had been pulled to his feet, restrained by her iron grip, and dragged protesting towards the stairs, and the inevitable visit to her quarters, a small group had gathered in the dining room at the beckoning of Griffiths, standing silently, but with a sense of awe, as he was marched away. Snowball smiled briefly at Sonya as he passed, even managing a brief wink before, as tradition dictated, feet not touching the ground, he disappeared into the stairwell with Halpin, and was not to be seen again for quite some time.

This was going to turn into a long running and painful saga, for both Snowball and Halpin. The problem for Halpin was that she only understood one interpretation of the rules: her interpretation. Her rules were based on basic, long established generics. All kids are the same, all kids can be beaten, all kids will respond in the same way to be treated the same or being beaten, all kids have the same needs, all kids like and dislike the same things, and so it went on. Snowball had internalised a different set of rules, a slightly elevated sense of morality, right, wrong and justice. Rules that recognised his differences, and those of others, his individuality, his ability to function independently within certain parameters, etc. He didn't fit, nor did he want to fit, in the 'one size fits all' box that they insisted on putting him in. He had no problem with being punished for things he had done. It was one of the fundamental cornerstones that underpinned life with his foster parents. It had been drilled into him by word and deed. His primary issue was being punished for things he hadn't done, or being punished on the whim of others, and being placed in a situation where it didn't matter whether he behaved or not, he was still likely to be punished at some time or another. The group punishment mentality, which was so pervasive in the homes, did not fit well with his developing intellect, nor his sense of fair play, and having determined that he could just about take most of what Halpin could dish out, it was a case of 'Game On'.

That was almost (bar the devilment of it) the entire reasoning behind the attack on Halpin, and the further attacks that would inevitably come her way in the future. She had, through her own malice, punished him indiscriminately too often. Whether in isolation, or group, she had singled him out for her amusement, malice and sadistic pleasures. She had pushed him into the corner, leading him to believe that there was no causal 'crime and punishment' link to her brutality. It was whimsical. Thus, for Snowball, in the absence of a credible defence, Plan A is to always go on the attack. Let them know you are in the fight!

In his own words, he had told her as much that day. As she'd dragged him from the kitchen, to the privacy and isolation of the staff quarters on the upper floor, she had remonstrated that she was going to beat the life out of him, and gleefully explained how he wouldn't be able to sit down for a week by the time she had finished (why is it always a fucking week?).

"You'd have hit me anyway," he had told her, resigned to what was inevitably coming his way. His words didn't sink in. She was too angry, too focussed on what she was about to do, but he was right. He knew the rules of the game and had developed a strategy to deal with it. He wasn't going to win the war, but not losing was the point. He knew that from the outset. He was a child in an adult world. Too small. Too weak. Too ill-equipped, and too often outnumbered. But he knew he could have fun on the journey, pick up the transient small win along the way, and there were clearly ways and means to get under her skin. She held all of the cards, that was more than apparent to him. But she only had one head of hair and he was holding a large chunk of it in his hand!

Although there was always a daily battle to be fought, life at The Manors did have some endearing moments, even if they were generally short-lived, and nothing to write home about, unless you were a child familiar with the level of social and emotional deprivation that Snowball lived in most of the time. Annual events were brought to the children, primarily as a means of ensuring that staff didn't miss out, rather than any overt sense of care and consideration for the kids in care, but they provided welcome respite. Birthdays always came along with a small, albeit worthless present, that ultimately found its way out of the birthday child's possession, and into the communal toy box. There would be a semblance of party spirit around tea-time, when a minor fuss was made of the birthday boy or girl, and everyone was compelled to sing happy birthday, as if they meant it, before sitting down to cold buffet food, knowing full well that it was a convenient replacement for the muchneeded hot offering that they craved, however poorly cooked it was. There would even be a homemade birthday cake, though there was no guarantee it would be edible.

Staff birthdays were occasionally celebrated, if they had been unfortunate enough to cop for a duty, on the given day, and been unable to roster swap. There were occasional day trips out during the school summer holidays, but these would be few and far between, as they often brought in more trouble than they staved off with bored children. The mini-bus could only seat around ten, including staff, so any trip usually meant at least two runs, each way. Catering for the age-range of the children, in terms of where to go, was problematic, so it was guaranteed that one group would be bored before they had departed, another before they had arrived, yet another within minutes of arrival, and everyone by the end of the day.

Many of the older children would use the trips as an opportunity to go shoplifting, which meant that most trips culminated in an hour long wait or more outside a police station, while someone was reprimanded and bailed with a promise to return at a later date, and brought shame-faced back to the bus, where they would mainly sit in silence, unresponsive to the adulation being poured upon them by their peers, as they contemplated the inevitable beating they were very likely to receive, upon return to The Manors. Before long, bonfire night would be enjoyed with attendance at a locally organised event, which was the only way that order could be maintained, and local pets protected from the annual attacks they endured, as fireworks became readily available, and shared between the excited, adventurous and sadistic in equal measure. Hot Jacket Potatoes, Treacle Toffee, Cinder Bars, and Fizzy Pop. All available in abundance, to be abused in a ravenous annual frenzy, which only served to highlight the levels of privation and disparity that were the norm outside of these events.

The cold, hostile November nights would transition into the decorative spectacle of Christmas. There would be visits to a grotto for the younger children, and the older ones were given some choice about what their 'Christmas Allowance' would be spent on. Santa was certainly a stingy bastard. Christmas Day would arrive. Excitement and expectation beyond the bounds of realism from the younger kids, supplemented by an air of stale resigned realism from the elder ones, as the 'excitement' of rushing to the end of the bed, only to see very little of what they wanted, and very little of anything else, hit home, and life as a child in care revealed itself yet again, as the utopian anti-climax they always knew it was.

The long and eagerly awaited Christmas dinner would arrive and disappear just as quickly. It was the solitary time in the year that two different cuts of roast meat were to be entertained on the same plate, as both beef and turkey, alongside all the trimmings, were served up to wide-eyed, nourishment deprived and hungry recipients. The whole spectacle followed up with a poorly cooked, relatively tasteless traditional Christmas pudding, and a home-made Christmas cake, complete with a spattering of coins, which were eagerly fought over, regardless of who found them in the slice they had been given. Christmas would turn into New Year celebrations for the staff, and then normal life would be resumed. Arseholes returned to being arseholes, bullies to bullies, self-harmers resumed their unhealthy preoccupation with all things harmful, and the brutal and sadistic nature of life in care rolled on, as did the unbridled beatings and abuse, as life once again picked up pace after the festive lull.

Yes, for Snowball and the others, there were times when life almost resembled normality, but the inequalities had a nasty habit of shining through. But there was always an air of uncertainty to these occasions, always an expectation that at any moment it could all turn sour, and it often did. He would often ponder why, it seemed that they couldn't just leave them alone to be happy. It wasn't as if happiness occurred often, so always spoil it. He wondered why happiness always comes at such a terribly high price. What was it that he and the others had done to deserve the life that they had been given? They went to church to learn of God, and yet God himself had abandoned and ignored them all, content that regardless of innocence, they suffered in hell. Where was this God when the beatings ensued? Where was he when the girls were being beaten, fondled and raped? Where was he when Emily had set fire to her bed and then laid herself upon it? Where was this God, when Halpin had brutalised him, day in and day out? This was a godless place by any standards, and he knew he would have to leave, before he became lost in the misery and succumbed to the innate desperation and self-harm like so many before him had done and continued to do.

It was shortly after one New Year that Halpin suddenly departed for pastures new. Rumours were rife that Halpin had been caught in a sexual liaison with one of the older boys, and it had transpired that she had indulged herself for quite some time, and with a number of the boys over the years. Snowball hadn't been so 'lucky' and the hypocrisy of Halpin attempting to instil behaviours beyond reproach in him, while regularly sneaking upstairs and being banged senseless by a juvenile, wasn't at all lost on him either. The boy in question was also moved to another home shortly afterwards, adding weight to the rumours, and life began to once again return to normal. Snowball was happy enough with the news. The strapping she had meted out to him the night before, was clearly the last she would deliver his way, and in being too young and under-developed to appeal to her in other ways, she may as well be gone from his perspective.

It all seemed rather ironic in many respects. They could, without rhyme or reason, beat and abuse children at will, male members of staff were sexually abusing, and often raping young girls in their care, and yet Halpin, illicit though it was, and as much as he had grown to hate her, was apparently hauled over the coals for having relations with consenting (as much as an under-age youth can legally be deemed to be consenting) young men. The irony wasn't lost on Snowball, even if her departure was the most welcoming of news he had heard in a long time.

Pleasure Precedes Pain (Occasionally)

Halpin was eventually replaced by a diminutively round little lady called Miss Blyth, who in time simply became known as 'the bitch', or 'the fucking bitch' depending on your linguistic capabilities, and whether you were saying it, or attempting to etch it into the woodwork with a pen knife. Miss Blyth was unremarkable in every sense. Middle-aged, singularly frigid, cold, intellectually stunted in many respects, and challenged in both figure and face. The only aspect of life she excelled at was her rigid, monotonous and religious zeal at applying the rules, and her unwavering enthusiasm for punishing transgressors. She was, in fact, just another Halpin, but without the propensity, nor feminine wares to attract the young male residents.

She was a woman wrapped in a shroud of her own perceived self-importance, and one who showed little interest in anything, other than harming children. She would constantly be seen enthusiastically patrolling the corridors and grounds of The Manors, in the hope of finding some unfortunate child, indulgent in the course of a misdeed, real or perceived, whom she could then physically exert her summarily sadistic authority over. To Snowball, it appeared there was a never-ending supply of brutal adults, wanting to humiliate, harm and subjugate children, for nothing more than their own perverse pleasures. How often he would feel that Emily was the lucky one. She had, at least in part, chosen her own destiny, wherever she was.

Blyth had been her maliciously rampant self, throughout the entirety of her weekend shift. Arriving early Friday evening, and not due to leave until late Sunday, she had made it plain that her mood was foul, and her temper short. Everyone, Snowball included, knew that she was to be given a wide berth for the ensuing forty-eight hours, but when a hunter prowls with the persistence that Blyth did, there was an inevitability about crossing her path that they all lived with, and were resigned to. Blyth administered, on average, three beatings a day, and she was known for her fearsome application of both strap and stick alike.

It was mid-Saturday afternoon, and many of the boys had been engaged in a game of football on the leafy front lawn outside the main entrance to The Manors. Blyth had insisted upon standing in the cold and watching, and it was apparent to everyone present, that she was on the hunt for the next half opportunity to drag someone away, and administer her worst, and there had been a few warnings regarding language, that had remained as warnings, simply because she had been unable to readily identify the verbally expressive user.

Snowball had been sidelined and was eagerly awaiting the arrival of another player to even up the odd numbers before he could get into the game, when the ball suddenly, and without warning, came hurtling towards the head of Blyth. It seemed like the whole world just suddenly slipped into a fretful slow motion movie, as the eyes of everyone present became transfixed upon the flight path of the errant football that was now heading towards the seemingly unaware Blyth, at a frightening rate of speed. The imagined flight path, becoming an horrific reality, as Blyth casually turned towards the game, and was smashed, full force in the face, by the oncoming football. The impact was as sickening as it was pleasing to witness, as her head jolted backwards, and almost spun around a full three hundred and sixty degrees, like a scene from The Exorcist.

Though there was little sympathy for Blyth, as she first stumbled backwards, and then collapsed to the floor, with a bright and raw pink mound beginning to swell up on the left-hand side of her face, there was, however, a simultaneous gasp for air from all on the pitch, the sound of which was only disturbed by the instantaneous burst of hysterical laughter that erupted from Snowball, as the sight of the prone Blyth was etched into his mind, and her jelly-like wobble on the floor electrified every ounce of sick humour in his body. He could feel his stomach crease and tighten, as the laughter sucked every ounce of air from his lungs. He began to gasp, eyes watering, fingers pointing, heart pounding, as the laughter continued to surface from deep within him. He had never seen anything like it, and it amused him. It was the perfect storm of time, place and circumstance, and for once, it was Blyth who was the victim.

However, pains always followed pleasures at The Manors. Blyth swiftly rose to her feet, indignant at the spectacle she had created around herself, but determined to show a steely front and solid resolve. She picked up the ball, and with her hand gestured to the boys that the game was over, and they needed to be heading indoors. Caressing her swollen face, she turned to Snowball, and instructed him to follow her. He knew what was coming and cared little for whether he deserved it or not. She would have her revenge, but he knew he would have many an amused moment, where he would recall her plight, and raise his own spirits and the spirits of those around him in the process. Small Victories meant everything, and he was becoming an avid collector.

In the consumption of her embarrassment, she had lost none of her ruthlessness with a strap, bringing it down, hard and fast across his lower back and backside. Caring little for where it landed, she swung the strap with sadistically wild abandon, until she felt suitably redeemed, and had ensured that he was appropriately repentant. And so, the day closed with each and all striving to avoid any further and unfortunate contact with Blyth, Snowball showing off his latest blister red badges of honour, and the football locked safely away in the office, ensuring that nobody had any real fun, until Blyth's shift came to an end the following night. She really was a miserable cow.

FORTUNE FAVOURS
THE BRAVE

There were times when, quite unexpectedly, life would spin itself around, and turn itself upside down. It was rarely for the better, but it happened, and when it did, on occasions it was the most welcome of surprises. Duggan had arrived at The Manors that morning. He was aggressive in look and demeanour and was clearly a young boy who had witnessed and been subjected to a few horrors in his life. He had spent most of the morning skulking around in the shadows under the trees in the garden, and had made little if any attempt to integrate, or familiarise himself with life and the home, or the people who lived there. It was obvious from the outset that he was going to have plenty of problems at The Manors, and most of them would probably result from his own actions. It wasn't that the staff needed an excuse to brutalise a child, but clearly there were options you could take, to mitigate the chances of being the subject of their attentions, if only you were capable of intelligent interface with the variables that were in play. Snowball knew exactly what Duggan was about. If nothing else, as he himself bounded from one conflict to another, he was at least learning how to survive, when to fight and when to walk away. Halpin had ensured that he paid a painful price for his attack on her in the kitchen, but it had also elevated his status amongst many of the other children, and his life was becoming much easier as a consequence, with more friends and less aggro, as his reputation as being one of those who was 'fucking nuts' began to grow.

Duggan was a bully. Snowball could tell straight away. It was the way he composed himself, the direct and confrontational way that he would approach people, the choice of words, and the manner in which he clearly circumvented all those whom he knew and were clearly beyond his physical influence. Snowball knew there would be problems with Duggan, and as the only black child in the home, he was well aware that Duggan would attempt to make his name at his expense. He also knew that he himself would be ready when it happened.

The Manors had a large internal laundry on the ground floor. It was an almost industrial set up, with large commercial sized washers and an industrial sized dryer to one side, a huge drying room to the other, with the two being connected by a row of large china look sinks that were utilised for hand washing, and cleaning larger items, which were deemed too big or too damaging for the washers. It also served on occasion as the 'Arena of the Caesars' where the gladiatorial amongst the children would assemble, to fight out their differences, in the knowledge that, if the machines weren't rolling, the chances are, the staff weren't coming.

The title of 'Cock of the Home' had been decided and changed hands on many an occasion in the laundry, when a pre-arranged fight between two protagonists was settled in the timehonoured pugilistic fashion that it warranted. Spartacus on one side, and a gladiator chosen by the Emperor of Rome on the other, battle would commence until one was defeated, and the hand of the other raised in victory to the baying crowds. Snowball had made several appearances in the arena, and though by no means a leading contender for the title, he had won more than he had lost, and that was enough to ensure that challenges became few and far between, as he navigated his way through life, one day at a time.

The laundry also served as a very convenient bolthole during the winter months, as both the drying room, and the industrial dryer that was often running, served to ensure that the heat on the inside far exceeded that on the outside. Snowball would also use it as somewhere he could go for respite from the general rough and tumble of life at The Manors, and as a place he could use to avoid the attentions of the staff, until a shift change had occurred. Taking some 'quiet time' at the right moments, was something Miss Bradwell had taught him, and it was a lesson that he had grown to appreciate the value of. He always thought how weird it was, that much of what she had taught him made very little sense at the time, as he had basked under her protective shadow. But now he was alone, and fending for himself, it all came flooding back, with a saliency that had him thinking about her on a regular basis.

It was during one of his self-imposed isolations that Snowball, warmly tucked up in the drying room with a book in hand, heard the 'newly dropped bollocks' wisp of Davidson, as he had entered the laundry, on the far side of the room. He silently rose to his feet, carefully controlling both movements and breathing, and with a precision crafted stealth, peered through the gap between the door jamb and the frame. He could see the odious little toad that was Davidson, his arch enemy on many an occasion, but recently more subdued and more willing to play ball, if for no other reason than a peaceful life. Davidson had wandered into the laundry, and then began gesturing to somebody else who had remained on the outside. He wasn't sure who it was, but they were clearly unwilling to enter at that point, and even when cajoled and tormented by the name 'chicken' had remained silently outside. Davidson was doing everything he could to entice them in, but they just didn't seem to want any part of it, so Snowball remained silent, hidden and waiting for events to unfold.

A few more taunts from Davidson, and then in walked Duggan, chest fluffed up, and full of the arrogance that had typified his demeanour since his arrival. For a fleeting moment, Snowball couldn't decide who he hated most, and given that they were most likely attending gladiator school, he would happily have seen both of them get a majestic life-ending thumbs down at some point. Then out of the blue it happened. Oi You Fucker right there and then in front of his eyes, as Duggan, barely in the room, and with the door still ajar, landed a ferocious punch into Davidson's face, Duggan 1-0 Davidson. The punch caught Davidson completely off-guard and sent him crashing to the ground. Sneaky fucker, he thought, as he witnessed Davidson, prone on the floor and struggling to overcome the shock of what had occurred, receive another crushing blow to the face, as the inflight Duggan had descended upon him, like a lion upon its prey. Duggan 2-0 Davidson.

Davidson was all over the place, arms flaying wildly in the air, as he vainly fought to stem the tidal wave of blows that were raining down upon him, as Duggan was now in full flow. Duggan 3-0 Davidson. Time and time again, Duggan landed blow after blow. Each punch hitting the exact target that it had been designed for. It was the most one-sided fight Snowball had ever witnessed, Davidson had been completely overcome in a matter of seconds, he wasn't even in the fight, but when push came to shove, it had all started unfairly, and despite the intense hate he felt for Davidson most days, that was something Snowball felt he simply couldn't tolerate.

And so, it was in that split second that Snowball decided who he hated the most that day, and it was Duggan. Now, under normal circumstances, it might not have been viewed as a monumental decision by any stretch of the imagination, but the significance wasn't lost on Duggan, who as the recipient of a well-timed and ferocious kick to the head had been sent sprawling in agony to the floor, blood dripping from his nose, and quite frankly, in mortal danger, as Snowball, fiery eyed and full of rage, swiftly descended. Duggan 0-1 Snowball, and in the timehonoured tradition, there was no intention of going to extra time.

Davidson remained on the floor alongside Duggan, by virtue of the fading sense of consciousness to which he had succumbed. Under normal circumstances, and for reasons of humanity, the ref would have stopped the fight, but these were not normal circumstances, and there was no humanity in the hell-hole in which they all survived. This was all about 'your place' in the order of things, and when that was considered, there was only one thing that could be done. Snowball continued to lay into his foe with a ferocity that belied his stature. It was Duggan 0-2 Snowball. Davidson was having trouble reconciling the fact that Snowball had come to his aid, while also trying to recover enough dignity to brush himself down and get to his feet, but nevertheless, the assault continued. Snowball momentarily glanced upwards and looked directly into Davidson's eyes. "Fucking let them know you're in the fight, you twat," he bellowed at Davidson, before resuming his assault on the unfortunate Duggan, who by now was crying out loudly, and begging him to stop. Duggan 0-3 Snowball. For Snowball, stopping at this point kind of seemed rude, as he had a point to make that he wasn't quite sure had been embedded in Duggan's mind, and so he continued onwards, as Duggan's pleas grew louder and louder, and Davidson simply remained an onlooker and in a stunned silence.

It was at this point that Snowball's guardian angel had seen enough and had chosen to abandon him to the fate that was silently strolling down the corridor in the rather awesomely attractive shape of Aunty Sharon. Aunty Sharon was your best friend and your worst enemy in equal measure. She was one of those people who simply just couldn't be read. There were times when she had a very black and white view of the world, which she clearly preferred, and as long as you conformed to that view, there was rarely a problem; and yet there were times when she could almost transport you into another world with kindness, a real world, where you felt wanted, valued, happy and occasionally loved. She was an enigma, and Snowball kind of liked that shit. Today was a black and white day, and she was about to be all over Snowball like an outbreak of teenage acne. As warm as she could occasionally be, she could also be the time specific version of the modern day 'the computer says no' advocate. She was often as dispassionate as she was compassionate, and her chosen implement of torture was a short pocket sized leather tawse, which she insisted her father had used on her on a regular basis, and it had done her no harm – and she was right, if having no friends, no social life, no long term romantic interest, being rigid, frigid, and having nothing to look forward to in life, other than a lonesome old age, was the definition of doing no harm.

Coinciding with the departure of his guardian angel, Aunty Sharon arriving on the scene was a classic Oi You Fucker moment in Snowball's life, and one he would very quickly come to regret, even if it had come riding on the back of another stunning victory that would add to his enigmatic persona and presumed psychosis that he was so readily cultivating. As she peered around the open door, the first thing that caught her eyes was the defeated Davidson, standing in the corner, covered in blood, and in proud ownership of a face that had clearly registered the surprise of her arrival. As she stepped further into the laundry, and witnessed Snowball sat astride a bloodied Duggan, her head, steeped in good Christian virtues, simply flipped, and she catapulted herself into action, grabbing him by the back of his t-shirt, and dragging him off his prone and helpless victim.

It at this moment that Snowball could really have done with a little help from Davidson, by means of an explanation as to what had occurred, but surprisingly he remained quiet, as Sharon, Snowball firmly locked in her vice-like grip, headed towards the office muttering words to the effect of how she had reached the 'end of her tether' which was an unfortunate term of phrase, given the full mouth of horse's teeth that she was the proud owner of (the only thing that spoiled her stunning visage), and instilling in him an immediate fear, as she rambled on about how much 'it was all going to hurt'. She momentarily paused in the corridor, to instruct London to 'take a look at what he had done in the laundry', and to clean the other two up, before she continued onwards to the office, where a swift and painful retribution was meted out. At least he could console himself with the fact that, as Sharon had told him while dragging him through the corridors of power, it was all for his own good!

SNOWBALL MEETS PAUL MCLARNEY

McLarney was a huge thug of a boy. Brutal by nature and appearance, and with a mean streak that would have been welcomed by the Nazis in concentration camps across Europe during the Second World War. Bright blonde hair, searing blue eyes, square jaw, and a huge bulbous nose that gave him the appearance of somebody who spent most of their waking moments buried knee deep in Whisky or Rum. He had muscles everywhere that muscles should be, and those muscles had, out of sympathy, adopted other muscles, which they proudly carried around for all to see. McLarney was one of those people that you always tried to avoid, but no matter where you went, he always seemed to turn up like a bad smell, if for no other reason than to torment or humiliate you in some mean-spirited, ego boosting, self-promoting game.

McLarney was another child from an abused background like Snowball, and he had come to appreciate that the best way to obtain compliance to his will was to brutalise people, in much the same way that he had been brutalised as a young child, before landing his sorry arse under the care and attention of the staff at The Manors, and various other institutions. His parents were clearly both psychotic and had kicked him around the home like a football, broken most bones in his body at one time or another, and left him battered, bruised, starving and close to death, before it had occurred to them that he hadn't been named or christened, and in a rare moment of sobriety and mental clarity, they duly decided to call him Paul McLarney, his first name after the former Beatle, and his last from his mother's side of the dysfunctional band of misfits and thieves she called family. They were a pair of cheesy twats. His entire family were cheesy twats from what they all saw, on the rare times that they had called in to see him on an escorted visit. But that's how it was for him. A life full of cheese and violence, and yet he remained emotionally attached to his mother in such a powerful way, that it belied the fact she had done jail time for harming him.

McLarney had excellent physical genetics, but a severe lack of acumen, which meant that his mouth would often write cheques that his body couldn't cash, when in the wrong company. Not that it really bothered McLarney, as Snowball and the other children all came to learn. For McLarney it was simply the thrill of the fight that mattered, and he fought often and ferociously. He had been on the wrong end of many stern beatings from the staff at The Manors, who over the years of his residency had taken plimsolls, straps, canes, belts, slippers, fists and feet to him, in an attempt to bring him to heel. But McLarney appeared to revel in it. He simply didn't care and was often seen to give as good as he got, before being temporarily subdued, only to rise like a Phoenix from the ashes of his own defeat and fight another day. For McLarney, any attention was better than no attention, and as long as his life was being occupied with a fight, it didn't seem to matter to him, whether he won or lost. Snowball held a begrudging admiration for McLarney in many ways. He epitomised the good fight. He was fearless, strong, and would always take it to his enemy regardless of the odds. But McLarney was also a brutal and intimidating bully, and as Snowball had found out to his own detriment on many an occasion, it was the black face that made the easiest target.

McLarney's favourite trick was to wait until people were asleep, before he launched his revenge attacks, or simply attacked out of pure malice. He would wait long into the dead of night, when all those around him were deep in slumber, and then attack. Silently creeping over to his intended victim, he would launch into a vicious two-fisted attack that would often leave somebody dazed, bloodied and bewildered, as they were brutally awoken from their deep state of unconsciousness. It had got to the point where most of the children in The Manors had been a victim of his assaults at one time or another, and as a direct consequence, many had found themselves unable to sleep properly, in the knowledge that they were potentially targets, for no reason other than the fact that he liked to hurt people.

Snowball himself had been attacked on numerous occasions, and spent many sleepless nights, sharing a room with McLarney and four others. The slightest squeak from a bedspring, turning of a body, or snore in the dead of night, proving to be enough to awaken him, in a sweat dripping fear, and to keep him awake for most of the night. It was a tiresome nightly routine for many, which inevitably had to come to an end in one manner or another, but the staff at The Manors, though expert at asserting their brutal authority over the weak, seemed powerless to stop the brute of a child that was Paul McLarney, and the attacks simply continued.

But like all good productions, the run comes to an end eventually. McLarney was a good act that had simply been on too long. And in the true tradition of a single straw breaking the camel's back, McLarney pushed his luck that little bit too far, and his house of cards came tumbling down around him. For Snowball, McLarney had been an unavoidable consequence of getting out of bed each morning. McLarney had spent hours tormenting him, and some of the other children the night before, and had only been stopped when he was dragged from his bed by a member of staff, and forced to stand, hands on head in a corner by the staff room, until he had quite literally dropped to the floor with exhaustion, before being quietly returned to bed in the early hours of the morning, where he subsequently fell into a deep sleep.

As morning broke, and children began to rise from their beds, McLarney took up from where he had finished the night before, and Snowball was his singular target, from the moment he awoke. It had started with a slap to the face as they both headed to the bathroom for a wash. The slap became a punch, and although Snowball had left the room, and headed to a bathroom further up the corridor, McLarney had chosen to follow him, and resumed the assault, until he had been stopped by several of the older boys, and warned of an impending beating, if he didn't desist. The torment continued throughout the day, all through school, and into the late afternoon and beyond, until McLarney suddenly became surprisingly conspicuous by his absence in the early evening. Snowball wasn't about to go looking for him, but in a surprising twist of fate, they would meet again, in much more favourable circumstances.

It was shortly after tea that Snowball noticed McLarney's absence, and there was a general lifting of tension that was felt by almost everybody. Things had gone quiet, and though nobody mentioned it, it appeared that everyone was enjoying the respite that McLarney's absence was providing. Snowball decided to grab some quiet time, and had slipped away, and headed for his bedroom. He came across Davidson in the stairwell at the rear of the house, who had nosily enquired where he was going, only to be told by Snowball to mind his 'own fucking business', and to leave him alone. It wasn't that Davidson had particularly done or said anything wrong, more that Snowball was reaching the end of a short tether, and the last thing he needed at that moment was Davidson jumping on

McLarney's bandwagon, and complicating matters. So, in Snowball's eyes, it was better to deter him before he started, than deal with the aftermath if he got into his stride. Davidson, clearly offended, but wary of another confrontation with Snowball, took the hint in good faith, and meekly followed Snowball upstairs and towards his bedroom in complete silence, as if he was clearly afraid to ask a second time, but couldn't help but satiate his inquisitive tendencies by following him to his end destination.

Snowball arrived at his bedroom door, with Davidson comfortably in his slipstream, and becoming something of a silent irritant that needed expunging. He gently pushed the bedroom door open, while sneeringly looking at Davidson, in a manner that informed him that he could go now. But Davidson wasn't looking at Snowball. He wasn't even interested in Snowball at that point, as he had just caught sight of the sleeping McLarney, lying on his back, in a state of complete vulnerability. It was an Oi You Fucker moment in the making, and one that Snowball simply couldn't resist (well, it would have been rude).

Snowball raised a finger to his pursed lips and indicated to Davidson that it was probably best if he remained silent. Davidson didn't need telling twice, and by now had begun to slowly back-pedal away from the bedroom door. Snowball flashed him a knowing smile, and beckoned him forward once more, the bemused Davidson, now standing still, with a look of total bewilderment sweeping across his face. "What are you doing?" he silent mouthed to Snowball. Snowball said nothing and simply pointed to the sleeping McLarney, and suddenly, once again, it was GAME ON.

Snowball crept towards the sleeping goliath, pausing only briefly to fully appreciate the irony of how the numerous cowardly attacks that this beast had perpetrated in the dead of night upon others as they slept, were about to be visited upon him in the most brutal fashion he could imagine. As he drew closer, he turned towards Davidson, smiled, picked up the small wooden bedside cabinet that stood alongside the sleeping McLarney, and raised it high above his head. Davidson's eyes bulged in terror, as he stood in the doorway, looking at the boy he had once bullied, about to formally exact a revenge upon the one person who, until that moment, had appeared completely untouchable to children and staff alike.

Snowball was now alongside McLarney, and as he calmly towered above his prone body, he called out his name, demanded he wake up, and then waited. McLarney remained motionless and silent, until at the second time of asking, he duly obliged, and momentarily opened his eyes, with an expression that first indicated a frustrated ire at being awoken from his sleep, before quickly changing to intense fear, as the realisation of his helpless predicament came into full cognition. It was the one thing Snowball wanted, and the only signal he needed. As the look of fear swept across McLarney's face, Snowball brought the bedside cabinet crashing down upon his head. Once, twice, three times, and then it shattered into what seemed like thousands of blood-spattered pieces that littered the bedroom floor, and laid testament to the brutality that had been inflicted.

"Not nice is it?" he muttered as he leaned over the tearful McLarney, callously adding that he should think twice about sleeping that night, before promptly leaving the room. There was of course a price to pay, when Aunty Sharon was informed of the carnage, but it was a small price to pay. Snowball was confined to a secure holding room for the following two days, which proved to be something of a blessing in terms of good sleep, and from that day onwards, McLarney quietened down and actually became quite likeable, everyone started to enjoy torment-free sleep, and Snowball found that his days as a victim in The Manors had finally passed him by.

WHO NEEDS FOOD ANYWAY (HILL ROAD, BOLTON)

'Here we fucking go again' and 'this will never work' were amongst the immediate thoughts cascading like a waterfall through Snowball's mind. The car he was in had just pulled up outside number 49 Hill Road in Bolton, and Paula was eagerly undoing her seatbelt, before turning to Snowball, and telling him to release his. Wary of his propensity for doing a 'bunk' at the traffic lights, she had cannily placed her handbag over the gap that housed his seatbelt fastening and the handbrake, in order to give herself some warning of the imminent. It probably wouldn't have made much of a difference in reality, but it clearly made her feel like she had taken all reasonable precautions.

Hill Road was described as a 'Family Group' home, but the definition was long lost on Snowball, who apart from his life in Farm Wood, had never come to view anywhere else as home, nor did he consider the occupants of these places as being family. They were all lost souls and transient guests of a care system that neither cared for, nor encouraged relationships of any kind, and they would all forget each other as quickly as night turned to day, under the right circumstances. Number sixty-six in Stockport had come a very close second to Farm Wood, but it had never quite reached the same cognitive heights, for the simple reason that in Farm Wood he had people whom he called Mum and Dad, he had brothers and sisters, he had a real grandad and nanna, and he had a whole host of 'aunties and uncles' whom he loved, and who loved him dearly. In Stockport he only had aunties, and to him, the difference was huge.

Snowball had sussed number 49 as a desolate place before Paula even opened her mouth. "Are you ok?" she asked, as she always did, while releasing him from the seatbelt death grip that had pinned him in place. 'Oh, fuck off, Paula, will you,

211

you asked me that last time you dragged me from a home, and the answer hasn't changed,' he thought to himself, the contempt in his eyes barely concealed, as he cast a weary glance across this 'limp lettuce' of a woman, who he would quite happily have punched, had he not appreciated the fact it would serve no useful purpose at all, and probably land him with another good hiding.

It wasn't that she didn't mean well, she was simply just 'wet through', naive and in need of the sort of enthusiastic slapping that could potentially project her into the real world in which he lived, courtesy of people, just like her. "You can fuck off," he told her, before feeling his hand grasped tightly by hers, as he flicked the seat belt buckle outwards, to stop it clipping him in the face, as it passed through. He looked her directly in the eyes, and silently implored her not to utter the words that were about to spew from her slowly revealed Hollywood white dentures, but unfortunately he was too late. "You won't be here long, and if you don't like it, we can always find you somewhere else to live, so just give it a chance," she stated, as he silently mirrored her words, and turned towards the doors, furious not so much with the blatant lies, as he had long since come to expect them, but the fact she thought him stupid enough to fall for that bollocks all over again. It was simply infuriating. If only he could land himself with a social worker who could tell the truth. Life would be so much simpler, so much easier to understand, and come to terms with. Why, oh why, he would wonder. Why the constant deceit.

"Grab my bag, will you, Paula, make yourself useful," he commanded, as his feet hit the pavement, and he headed to the gate with a nonchalant gait. He could hear the depth of her belly sigh as she emerged from the car, but he knew she would say nothing, as right now, the only thing on her mind was getting him from the street to the front door, without him taking off into the distance, like he had done previously, and much to her personal embarrassment. Carrying his bags was therefore the least of her immediate worries, and an insignificantly small price to pay, if all else went smoothly. But when does that ever happen.

The door of number forty-nine opened, and they were confronted by Mrs Betty Marsden, a pug ugly, grotesque and incredibly bulbous looking woman, who was clearly no imminent, clear or present threat to the salad tray that had been designed into her aging kitchen fridge. Nor was she a complete stranger to the cake tin, which he would later find secreted in one of the living room cupboards, in what appeared to be a quite juvenile attempt to hide it from all but herself. She had a large, flat, squared off bottom, that looked like a small billboard, and appeared to move in the wind, completely independently of the rest of her body, as she swaggered her way around the house. She wore old-fashioned, dowdy, ill-fitting clothes, that hung off her, like the limp unpegged canvas of a tent, and Snowball couldn't help but think that she looked, and was as a point of fact, a complete fucking mess. There was a violently red, protruding inflammation on one cheek, which looked like it had been freshly squeezed just for his arrival, and a large black beauty spot on the other, which was clearly failing in the only job it had been put there to do. The trusses of blonde hair and traces of a black moustache were in contrast to each other, as was the faint odour that lingered with each sway of her enormous belly, alongside the air freshener that she had obviously sprayed just prior to their arrival.

All in all, as far as first impressions went, Mrs Marsden was a walking disaster that wasn't so much waiting to happen, but had actually happened on Groundhog Day, and was an ongoing nightmare, from which she couldn't extricate herself. She extended a hand in his direction, which was a trick he had vowed never to fall for again, and it was promptly ignored as he attempted to place a less than reluctant and disdainful foot across the threshold. The stony silence that followed his 'rudeness' was only interrupted by the limp bundle of Cos leaves behind him, as she found herself stepping forward, and boldly announcing her name to the indignant caricature that stood before them, while vigorously shaking Mrs Marsden's hand, and hoping that Snowball was actually going to enter the house, without any further issue.

Mrs Marsden looked down at him, as they strolled through the small external porch, and into the main house, where they headed directly to the front living room (yeah, well done, you remembered. The adults only one, spic, span and under used). "You're a little charmer," she said, tapping him on the shoulder, in the hope of eliciting some form of a response, even if it was likely to be a torrent of abuse, that the pug-ugly look on her face deserved. 'You don't know the half of it, fatso,' he thought, and continued to ignore the monstrosity that was casually passing itself off as human being.

It was a large open living room, painted in faint, faded pastel colours, and home to a three-seated floral settee, two identical armchairs, and a large oak coffee-table, sat upon which was a china tea service, comprising cups, saucers, matching kettle, kettle stand and a series of teaspoons. Snowball again picked up a faint whiff of body odour that was lingering in the room, the same odour that he had come across as Mrs Marsden had presented herself at the front door, and the one that subsequently seemed to waft around him, with every step she took. He considered enquiring about its origin, but thought better of it, while she proceeded with a well-rehearsed welcome, and introduction to the family group.

There was a tall, thin antique looking cabinet propped up in one corner, and a smaller white vase housing what looked like dried out swamp reeds in another. The only other thing of note was the electric organ that seemed to have pride of place, and totally dominated the far wall of the room, with its accompanying chair, and smattering of musical scores that looked well thumbed, and were spread around the floor underneath it. Mrs Marsden had also laid out some biscuits on a china plate, which immediately caught both the eye and hand of the hovering Snowball. They all sat down and began to go through the standard format of half-hearted introductions, followed by a discussion on 'how things were, and were going to be' at the home, what was expected, and could be expected, and the usual assertions from Paula and Mrs Marsden alike, that everything would be fine just as long as he gave it a chance. And they were right. If you didn't have a personality of your own, were willing to be led like a lamb, if you dressed as they did, did as you were instructed, pretended to like everything they liked, ate and watched, then everything would be fucking fine, because that was called conforming, but Snowball no longer did conformity, there was no fun in it, and he wasn't about to be told how things were going to be, by a complete fucking stranger.

As Paula well knew and understood, Snowball wasn't interested in being indoctrinated, nor burying his sense of self, in order to meet the aspirations of others, who he rarely saw as being noteworthy enough for him to aspire to. He had developed finely tuned instincts as a matter of survival, and as a result of those instincts, he had taken an instant dislike to Mrs Marsden, and the aura (not the odour) that she was giving off, and besides that, he had heard it all before, and knew nothing was going to change. Mrs Marsden had abuses written all over her. She was sweating them as they sat and listened to her speak. Her excessive use of the word 'I' gave him the clearest indication needed, as to what life at number forty-nine was focussed upon, and he knew it wouldn't be him. He could see abuse and hate oozing from every pore of her sweat dripped face, and it was clear they weren't going to get on regardless of whether he gave it a chance or not. It was only a matter of time before everything went south in his eyes, and it was just another stop on the road to his eventually abandonment.

Eventually, the time came for Paula to leave, and she rose from her seat, with one of those supercilious smiles on her face, that laid bare the fact that she had no idea as to what she was abandoning her charge into, nor any understanding of what he thought about it. She was content that her job had been completed and made the standard promises to return for a visit in the near future and see how he was getting on. She probably really did think that everything would be OK. Snowball didn't know whether to laugh or cry, but the one thing he was certain of, was that it was better if she left than stayed, as she wasn't adding any assurances that were worth the breath she had used to utter them.

Once Paula had departed, Mrs Marsden began to introduce him to the other children at the home, as they slowly began to arrive back in the early evening from various activities. The most prominent of introductions was to Prunes, so nicknamed by her friends because she apparently adored the things, and could regularly be seen eating them, often directly from the tin, which invariably she had stolen from either the house, from the home of a friend, or one of the nearby shops on her way home from school. Snowball couldn't stand the things, but Prunes herself looked like a dream girl, and so he was sure he could find forgiveness somewhere in his heart, for her culinary indiscretions. Mrs Marsden had told him that he would do well to stay clear of her, as she was 'nothing but trouble, and a little trollop', which to Snowball was the biggest indication that he could have been given, that he and Prunes were likely to get on just fine.

Prunes was the same age as Snowball, but in terms of maturity, she was streets ahead of him as dear Emily had been, and she both knew and acted it. She had the body of an adult, and she knew just how to carry and use it to her own advantage. She would inevitably grow up to be the 'Jolene' of the Dolly Parton lyrical waxing, as women from all walks of life begged her to take her stunning good looks elsewhere, and leave their men alone. By all accounts, she had at times been pimped out by her parents, well before her age had reached double figures, and as a result had been made subject of a care order in the courts, and her life had spiralled downwards from there onwards, as she developed a disturbing and unflattering level of promiscuity, which had boys and men alike clamouring for her attentions, and indulging in often paid for illicit interactions.

There was always a sense of tragedy surrounding Prunes, as she seemed to revel in the illicit attention that was heaped upon her, completely oblivious that she was in fact being used and abused, to satiate the sexual whim of others. At times she appeared to be the one to follow, for her worldly-wise demeanour, and her unapologetic and acutely focussed sense of being, only for those occasions to pale away into the darkness of her own insignificance, as the frightened, tearful, used and abused child that dwelt deep within her, reared its fretful head from below the parapet, stumbling and faltering in the adult world, into which she had so willingly gate-crashed.

Snowball never really knew what to believe with Prunes. If only half the tales about her were true, she'd had a frightful and often painful life to date. She was a girl who had clearly lived beyond that which her years would normally have facilitated, and she had and could recite many an interesting story, which from the mouths of others would have appeared as nothing more than childish flights of fantasy, or outright bullshit, but from Prunes, one never really knew whether they were true or not, because the simple, inescapable and painful fact was, however outrageous the tale, there was always the possibility with Prunes that it was indeed factually correct.

Prunes was the product of everything bad that society had to offer a child. She was inequality, deprivation, abuse and lack of privilege all rolled up into a neat and tidy little bundle of exploited flesh. She had nothing at all going for her, bar that which she formulated and orchestrated herself. Abandoned by her parents, her extended family and the system alike, she was a young girl on the path to a dimly lit future in the seediest enclaves of life, if things couldn't be turned around. None of it was her own fault, she was just a victim like the rest of them were, and she would continue being a victim because she knew nothing else. She was the living epitome of the notion that any type of attention was better than no attention at all, and this notion seemed to lead her from one pathetic relationship to another, one abuser to another, and inevitably led her to more harm than it ever led her to good. She did, however, at times have a most enviable personal strength and aura of character. But she was a classic example of how the system had, could and would fail children that were placed into its care. As mentally strong as she often was, and regardless of her unbelievable character, and her street wiles, she was simply never going to beat the system. She just didn't know it. She had absorbed all the negative commentaries that had been placed in front of her, and she had at some point chosen to believe them. Where Snowball was determined to prove people wrong, she simply opted to ensure that her stated destiny became a reality. She had given up the fight and settled for what was in the pantry.

Mrs Marsden and the care system had often told Prunes, like they'd told so many other girls, that she didn't have a future, that she was no good, that her only usefulness in life would be lying down on her back for money, to be used by men, and to have their babies, and she like so many others, believed and internalised every word. She had been burdened with the guilt of others, and been bounced into accepting it in many ways. She was a tragic standard bearer, of a system that gave children nothing, expected nothing from them, and ensured that they aspired to be nothing. Just like Snowball, she was an outsider in a world of outsiders. An underdog, in a world of underdogs, in a world that rarely seemed to value a child, let alone value 'children like them'. They were the most undervalued of all. One black. One promiscuous. Both apparently trouble. Abandoned into an uncompromising and violently abusive world, they were survivors of their own making, doing it their own way, in the only way that they knew how. Alone.

The regime at Hill Road was simple, brutal and stark, for both children and staff alike. Some good people worked there. Decent people, with conscience and morality, but who, like the children who resided there, had been intimidated and silenced by the despotic regime that Mrs Marsden overtly operated. There was a pervasive and tangible climate of fear, which consumed every waking moment of life at number forty-nine. Everybody succumbed to it. It was akin to a virulent disease sweeping through a health impoverished region and infecting all those who came into contact with it, directly or otherwise.

Children were not permitted in the front living room, and by default not permitted to use the organ that Mrs Marsden had so proudly demonstrated in the company of the social worker, upon Snowball's arrival. They were not allowed in the rear living room either, which she kept for the sole independent use of herself and her limp wristed husband. They were not permitted upstairs, unless they were bathing or in bed. They were not allowed to touch or use the TV, nor the books that were displayed, not for their use, but for the purpose of creating an appropriate impression for visiting social workers. They were forbidden from touching the ornaments, nor were they permitted to sit on the furniture. It was an austere existence, enforced with violence. They were forbidden from interacting with almost everything tangible. They were to touch, eat and drink absolutely nothing, unless it had specifically been given to them by Mrs Marsden, or her effeminate husband, who would often sit silently in a corner, like a chastened child, awaiting some morsel of comfort from the ogress who dominated his pathetic life.

Regardless of the external weather conditions, every child was forbidden from remaining in the house during the daytime, unless they were being fed, or prepared for bed. Mrs Marsden insisted upon silence at all times, and life in Hill Road was managed according to her seemingly endless list of rules, needs and desires. She also retained a callous disregard for the staff who worked under her and ruled them with an iron fist of both intimidation and verbal abuse, which ensured they remained silently obedient to her escalating abuses, and indifference, which she duly extended to the children under her charge, by adding the 'benefits' of physical chastisement as and when she saw fit. For all intents and purposes, Hill Road was an oppressive Gulag, where the inmates were so highly regulated that the only thing they retained full control of, was the ability to simply breathe unaided.

Mrs Marsden was a serial abuser. She was by no means as prolific physically as many who Snowball had survived, but habitual and prolific in more subtle ways, and physically abusive nonetheless. For her, children out of sight were children out of mind, and that is exactly as she preferred it. At every opportunity Snowball was forced outside into the cold, with the singular remit of not returning until the next scheduled meal time. Be it an oppressive summer heat, or a freezing cold winter, the remit remained the same. STAY AWAY until you are called for. It was a simple mantra that was enforced with subtle brutalities, which would leave no marks, bar the imprints of hate that festered in the minds of young children, upon whom they had been inflicted.

By no means averse to slapping him viciously across the face, Mrs Marsden deployed many tactics from an extensive repertoire, in determining how she would try to eventually break Snowball, and all those around him. Her favourite tactics were food deprivation, alongside heat deprivation and the removal of shelter. Food deprivation was a useful weapon in her twisted psychology, and she readily deployed it with a frightening regularity. Meals were often as infrequent as one per day and consisted of nothing more than a piece of fruit and a packet of crisps. The regime would be ruthlessly deployed for days at a time, in order to bring the children to heel, and would often prove so debilitating, that Snowball was left with no other options than to sneak downstairs in the dead of night, and steal food from the fridge and cupboards, before returning to the bedrooms and feeding the other hungry children, as well as himself. Nights were occasionally spent huddled together under the same blankets for warmth, only returning to their own beds upon hearing the footsteps of their primary tormentor climbing the creaking old staircase, which proved to be the most useful of early warning systems they could have ever imagined. There were countless nights spent listening to the muffled cries of the suffering children, as they slowly rocked themselves to sleep, and all the time, the hate and anger within Snowball grew more potent, as each abuse, each day without food, and night without sleep, rolled into one endless battle for basic survival.

When it suited her aims, and her burgeoning gratuitous sadism, she would confine their movements to the back yard of the house, where they would suffer in the freezing cold for hours at a time, isolated from all human contact, freezing and physically diminished. They were expected to simply stand there and wait. To wait for nothing in essence, other than the undeniable certainty of more degrading abuse, but waiting was all they had, and wait they did, the slow march of time showing no compassion and providing no solace from the never-ending cycle of institutionalised abuse that she inflicted upon them. From the youngest to the oldest, nobody was immune from her attentions. And so here it is, number 49 Hill Road. Parkland to the right, town centre to the left, and nothing but misery inside.

It was only a short downhill walk to number twenty-two, another Family Group Home, managed by a different set of staff, and which implemented an entirely different regime than the one Snowball was enduring. At twenty-two, the children were well dressed, clean, well fed and had the appearance of being looked after. It was all a far cry from what was taking place less than fifteen doors further up the road, hidden from public scrutiny, and largely ignored by all those who were complicit to its tyranny. Another short walk, and Snowball would reach a small row of local shops. There was a greengrocer's and a butcher's where Mrs Marsden would spend the food allowance allotted for the home, before sub-dividing the better items, and shipping them off to family and friends to enjoy 'on the house'. It was food that should have gone back to the home, to the mouths of the hungry children imprisoned within, but who simply marked time in the cold back yard in which she had so callously confined them.

There was also a small lack-lustre looking newsagent's shop, where the children from twenty-two would spend their pocket money, but the children from number forty-nine rarely ever frequented, as their money was rarely their own for the keeping, rarely handed over, and rarely found its merry way to a sweet shop of any kind. There was also a fish and chip shop. Regularly used by the Marsden family, but again, rarely enjoyed by a child at number forty-nine, bar the exception of smelling the recently purchased steaming hot food, as it was taken, plated and ready to eat, from kitchen to back living room, where, in isolation, the Marsden family would devour it, before returning empty plated to the kitchen, hunger satiated, and completely dispassionate to the hunger around them.

School was a one and a half mile walk from Hill Road. Mainly uphill on the way there, and mercifully, at the culmination of a tiring day in the books, and on the sports fields, a relative canter downhill on the way home. Moorcroft Road Secondary Modern was a sprawling single level building, located on the fringes of town, although there was very little that was modern about the dilapidated structure, nor the internal design and fitments, but it served its purpose, and was school to several hundred pupils and a small band of dedicated teachers, led by Mr Brady, a one eyed, height challenged and aging man, who attempted to educate them in the main, or keep them subdued if and when the glories of education failed.

Snowball enjoyed his time at Moorcroft Road, and was keen to attend most days, if for no other reason than the respite it offered from life, and the brazen mistreatment that he suffered at the hands of Mrs Marsden. He fought his way into the form football team, although he could never understand why he needed to fight for a place, as they were shit at football, and got stuffed in just about every game they played. In all honesty, they never really played a game of football. It was more the case that they were transported to various grounds around the town, got changed into their strip, stood in various formations around the pitch, and then watched the opposition display a vast array of skills that they could only dream about having, before succumbing to the inevitable defeat, and incoming humiliation, as the opposing team basically took the piss at their ineptitude. On a good day, the opposition were kept to a single figure goal tally, and on a bad day, which invariably it was, the score sheet could easily be misinterpreted as a cricket result.

He also found his way into the school cricket team, for no other reason than he was black, the cricket coach was a huge West Indies fan, and had assumed as you 'obviously' would, that in being black, he was most likely a fast bowler and an excellent batsman. Even after a poor first outing, where he had bowled four overs, been hit for approximately ten runs an over, and taken no wickets, before being ducked at the crease, he still remained in the coach's favour, and an automatic shoe-in for the next match the following week. When it reached the point that it became inescapably apparent that he didn't know one end of a bat from the other, he was still selected for the team on the basis that the sight of a West Indian looking player apparently worked wonders at destabilising the opposition's psyche, to the point that they invariably had lost the mind game, before they had taken to the crease, and a ball had been struck.

There were many other sports to participate in at Moorcroft Road. Dodging Mr Humbley was a very popular sport amongst the children who attended. He was a tall, thin teacher. Elderly in comparison to most, with a faint hint of Tony

Benn about him. He wore thick rimmed glasses, with even thicker lenses, and was an avid member of the 'Tweed and Brogues' fashion set. He looked every inch a military officer and ran his classes accordingly. He was a man with very rigid standards when it came to controlling children, and was the sort of teacher who would rather cane you than teach you, as he was a firm believer that you could teach someone far more with a rod in your hand, than a book. Weirdly as it happens, given his propensity to beat children for randomly obscure offences against his code, Snowball actually quite liked him. There was a certain 'persona' about Humbley, who was just as likely to pass on some startling revelation, or humour laden ditty, as he was to challenge your behaviour and ability to sit comfortably in his classes.

It was the intellect and his difference to others that appealed. He was out there on his own, and he didn't care what anybody thought about it. There were times when Snowball was the same, and he identified closely with that characteristic. He knew he was a dying breed, a dinosaur to many, but Humbley was equally aware that he had something unique to offer, something mysterious, something unusual and enigmatic that you couldn't get from any other teacher at the school, and all you had to do was be ardently open to listening.

There was also Miss Bealeton. A porky, red-headed harridan, who taught swimming and physical education, and whose favourite hobby was lining up the entire class alongside the edge of the pool, forcing them to touch their toes, and slippering them with a plimsoll, in such a fashion that they were forced into the pool, where she would keep them swimming and treading water, until such time as the lesson time expired, or she was in literal danger of killing a child, who through sheer physical exhaustion was about to go under.

However, Miss Bealeton wasn't so much of a problem, as the lesson itself was for Snowball. One slap of a plimsoll was considered a 'let off' for a child with his background, but the swimming lessons exposed him to ridicule and abuse, as his scarred limbs and feet were exposed for all to see. It was a weekly ritual that would last for the remainder of the day and caused him great misery. It was also inescapable, as Miss Bealeton would always insist that any child, with any reason whatsoever not to swim, should still be seen to attend the class, get themselves changed into their swimwear, and then sit on the edge of the pool and watch the remainder of the pupils suffer at her hands.

Most would eventually give in, and end up swimming at some point in the lesson, and in fairness to her, the 'notes from mothers' dried up within a few weeks of each new intake starting, and resulted in a high percentage of the school's pupils being submitted for Bronze, Silver and Gold swimming awards, which in turn, no doubt saved some unfortunates later down the line, as they ventured into lakes and lodges around Lancashire. For Snowball, however, it would remain a weekly torment that he would have to endure, and if nothing else, he could always revert to directing a random aggressive outburst at her, and storming off, which was a strategy that had worked in the past, even if it did result in a caning later in the day. You get the picture – lesser of two evils and all that bollocks.

Miss McClintock was another woman at the school with a striking red head, and a great deal of athletic prowess. A sports teacher like Miss Bealeton, but unlike her porky counterpart, she had been endowed with the most charming of feminine assets and was the stuff of adolescent fantasy for most of the boys in the school. She was slim, athletic, keenly sports orientated, wore short sports skirts, which afforded the occasional flash of her regulation sports knickers, and wore her hair in childish pigtails, which for some strange reason only added to her Pippi Longstocking type charm. She had been rumoured to have had or been engaged in affairs with a number of the more prominent male teachers at Moorcroft Road, and regardless of whether it was true or not, that seemed to be enough to embolden every boy there, with the belief that they 'had a chance with McC', if only they were afforded the opportunity and enough time to work their limp-dicked magical charms.

However, she would unfortunately remain one professional step above and ahead of each of them, and it soon became apparent to most of the boys that the only place they would be seeing McC outside of the classroom setting anytime soon, was in their own imagination, where they would no doubt be undertaking all manner of sexually athletic games with her, only to awaken in a soggy yellow-stained bedsheet, with the dawning realisation that it had been nothing more than damp slumber. Most of them probably wrote to Jim'll Fix It with their 'McC Aspirations', not knowing that it was just the sort of thing he might happily have arranged for them, if only their letters had gotten past the initial sorting process. But alas McC was out of bounds, and like the rest of them, Snowball would just have to wonder what might have been, or take up Badminton, where he could sit on the side-lines, and await the regular flash of her green gym knickers, as she overstretched for the cock of the shuttle variety.

Science and music were taught by the Divers. A most likely rare husband and wife combination in schools around the country. They were remarkable, only for being unremarkable. They were built like beanpoles, and towered above everyone they came across, and as far as anyone could discern, apart from the tyranny they brought with them, they would have arrived into this world, done their thing, and subsequently departed, without even being noticed by him or anyone else for that matter. She was painfully thin, gaunt, anorexic looking to the extent that it gave her a manly jaw-line, and patently was as much in dire need of feeding, as Snowball was most days.

She was a prickly character, educationally self-confident to the point of being aloof, and possessed angular bones that protruded from all over her taut anaemic skin. Unlike her rather mild-mannered husband, who looked equally as malnourished as he was prickly, she (alongside Humbley) also was a woman with a real-time penchant for teaching pupils with a plimsoll, rather than a book, and was often to be seen marching an unfortunate transgressor from her classroom to the Deputy Head's office, where she would administer her punishments, before dragging the tearful recipient back down the corridor for the ritual humiliation in front of the class.

Back at Hill Road, things were no better on the food front from day to day. The presence of the wafer-thin Divers at school was a constant and tormenting reminder to Snowball of the hungers he was experiencing back 'home'. As if life wasn't hard enough, he had to look at two people every day, who had the means and resources to feed themselves, and yet appeared to be indulging in a self-imposed hunger strike, which he just couldn't understand. If only they knew, he would wonder constantly, if only they knew.

His hunger wasn't funny, it wasn't a laughing matter, but it did provide for the occasional funny moment, which resulted in an abundance of laughter when the stories spread. On one such occasion, Mrs Marsden had delivered the usual poor standard of food for the evening meal and left most of the children hungry and frustrated. It was turning into one of those 'last straw' moments, as the younger children began to look towards Snowball and Prunes to help them out. Prunes was an occasional help, but the problem was that her help only came when she herself was also in need, so she was unreliable in the general context of life at Hill Road. Snowball informed the kids that he would take care of things later, when the Marsdens were watching their TV, alone in the rear living room, and they were all in bed. It wasn't ideal in terms of the immediacy of their hunger, but they appeared to appreciate that it was the best he could do for them, and the evening rolled on without incident.

By eight o'clock, they were all in bed, and Mr and Mrs Marsden had settled down to an undisturbed night in front of the television. Mrs Marsden had spent the afternoon baking, and Snowball knew that there were tins in the kitchen, bulging with fresh cakes and confectionery. There was a veritable feast down in the cupboards, and he was intent on alleviating them of it. He had given them a good thirty minutes to settle down both upstairs and down, before making his way with military stealth, down the creaking stairs, and into the kitchen at the back of the house. As he passed the living room door, he paused and giggled as he could hear one of the Marsdens snoring like a pig, before continuing on towards the bounty that awaited.

The large door that separated the hallway from the back of the house and kitchen was his next big hurdle. It creaked and strained with every movement, and while it could eventually be opened in silence, it took an abundance of very carefully executed small movements, which inevitably took time. Now, time was something that he had plenty of, but that wasn't an issue. What was an issue, however, was that it was the one point where he was exposed and vulnerable if either of the Marsdens stirred from their porcine-like slumber. If they opened their living room door, the first two things they would see would be the kitchen door he was stood at, and the mid-point of the staircase, thus preventing him from escaping upstairs, unseen. Bolting into the front room was impossible, because the noise incurred in doing so would immediately divulge his nefarious presence, and so his only points of escape and places to hide were on the other side of the kitchen door.

Regardless of this he carried on, slowly pushing the kitchen door open. Pausing only to silence the constant creaks as the door whined, and listening to the continued snoring that filled the ground floor of the house. Ten minutes of sweat, stress and anxiety later, and he was in. The feast awaited – all he had to do was grab it. He knew exactly where to go, as the Marsdens were methodical in ensuring that they separated 'their' food, from that which was begrudgingly allocated for the children. If there was anything good to be had in that kitchen, he was all too aware that it would be in their half of the cupboards, and they didn't let him down. The cake tins were brimming, and so it was back upstairs, cake tin in one hand, bottle of cold milk in the other. Past the porcine pairing, he crept. A cheeky smile flashing across his face at the thought of her anger, when she eventually came to realise what had taken place that night, and that all her efforts the day before had gone to waste. He slowly mounted the creaking stairs, and called into the girls' room, where he distributed some of the spoils, and decanted some of the milk into a cup for them to share between them. They seemed happy with his efforts, with Prunes grinning broadly as he departed the room, and she quietly closed the door behind him.

Next stop was the boys' room, where he was confronted with an equally happy and enthusiastic band of hungry infant starlings awaiting the return of their food laden parent. It was the smiles on the faces that made it all worthwhile, though Snowball was acutely aware that the smiles only lasted as long as the hunger in their stomachs was abated. He knew it was a case of 'one day at a time'. At least tonight they would sleep content and happy, he thought. He would have to wait and see what tomorrow brought. He sat and watched his hungry birds fill their stomachs, before coaxing them back into bed, and off to sleep. That night there were only two more things that remained for him to do. Firstly, he sat quietly and enjoyed some of the fruits of his labours, then he quietly crept back downstairs, and returned the cake tin to the cupboard, but not before sealing in a signed note, that cheekily read, 'Fill this up, I will be back tomorrow'. He knew Mrs Marsden would know it was him, but that was the whole point. Their attentions would be focussed upon him, and that kept the others free from the hostilities that would follow.

The aftermath of the cake stealing incident lasted several weeks. Food rations became noticeably smaller than they already were, as she sought to continuously punish him for stealing her cakes. She was more openly hostile, and constantly castigated him for 'stealing', and being a bad person, though it never occurred to her to address the issue of why the children in her care were forced into stealing food from the cupboards in the first place. She continually reminded him that he had no future, other than a life behind bars, because he was simply a very bad person, from bad stock, and nothing could change that. After all, as she so openly told him on numerous occasions, what more could she expect from a black person?

It was almost as if she was presenting herself as a rejected role model, and the irony of her protestations and vitriol wasn't lost on Snowball in the slightest. It made little difference overall to Snowball. He was generally in a state of hunger as it was, and he had long ago undertaken to have no dependence upon what she provided, choosing instead to lift what he needed, when he needed it, and to supplement his diet by eating at the homes of friends, if and when he was invited to do so. He knew he would continue to suffer hunger at her hands. That was a given. Food was one of her chosen weapons, and she deployed her arsenal frequently. But ultimately, his own plight concerned him far less than that of the others, as, unlike him, they had no independent means of addressing their predicament, and so their issue became his issue, and they had become totally dependent upon him to fulfil their needs. It was a constant source of pressure, but what was he to do, other than step up to the mark, and take care of what he could?

Mrs Marsden tightened up on her 'food security' measures, and Snowball noted that she now assumed the seat by the living room door, which she always kept open, and which afforded her an unobstructed view of the stairs, in order to catch him on his next forays. Little did she realise that she was simply making life easier for Snowball in the general scheme of things, as the noise from the television would disguise the sound of him creeping across the landing, into the girls' room, where he would alight through the window, onto the kitchen extension, and make his way to the chip shop, where he would occasionally purchase food, finances permitting, which he then took back to the others. He knew that one day she would twig onto the chippy runs, but while it lasted, he would make the most of it, before formulating another strategy, if and when it became needed. It also became noticeable that Mr Marsden had assumed a more prominent role in his torment. It appeared that Mrs Marsden had conceded to the fact that she was making no inroads with her abuses, and that Snowball needed something firmer to stop him in his tracks. She had therefore invoked the assistance of her husband, who had been deployed to handle the physical intimidation, as she persevered with the mental stresses, and the implementation of the regime in general.

Snowball soon found himself being physically beaten on a regular basis by Mr Marsden. As the weeks passed, it almost became a daily occurrence, as Mrs Marsden would eventually give in to her exasperation and lose her temper, before storming into the back-living room, ranting wildly about 'sambo', only for Mr Marsden to spontaneously appear, and assault him. It got to be so frequent that Snowball once followed her into the back-living room, before explaining to Mr Marsden that his presence saved him getting up. Mr Marsden subsequently flew into an uncontrolled rage, and dragged him upstairs, where he was repeatedly beaten with a belt.

It was the culmination of all these beatings, the torments, and the abuses, that would finally lead to the downfall of the Marsdens, and the regime that they had so ruthlessly implemented and exposed him to. As the unfairness of it all struck home with Snowball, he began to seriously consider what he was able to do, to bring it all to the end that it so desperately needed to come to. He knew he couldn't continue to withstand the beatings, the intimidation, the hunger, the abuses, and he could no longer reconcile doing nothing, alongside the concerns he had for the other children, who were far more vulnerable than he was. As he once again walked the long winding road to Damascus, hate and conscience as his only companions, he began to think the entire thing through, and put together the semblance of a plan, that would ultimately free them all from the tyranny of the Marsdens, and life at Hill Road.

In the end, it boiled down to a staggering piece of simplicity. Mrs Marsden had one serious weapon of deployment, which she essentially relied on to cure all ills. That was food deprivation. She used it daily, with malice, and with no regard for the impacts it was having, as long as she could be seen to be getting her own way. She had legitimised the use of starvation as a disciplinary measure, and it was that which Snowball determined to use against her and bring her down once and for all.

WHEN FOOD IS THE WEAPON

Snowball was sat on his familiar perch in his bedroom window. Night was turning into morning, as the darkness was transformed into various shades of grey, after which, the brightness of the morning would begin to shine through. It was obvious the Marsdens had entertained visitors the night before, as he could feel the last remnants of heat rising from the radiator under the window sill, as it slowly warmed the underneath of his thighs. He would also soon bear witness to the remains of the food they had enjoyed, having been cast into the bin in which he frequently rummaged. There had been a general warmth around the house, as he had returned from his mandatory exclusion earlier in the evening, although the warmth hadn't been extended his way, and he had been sent directly upstairs to change, and make himself ready for bed. Returning from one of his nocturnal sorties had also been a close call, and one he didn't want to repeat, as he mulled over the potential consequences, not just for himself, but the remainder of the children, who had a vicarious dependency upon his ability to move freely in, out and around the house, in the dead of night.

The night had come to its usual end. He had been seen taking fruit from the bowl while passing through the dining room, he had argued with Mrs Marsden, after which he had thrown the fruit at her, before storming indignantly from the room. Mr Marsden had subsequently struck him several times across the back and head, before they had all simmered down, as they dispersed to various corners of the house, expletives uttered, and both contempt and disgust at his seemingly uncontrollable behaviour, which was clearly being exacerbated by the colour of his skin according to Mrs Marsden, articulated forcefully. It was a constant source of amusement to him that they expected to be treated any better, given how they treated him and the other children, but it was what it was, and he just came to accept it.

The boys in his room were hungry, and had pleadingly asked him if there would be any food that night. The girls were probably in a similar state of being, as life at Hill Road mercilessly rumbled on. As usual he had assured them he would take care of them, and that he just needed them to settle down quickly, as the sooner they appeared rested, the sooner the Marsdens would feel they could retire to the solitude of their beds, and then he would take care of things. It was an overwhelming feeling of responsibility that he cared little for. Responsibility that wasn't his, but that he unwillingly assumed, as a mixture of ill-placed guilt in relation to their plight, and the presumption that as one of the eldest amongst them he had a duty to help, regardless of the personal sacrifice it entailed. He knew it would have to come to an end one day, and that they would all be on their own, but he had made a silent vow to himself, that he would continue for as long as he could, for as long as it lasted, and in reality, part of him got a perverse sense of pleasure from knowing that most days, he was getting one over on the Marsdens, and they hadn't seemed to see it coming.

The Marsdens had duly settled that night, and an hour afterwards Snowball risked all, and sneaked downstairs to the kitchen. He had rifled through a few of the cupboards, and had taken a quick look in the fridge, but to his dismay there seemed to be nothing appropriate that he could take back to the hungry kids upstairs. It was a rare set of circumstances, but everything he touched, everything he came across, needed to be cooked, or warmed in some way, and that was something that he simply couldn't risk doing. Even the biscuit tin was bare, bar a few broken fragments of some long-time stale confection that had neither the volume nor appeal to satisfy the needs they had. The forage came to an end, and he returned upstairs to disappointed faces that had waited in eager anticipation of his return. The sense of disappointment was clear, and the burden of responsibility growing increasingly more cumbersome and fraught.

"Give me five minutes, and I will go to the chippy before they close," he told them. It was something he had done often, but even that was proving to be more and more infrequent, as because of the smell, he could only do a chippy run, if the Marsdens had also been there that evening themselves, and as the colder nights closed in, he had noticed that they had become much more reluctant to make the cold walk down the road. Little faces began to light up, as he fumbled through the coins at the bottom of his drawer, which he had hidden for just such events. Mrs Marsden's petty cash tin had its uses. He needed constant buy-in from the girls, in order to cross through their room, and alight through the window, but that was rarely a problem, as they were often as hungry as the rest of them, and the simple fact was, if Snowball didn't feed them when they were hungry, they weren't being fed at all.

And so, with the familiar sound of the porcine pillocks sleeping in their chairs ringing out across the downstairs, he took the few short steps to the bedroom opposite, climbed through the window, traversed the kitchen roof, and dropped silently down into the back street. As his feet touched he floor, he broke into an immediate sprint. It wasn't that he was so desperately in need for nourishment, but the draught ploughing through the slightly open window would rattle the bedroom door in its ill-fitting frame. That in turn ran the risk of awakening the Marsdens, and so he had been forced to concede to the necessity for the window to be closed while he was away, leaving him dependent on somebody remaining awake until he returned. It wasn't normally a problem, but on occasion, he had spent a few uncomfortable minutes trying to waken the occupants on the inside, while attempting to remain quiet enough not to awaken the Marsdens, who on occasion had retired to the adjacent bedroom, which had a window that looked directly onto the extension roof, on which he was precariously perched. It all added to the sense of adventure on most occasions, and was even funny at times, but his patience was being tested, and thus he thought better of incurring any delay, and aimed to return as quickly as possible.

He arrived at the chip shop minutes later and entered to find a sizeable queue had already formed. It appeared that certain items were being 'cooked to order' and both to his dismay, and according to the drunk mid-way up the queue, who was in the process of explaining to his wife at the door, they were all 'waiting on fucking chips'. It was unusual as well as inconvenient, but he figured he was there now, and a few minutes waiting couldn't really do any harm. He had been stood there for only a few moments, before, upon hearing a familiar voice, looking up to see Aunty Liz from number twenty-two, the sister home to his own, standing at the front of the queue, and placing her order. His entire world was immediately transformed into a 35mm, slow motion cinematography exercise, as his heart became the only thing he could hear, and everything bar himself and the chip guzzling Aunty Liz became a peripheral blur.

He moved slowly towards the door of the chip shop, glancing upwards and across at the counter, to see her head, slowly turning towards him, and at a pace not too dissimilar to his own. He figured he was on the periphery of her vision, and as long as he kept moving, they would likely pass like ships in the night, having failed to catch proper sight or sound of each other. He had reached and exited the door, before she had fully turned around, and was half way across the road, before raising the courage to glance back at the chip shop to see if he had been caught. He could see her squinting in the window, her view obscured by the steam clouds emitted from the fryers. There was no way of knowing whether he had been seen or not, but it wasn't the time for static wonderings, and he set himself in flight, and headed back home. It had been a long day and was proving to be a long night.

The children were going to go hungry, but that was the least of his immediate worries, as he turned into the back street at the rear of his home and began to scale the extension at the back of the house. He reached the bedroom window and tapped lightly on the glass. It had taken a few minutes to elicit a response from the girls, but on the fourth or fifth time of knocking, Elaine gingerly opened it, and as he climbed in through the open pane, she began frantically pointing down, at the light that was shining under the door frame. "She's on the phone," Elaine informed him in a muffled voice, that was mixed with both fear and amusement. "I didn't want her to hear me get up," she said apologetically, as if that was going to make him feel better about being stuck on the roof. Snowball immediately headed for the bedroom door, while quietly explaining what had happened in the chip shop, and despairingly apologising for the fact there was no food that night. The other girls were asleep, so it didn't really matter that much, as Elaine clearly understood, and was happy just to be closing the door and window behind him and getting back into the relative safety of her bed.

Snowball crossed the landing, pausing only momentarily to hear Mrs Marsden declare with a flourish on the telephone, "No, you must be mistaken, Liz, they've been in bed for a while, it couldn't possibly be him". Though the excursion had ended in an abject failure, it was at least time for a smile, albeit one of defeat. He heard Mrs Marsden replace the phone, and then her feet hitting the bottom riser of the stairs, as she began to make her way back to bed. Fully clothed, he jumped under his blankets, pulled them up to his neck, and turned to face the window, as the bedroom door opened, and Mrs Marsden popped her head through the gap, before glancing around the room. It appeared that nothing was out of order. Everyone was asleep, and it looked like Aunty Liz had clearly got it all wrong.

As the light of day slowly began to rise over the top of the house opposite, Snowball knew that things couldn't continue as they were. It was too much. Too much hostility, too much abuse, too much responsibility for his young shoulders to bear, and too much hunger too much of the time. He glanced knowingly at his roommates. Knowing that the day they were about to endure would bring them nothing better than the day they had just fretfully slept off. There would be cold baths for the bedwetters, and little if any food for them all. Life and then abuse that came with it, would just roll on unhindered. He knew that he couldn't continue to watch the kids go hungry, and he couldn't go hungry much longer himself, and yet he felt so helpless to act. He needed to act, and he vowed to do so, but he was fearful of where it would all lead.

SUFFER LiTTLE CHILDREN

From that morning onwards, Snowball began to collate a secret food diary. He noted every meal of every day, every morsel of food that was provided, every drink and when it was provided, who ate and who didn't. He covered the entire diet and regime from start to finish every single day. Ironically, he had got the idea from the Marsdens themselves, having seen the food diary that the Marsdens kept, and which they furnished to inquisitive social workers, if they ever had the temerity to be seen to care about the children they were ultimately responsible for. It was a requirement of social services departments across the country, that every home in their authority area logged what the children ate on a daily basis, with the log also acting as a form of surface level audit, when it was married up to the receipts that they submitted for the food that they bought.

He had been completely outraged when he had read their diary, having taken it to the toilet for a sneaky read after it had been left out in the kitchen one evening. It bore no resemblance to the reality of their daily diet and was nothing short of an outright deception on a grand scale. It was possibly the most flamboyantly deceitful piece of creative writing he had ever read, and Mrs Marsden had excelled in her description of the food she had provided, to the point where there were meals being represented that he had never even heard of, couldn't possibly describe, let alone having ever eaten. He had wanted to hunt her out, and smash her across the head and face with the diary, but he was also learning the value of 'biding one's time', choosing one's battles, and utilising attrition as she did so well. He was rapidly beginning to appreciate that wars were won through the consistent attainment of small victories, across time, rather than the all-out onslaughts that he much preferred, but which had served him so poorly and painfully in the past. No, this was going to be a long haul, he knew that much. But it was also a golden opportunity, because, if nothing else, the Marsdens were a particularly diligent pair in the maintenance of their deception, as well as the concealment of their abuses, and that is what he would use against them. Day after day, he would sit and memorise each meal, before spending some quiet time in the toilet writing it all down, prior to stashing his diary away until it was next needed. It wasn't a particularly onerous task. After all, meals were infrequent, simple, repetitious and small.

Monday – Breakfast: half a slice of toast, glass of water (The Marsden Diary: bacon, eggs, sausage, toast, hot/cold milk or cordial). Lunch: Bag of crisps (The Marsden Diary: ham sandwiches, fruit, chocolate bar, pop). Dinner: bread and butter, an apple, milk or water (The Marsden Diary: beef, potatoes, vegetables, apple pie, ice cream, hot/cold milk or cordial).

Tuesday – Breakfast: Glass of water (The Marsden Diary: cereal, bacon, eggs, sausage, toast, hot/cold milk or cordial). Lunch: Nothing (The Marsden Diary: corned beef sandwiches, fruit, chocolate bar, pop). Dinner: an apple, milk (The Marsden Diary: chicken, potatoes, vegetables, fruit crumble, ice cream, hot/cold milk or cordial).

And that is how it went day after day, week after week, and into the following months. He continued to watch as the children suffered and starved. He continued his regular sorties to the local shops and chippy under the cover of darkness, and he continued his almost nightly raids on the fridge and the biscuit tins, as he waited and collated his evidence. He knew he couldn't strike early, no matter how much suffering he witnessed. Everything was contingent upon a credible amount of evidence, which covered a credible amount of time, and it had to be irrefutable. He needed to ensure that there was no way out for Mrs Marsden when he finally struck. There had to be serious discrepancies between her story and his, to such an extent that he had to be believed, if for no other reason than the sheer volume of evidence that he had provided. And so, the children would have to suffer as they did. It was all in the timing, and he had to get that right.

The day of reckoning was long and slow in coming. When to act was a difficult decision, and the balance between the turmoil of seeing the suffering involved, and the need to be as comprehensive and detailed as he could, was a difficult and emotional one to strike. But the time had arrived. The evidence was there. He had seen the Marsden Diary, and he knew at that moment that all he needed was a large fan to throw the shit at.

That morning he decided that school didn't matter, and took the bus into the town centre, before jumping on a second bus out to the offices where his social worker was based. He strolled into the reception area, announced his presence and demanded to see his social worker. She was rightfully surprised to see him, not only because he was expected to be at school, but the distance and journey to her workplace was considerable for his age and awareness. Or so she thought. Naivety can be a wonderfully cute thing in an adult, and Paula never failed to impress. She was completely unaware of the knock-on consequences that were about to unfold, when she asked him if there was a problem, and he replied that there was indeed. But ask she did, and the answer began to slowly unfurl and ruin her day. Oi, you fucker. Here we go.

"You know when you always ask me if I'm fucking OK, Paula?" he asked, looking her intensely in the eyes, and witnessing the dawning of an awakening beginning to kindle as her facial pallor rapidly changed. "OK," she replied, hesitant both of his next potential outburst, and the possibility that he was about to come flying across the desk in a befitting outburst of pique. "Well I'm not fucking OK, and neither are any of the other children in that fucking shithole you placed me in," he continued, as a hushed silence descended upon the open plan office, and bottoms started to uncomfortably shift in the seats around him. "And don't say ok again, Paula," he mumbled, as her lips began to part, then snapped closed in an act of contrite submission to his will.

He knew her so well, but this was not the time for tolerance, as he had a point make, and was intent on making it. He began to outline the series of abuses that were being inflicted upon him and the other children in the Marsdens' care, making the provision and precision of his detail so eminently clear that it was almost impossible to refute, no matter which angle they chose in their attempts to demolish it. He culminated with the provision of the food diary, and by laying down a simple challenge to Paula, before leaving the office, in the same defiant mood he had arrived. "Go there, and ask for the food diary, then compare it with this – it really is that simple," he told her, as once again she shuffled nervously in her seat. "Go and have a fucking look." And with that he was gone, school would be expecting him, and he had a football game to catch, as well as a slippering for truancy.

The fallout was immediate and intense. He arrived at school in time for the game, but mid-afternoon he was called to the Headmaster's Office, where a small group had congregated. His form teacher was there, as was Paula, a plain clothed police officer, and another lady he had never seen before, but who introduced herself as being from the social services department, and by all accounts it was her responsibility to investigate the complaints he had made. Initially he presumed it was all about his late attendance that morning, but on seeing the assembled great and good, he soon realised that it was all about Mrs Marsden. The Headmaster opened up the conversation, almost in a tone of appeasement, as he outlined why everyone was present, and asked Snowball to take a seat. Snowball wasn't impressed. He had spoken to him on previous occasions, and he had referred to the abuses in the past, but he had been ignored or disbelieved, and the Head had chosen to do nothing. Just another black kid with a chip on his shoulder, wanting to cause trouble had been the assumption, but it was all different now, when the possibility that it might just spill out into the public arena was a very real threat.

Next up was Paula, who chose to explain the presence of the police. "They need to check the details of your allegations," she said. "Why?" replied Snowball, staring intensely at the short-sleeved officer in the seat to his immediate left. He was wondering why he had short-sleeves on in the dead of winter, but he couldn't hold the thought, as almost without conscious effort his response to Paula came splurging out in a rapid-fire torrent. "It's the same story, of the same abuses I told them about, when they picked me up for absconding," he continued. "And it's very similar to the stories I've told other social workers and the police in the past, as you very well know." Paula bowed her head in an acceptance and resignation to the facts and took a deep inward breath before continuing. "The allegations are serious, very serious in fact. You need to understand that. We need to be absolutely certain that you have this right." "Oh, Fuck Off, Paula," he mumbled, much to both her bemusement and embarrassment.

In Snowball's mind, this was the beginning of the cover-up that he expected, and he verbally launched into Paula, and stopped her dead in her tracks. "So, your assumption is I'm telling lies, rather than the truth?" he queried. "No, we just have to be sure. Don't make it any more difficult than it needs to be, please," she replied. Snowball was left wondering how much more difficult it could be. It was him living with the abuse, the brutality and the hunger, not them. They were all going home to families, and warmth, to food on the table, and to restful nights of sleep, and it wasn't as if they could stop the food he wasn't receiving anyway, but he immediately realised what their game was, and he shifted back into his seat, to await the inevitable attempt to deconstruct his allegations.

"You do realise that you may have to go to court and repeat these allegations under oath" asked the policeman. "Do you know what perjury is?" he continued. Snowball smiled. It had started in his first sentence, and he had played his hand too early. "It won't go to court though, will it, so you can just fuck off," Snowball countered. "I know that, and you know that," he continued. Brady was indignant at his lack of respect, not least because, in his opinion, it reflected badly on the school. But both he and Snowball knew exactly what the aims of that afternoon were, and he needed to keep it on track regardless of Snowball's belligerence. Between the school, police and social services, they were going to try and dissuade him from taking things any further, and Paula, sat there like the limp wristed withering coward he always knew she was, seemed intent on helping them. Arriving so soon at the school and opening up the conversation with a talk about perjury, indicated if nothing else that it was something they were being forced to deal with, and the need for him to retract his allegations, indicated that they needed something that he was never going to give them. His cooperation in burying it all.

"You do realise that I'm not going to change my story, don't you?" he asked, glancing around the room, and making eye contact with everybody present. "I'm not expecting that you will do anything, but I'm not changing my story," he continued. That statement alone brought a deep inward sigh from Paula, as the ramifications of what he was saying, and the action he was proposing, signalled a continuing nightmare from which she wasn't going to extricate herself, anytime soon. It amused Snowball for numerous reasons, not least of which was that she was so visually expressive. There was never any need to try and read Paula. Her thoughts and feelings were always agonisingly etched across her face for all to bear witness to. She was the worst poker player in town, and Snowball knew it. He had long ago learned that he needed to conceal his mood, simply to avoid being taken advantage of, and here was Paula, making school girl errors in demeanour, that frankly he found to be as much an embarrassment, as it was an amusement.

There was more than ninety minutes of toing-and-froing, as they examined his allegations in detail. Each, and every line scrutinised, each and every allegation queried, and each refusal to retract met with a stony silence, or direct intimidation. By now the Headmaster was twitching at the prospect of this continuing past school hours, as it became apparent that the issue was not going to be resolved that afternoon, or indeed any time soon. "You do realise that you will have to come to the police station, and be formally interviewed by detectives, don't you?" came the interjection from the wannabee 'Jack Regan' who by this time, was on his feet, and proposing that the meeting be adjourned until a later date. Snowball treated the comment with the contempt it clearly deserved, choosing merely to glance across at Paula, and throw her a sarcastic smile. "Can you make the arrangements?" Paula asked, as the officer made his way to the door. "We'll be in touch," he replied, before banging the office door closed, in a clear display of his discontent. Snowball rose to his feet and moved towards Paula. "Are you taking me back?" he queried, as she rose to her feet, and thanked the remainder of the assembly for coming. "Yes, I am." And with that, they headed out of the office and into the car park, where the conversation continued.

Snowball asked Paula to drive the long way back to the home. He was still furious with the events of that afternoon, and needed time to compose himself for the awkward reunion that was about to take place with Mrs Marsden. He queried Paula about how long he would be staying there, now that this was all out in the open, and he wondered openly about where his next move would be. She replied by asking if a move was the reason that he was 'doing all this', which was another comment that he chose to ignore and treat with a familiar contempt that had been the hallmark of the afternoon so far, and his relationship with Paula overall. 'Doing all this,' he thought. Telling the truth, and exposing the abuse, was classed as 'doing all this', as if somehow he had caused an affront to humankind, or was responsible on a personal level for all the starving kids in fucking Africa. He could have choked the life out of her there and then, but for the fact the car was moving on a busy street, and he didn't see her as that much of a worthy challenge anyway. "The reason I am doing it, is because I'm tired of it, Paula," he eventually countered in a calmed tone that belied the rage inside him. "Tired of seeing the abuse, tired of being abused, and tired of people like you doing fuck all about it, other than asking me if I'm O-fucking-K, when you know what I am going through," he continued, before turning sideways in his seat to face the passenger window and remaining silent for the remainder of the journey.

His mind wandered back to Miss Bradwell in Preston, and all the lessons she had endeavoured to teach him. He knew that he would need to call upon every piece of wisdom that she had imparted, and he was somewhat appreciative of the time she had spent with her sometimes unwilling pupil, as she sought to equip him with the skills and wisdom she knew he was clearly going to need many times in his future. How he longed to be back under her tutelage, safe in part from the harsher excesses of a system that seemed designed to subdue and defeat him. But as the car made its way through the darkening street, he knew that, for now, he would have to stand alone, and deal with life as it came at him. Alone again. Nothing new. Same shit, different abusers.

His arrival back was surprisingly warm, but in the presence of his social worker, and with another one en-route, it could hardly be anything else. Mrs Marsden smiled on cue, made all the right noises when they needed to be made, patronised and teased where she thought it would add value to her position, and generally acted as if everything was simply ok. Maybe it was all just a big misunderstanding, and something that could be sorted out to the satisfaction of all present, over tea and biscuits in the front room. She had even organised for the other children to be eating a hearty tea, tactically served up in the presence of the social workers, and with great effort made to ensure that everyone was eating up, and all plates were 'cleaned'. The charm offensive was in full swing, and was even supplemented by Mr Marsden, assembling all the children in the front room for an impromptu musical session on the organ, where they duly performed like fairground monkeys. The whole charade was so transparent that anyone witnessing it should have immediately assumed that something wasn't quite right. The Von Trapp children clearly weren't happy, nor aware that their role was to look so. But Paula being Paula, it was all soaked up like water into a dry sponge, and duly noted for future reference. It was well over an hour before Paula left. The longest period of time she had ever stayed, and it signalled the start of the verbal and physical onslaught that the Marsdens were waiting to deliver.

It started with a vicious blow across the back of his head from Mrs Marsden, followed by a promise that, 'one way or another, he would retract those allegations' and apologise for all the trouble 'he had caused'. The irony that she was verbally and physically abusing him, in an attempt to get him to withdraw allegations that she was verbally and physically abusing him, seemed completely lost on her, during her sudden bout of pique, but she continued nonetheless. Mr Marsden soon joined the fray, laying all manner of accusations at Snowball's feet, none of which were true, but he apparently felt compelled to 'tell the police all about it', if he refused to withdraw his allegations. Snowball simply sat through the onslaught, until it became apparent to the Marsdens that they were making no inroads into his resolve, and he was ordered to bed. It had been a long day. Another day without much food as it happened, but the ball was in play, the back-field were in motion, and the quarterback was in full control. All-in-all, quite a success he thought, as he dimmed the light, and pulled his blankets up and over his head. It wasn't that he was unaffected. He still shed tears under the blanket. He was still fearful of how events would eventually unfold, and where this would all lead, but he had started something he was proud of, and he resolved to see it through to its completion, whatever that was to be. And so, with a lightly tear-stained face, and hunger in his stomach, he wearily closed his eyes, and slipped quietly into a deep sleep that brought his contentious day to an end.

FOR EVIL TO PROSPER, ALL THAT IS REQUIRED, IS.........

Snowball arrived at Ampstey Ridge Police Station mid-morning, on a typically dull, grimy, northern winter's day, and little did anybody know that he wouldn't be leaving until late in the afternoon, as events would unfold that were apparently to nobody's planning. It had been a short sullen drive from the torments of Hill Road, with Snowball sitting quietly in the car, as Paula drove the few miles across town, and into Ampstey Ridge. He had arisen that morning to a stone cold Mrs Marsden, whose pugfaced visage was a picture perfect vision of barely contained satanic hate. She had ensured that he remained isolated from all the other children at breakfast, through fear of his 'sedition' spreading like a virus, and had half welcomed the arrival of his social worker, even though she was fretful of what allegations would be laid bare in her absence at the police station.

It was potentially her day of reckoning. A day she neither expected nor dreamed would ever arrive, as she reigned supreme and unchallenged in her own, private, ungodly domain. The dossier that Snowball had compiled right under her very nose was now public knowledge, in the hands of social services, and he was about to be formally interviewed by the police, in relation to its contents. On the one hand she desperately wanted to strike out, as she had on so many previous occasions, but on the other hand, she was more than well aware that any further abuses were only likely to make the immediate matters worse. And so, through gritted teeth, she had been forced into a barely contained silence, forced to feed him properly, and ultimately ensure that at least he was happy and harboured no further indignation, as the doorbell rang and he was escorted to the awaiting car outside.

It would turn into an almost day-long stay at the police station. It wasn't really planned that way, as the police were probably of the mindset that, with the right amount of coaxing, shouting, intimidation, and physical abuse, they could probably wrap things up relatively quickly, and have him on his way, case closed, within the hour. However, as the day would eventually unfold, it perhaps became more and more apparent that they hadn't fully accounted for the resilience that a life of abuse instils in a child, and they clearly weren't happy that they were still being forced to press ahead with questioning, as the clock turned from morning into the afternoon, and onwards.

Snowball had been left at the station by Paula, and in the intervening period, alone, isolated, and in clear contravention of the law as it applied to juveniles, had been bellowed at, physically and verbally abused, racially abused, intimidated, stripped naked, threatened with a body search, redressed and stripped again, struck across the head several times, and threatened with a spell in a detention centre (for taking an apple from Mrs Marsden's fruit bowl without permission) if he continued to press ahead with his allegations against 'those good people' who had, according to the two detectives who had taken it upon themselves to coerce a retraction, 'done all that they could' to ensure he had been the beneficiary of a 'safe, secure and caring' upbringing, within an environment some kids would apparently have happily died for.

The onslaught was cowardly, vicious and unyielding, and had lasted several hours, with Snowball stood naked in a corner while the detectives took turns at haranguing him verbally and systematically in an attempt to deconstruct his story from top to bottom. His mind was in a state of turmoil as, stood naked in the corner, he physically shook under the continued duress. Truthfulness, as he had been told so many times before, was what society expected, and yet truthfulness was not serving him well. The truth had abdicated itself to his further abuse and humiliation at the hands of those who were charged with protecting his interests. It seemed like the entire system was against him, and in the naked immediacy of his reality, it was. For all intents and purposes, he was being condemned to a life of incessant abuse and misery, and he would begin to ponder whether he would simply be better off dead, than to find himself forced to live through this nightmare that had no discernible end, unless he took the bull by the horns, and ended it himself. Maybe that was what they wanted, he thought, mind flipping between conscious thoughts of obliging them, and bouts of formidable resistance, as the 'fuck you' mentality kicked in, only to be verbally and physically beaten to the ground, and back into despair. They were playing 'Good Cop, Bad Cop' with him, and his mind was doing the same.

He had been repeatedly asked to sign a piece of paper, declaring that the dossier he had written was in fact untrue, a load of selfish dishonest bollocks that he had made up, in order that he might ultimately discredit the Marsdens, because he was unhappy staying in their home. He had repeatedly refused to either agree with them or sign the document, and with each refusal had come a fresh onslaught from the detectives, which grew in both intensity and physicality as their 'limited amount of patience' as they referred to it, was being blown around like leaves in the wind. It was clear to him that the report was going to get buried, and buried somewhere deep, but they would have to bury it without his assistance, and so, in the same resolute manner, in which he had entered the police station, he opposed the internal voices of dissent that filled his head, maintained his position, and stood firm. Detention centre or not, he wasn't going to buckle, and Mrs Marsden could stick her manky apples up her fucking fat arse as far as he was concerned.

Snowball's confidence eventually started to bloom in the face of ineffective harassment and intimidation, as did his outright refusal to play ball with the increasingly desperate detectives, who were, by now, working much harder on this 'open and shut' case than either of them had anticipated as they strolled into the office that morning. It was clearly a frustrating time for them both, and something Snowball was inwardly relishing, in the belief that his obstinance was perhaps something that they hadn't come across before in someone so young. However, things suddenly reached boiling point when, after unsuccessfully playing out the 'Good Cop, Bad Cop' routine one more time, one detective noticed a fleeting smile wash across Snowball's face, and immediately flew into a rage.

It was the sort of rage that, when witnessed from the opposing side of the discussion, clearly signals that 'you have just won', even though things are about to go seriously tits up, and out of your favour. The detective quite simply lost it, alongside all personal control, and at that moment in time he unwittingly succumbed to the reality of defeat, in an overt and outward display of adult petulance. He raised his hand and brought it crashing down on the side of Snowball's head, sending him from one side of the room to the other, where he promptly fell, naked, dazed and limp to the ground. "Not funny now, is it?" yelled the detective, as he towered above him, before being quickly pushed aside by his 'good cop' sidekick, who pulled Snowball to his feet, and pushed him unsteadily back into the corner. Snowball looked up at the wall behind them and smiled again. It was all he could do in the face of such brutalising adversity, and it was all about the small victories. "Fuck Off," he yelled, tears flooding from his eyes, as in total disbelief and unison, both detectives turned around and looked at the wall as well.

Snowball pointed to the clock. "Look at the clock, you twat," he said. They were both now looking at the unremarkable clock that hung on the wall opposite Snowball, positioned centrally above the interview room door. It was four o'clock in the afternoon, and the significance was completely lost on them. Snowball couldn't help but smile again. It was a smile of defiance, a smile of knowing, a smile of victory in some strange sense, and it was a smile that heavily disguised the pain and anguish that the battle had inflicted. "Paula finishes at four-thirty, she'll be back for me soon," he said, knowing that he clearly had the resilience to wait another thirty minutes, and that it was the detectives who were now feeling the overbearing frustrations that he had felt most of the afternoon. He needed nor wanted anything from them, and before too long his day would be closed out, and they'd have to start all over again another time.

It was at that point that 'Bad Cop' decided he had heard enough, and promptly stormed from the room, while 'Good Cop' instructed Snowball to get dressed and follow him once he was. Snowball could vaguely hear the muffled conversation that was taking place in the corridor, as he quickly pulled on his underwear and clothing, before he headed for the door. 'Good Cop' could be heard explaining to a colleague that, 'he was probably telling the truth, as the kid hadn't wavered all day', and in fact, he hadn't 'seen a kid as determined as that in a long time'. The expletives that followed indicated that it was a message the recipient neither wanted to hear, nor had the patience or time for, and as Snowball entered into view, the muffled discussions turned silent, and he was led to a small waiting room, while arrangements were made for his collection.

It was forty-five minutes before his social worker arrived, and another fifteen before she emerged from a 'huddle of complicity' with the detectives, which Snowball had witnessed through the large glass windows that separated the waiting area from the office in which they had met. There was a shaking of heads, and fleeting glances of dismay in his direction, before 'Good Cop' emerged from the office with the complicit Paula in tow, and boldly announced to all within earshot that he was 'leaving it with her, and if there were any further problems, to get back in touch'. He may as well have walked over to Snowball and admitted defeat, because that's exactly how Snowball had viewed his outburst, and whilst he was fully aware that between them they had just buried his dossier, he was content in the knowledge that they now knew what was taking place and could never deny that they knew. The treacherous female flunky that had abandoned him to the mercies of the detectives that morning, drove him in silence back to Hill Road, where she promptly left him on the doorstep and quickly departed, clearly unable to face Mrs Marsden and admit that he had defeated them all, and that the game was probably still on in some form or another.

Snowball spent the remainder of the day and night with a debilitating hate smouldering deep within his soul. He had been betrayed by everybody who he should have been to be able to trust. They were all complicit, his enemies were everywhere, and the sense of betrayal cut deep. They were complicit to the abuse, complicit to its cover up, and complicit to its prolongation, as it would surely materialise. It was a psychological as well as a physical war of attrition, and while he was aware of his propensity to secure the occasional transient victory in the heat of the battle, he was also cognisant of the fact that, in a war of attrition, you need the resources of battle to be stacked in your favour, and in this war, he had precious few resources to call upon.

Mr and Mrs Marsden, the police, the social services, school, teachers and carers alike, everyone who should have known better, had conspired to ensure that he would remain unheard, a solitary voice screaming out in the darkness, praying and hoping beyond all hope that someone out there would hear his calls, but in the orchestrated certainty that his voice was destined to call out in vain and reach nobody. A solitary black child, standing alone, with the burden of every ethnic stereotype they could muster being carried on his shoulders, every slur to his character, and besmirching of his name. They stood and watched him drag the rotting corpse of their own integrity in front of them, never once seeming to understand the point that was being made. Because for Snowball, it wasn't about them doing something about the abuses, it wasn't about them acting, or challenging Mrs Marsden, or changing the regime. It was simply about denying them the cloak of privilege that they had long assumed, in being able to say, "we simply didn't know", because they did know, and by their inaction and deliberately inattentive behaviour they sanctioned the abuses. They turned a conscious blind eye to the abuses, and as predictable as the sun rising in the east and setting in the west, they covered up those abuses, and abandoned generations of vulnerable and desperate children, to a life of turmoil and harm.

Snowball sat quietly at his bedroom window that night. Long after darkness had fallen, and the house had descended into a familiar night time hush, he sat and pondered the outcomes of the day. Two bedrooms away, he could hear the ogress snoring in a deep contented slumber, resting peacefully in the knowledge that criminal accountability had been averted, and that the regime which she had so callously implemented, manipulated and used to abuse children for years, was now free to continue, 'officially' sanctioned by social services, 'approved' by the police, and the only voice of dissent had been silenced and humbled.

The faces of the day flashed in front of him, pausing only long enough for him to re-acquaint himself with the treachery that was concealed behind the smiles. There was Mrs Marsden, who had smiled through gritted teeth and deep rooted anger, as she had fed him breakfast and escorted him from the house that morning. Paula, who, grinning like a Cheshire Cat, had driven the short distance across town, and callously abandoned him into the brutal custody of a hostile police station. There was 'Good Cop', 'Bad Cop'. Faces beaming with an overt confidence, before descending into hate filled anger, and ultimately violent rage, as their confidently predicted outcomes began to slowly slip from their sweaty grasp. And there were the silent, fear-etched faces of the other children, who had been forced, in his absence, to listen to the raging torrent of anger that Mrs Marsden had directed towards them, in an overtly hostile attempt to ensure that nobody else had the temerity to break ranks and complain about their treatment. They had all at one time or another looked up to Snowball. He had tried to protect them, stolen food to feed their empty stomachs, wrapped them in his own bedding to keep them warm, and reassured them that, one day, things would be better, and that they would all be free of the nightmare they unwillingly shared.

But as he gazed through the bedroom window, and down into the streets opposite, his emotions began to subtly dissipate into the silent darkness that cloaked Hill Road, and consumed the streets outside, only to be replaced by a fresh unnerving uncertainty, amidst the almost certain continuation of the abuses that they all suffered. He could hear the troubled breathing of the new boy in the bed opposite, and the constant tossing and turning of Stephen in the corner, as he flayed his way through a disturbed sleep, that would see him rise and fall, in semi-conscious fear, as his demons paid their nightly visit to his bedside, and he relived the horrors of his childhood. In the fourth bed was Andrew, young, frail and almost ghostly in appearance. It was almost certain that he would shortly awaken screaming like he would each night, as if his very life was under threat, which for a large part of his short, sad life, it constantly had been.

It was fast becoming one of those nights when things were simply just too much for him to handle. Again, he pondered why he was so often shouldering a burden of care, for the younger children, that clearly should have fallen to others. Why did he need to steal food to feed, or sneak water to them when they became thirsty? Why couldn't somebody else just keep them fed and fucking watered. He had no answers, and there was nobody to stand between them and the onslaughts that the Marsdens perpetrated. There were so many people coming and going, and yet none of them seemed to have time to care about the overt misery and suffering that they were all enduring, and which must have been so visibly apparent. He wondered how many more times he could sit with Andrew, and coax him back into a slumber, before being allowed to fall exhausted into his own bed, to grab whatever remained of the night to himself. How many more times would he be expected to simply lie there and listen to their stomachs rumble, as they waited for the Marsdens to go to bed and descend into their contented sleep, before he could silently sneak across the landing and down to the kitchen, searching for something that they could eat. What more would he be expected to do, and where would it all end?

WHEN HEAVEN CALLS,
NEVER ANSWER...

Weeks later, Snowball was still living with the Marsdens. They had been traumatic weeks, with a continuous onslaught from his hosts, supplemented almost daily by visits from the social services, 'interviews' with his headmaster, or interrogations at the police station. It wasn't the case that any of them were investigating his allegations. They had long ago decided that whether he was a liar or not, they were going to defend their patches, and by definition that meant they had no other option than to defend the Marsdens. It was a simple matter of accountability. If the allegations were proved to be right, it wasn't just the Marsdens that took a fall. The shit would start rolling at the top and slide downhill. All those in the way, anyone who had an ounce of identifiable responsibility towards Snowball and the other children, would be pulled into the passing mess. Paula, his headmaster, the police, and anybody who had ignored his previous complaints, all bit players with a great deal of professional credibility at stake, if Snowball continued with his allegations, and they could be proven. Each and every one of them knew that he somehow had to be stopped, and stopped quickly.

They could have opted for the 'passage of time' approach, but gullible Paula had informed them that Snowball had made a copy of his dossier, and had threatened to post it to the press. He had no such thing, and had only told Paula that, because he knew that in the first instance it would scare the life out of her, and in the second, she couldn't hold her water, and would pass it on, putting the fear of god himself into most who touched the case. It was a strategy that worked with the Marsdens, as on several occasions he returned home to find that his few belongings had been rifled through, in the search for the document. He had even tormented them, by stating they needed to stop looking, as it wasn't even in the house, which had infuriated Mrs Marsden, making the deception all the more fun. Paula clearly had her uses, it was just a shame that being a good social worker wasn't one of them.

However, the weeks of frustration, turmoil, mental and physical abuse were taking their toll. Snowball was becoming introverted, sullen, distant and fractious. It wasn't just life at the hands of Mrs Marsden that was the problem. It was the culmination of years of systematic abuse, and the relentless struggle to simply exist and have a childhood. He had matured too soon, was aging too fast, and had seen, experienced and been party to things that he should never have witnessed. He was an aging adult in a young body, and his maturing years had been nothing but hardship. Then there was the societal deception. The placement into care, which turned out to be anything but caring. The misconception that truth, integrity and decency were virtuous and worthy traits, when they were absent in all who interacted with him. There were the protectors who didn't protect, the carers who didn't care, teachers who didn't teach. It was all just a fabrication, a lie, a trick. None of them could live up to their own expectations of him, nor his expectations of them. Society was a con trick, a sleight of hand, and they were playing him, in a relentless, unyielding game of cat and mouse, and all he craved was liberation from his nightmare.

It was approaching midnight one winter's Saturday, when Mrs Marsden made the frantic call to the police that resulted in a blue light attendance outside the house. She met the attending constable at the door, and ushered him into the house, and upstairs to where Snowball should have been sleeping. He had been isolated in his own bedroom for some weeks, in order to 'keep him from influencing' the other children, and she had sent him to bed early that night, as it had all kicked off again, when he'd tormented her about another report that he was writing. That had been four hours earlier, and she had only noticed his absence as she had popped her head around the door, while making her final checks around the house before retiring. However, the absconding wasn't the key issue for her, as she fearfully explained to the constable. No, Snowball had gone numerous times before. It was an ongoing issue, but nothing that anybody panicked over. But this was different. He had left a note, alluded to suicide, and emptied her medicine drawer of tablets before he'd left. Not only that, he had laid the blame for his actions at her feet and hers alone, and asked her to live with that, because he wouldn't have to. If nothing else, she had taught him the value of a good mindfuck.

She was in a state of panic. The one thing she knew above all else about Snowball was that the 'little golliwog' as she had so often taunted, was not one to make idle claims or threats. In fact, it was as she knew only too well, and to her personal cost on numerous occasions, the complete opposite. He would prefer to cut off his nose to spite his face, rather than be seen to step back from a promise to act, whether that promise be good or bad. He had lived a hard life for someone so young, and he had learned the value of 'putting up or shutting up'. He knew only too well that if you couldn't deliver, don't make the threat, because it looks weak, it is weak, and the weak get punished by the strong. Mr Marsden had tried to calm her down, but had been summarily rebuked and pushed to one side, as the unfolding situation consumed and tormented her. The other children had been awoken, and quizzed about anything they knew, but it was a fruitless exercise. Snowball knew better than to include them in anything that might bring trouble to their doors. It was trouble he knew they couldn't handle, nor wanted them to. As he had once been told, 'the only way three people can keep a secret, is if two of them are dead'.

The constable put out a call to his control centre, who subsequently informed patrols of his absence, and the possibility that he may require medical attention when found. It seemed that everyone was now looking for him, and perhaps for the first time, they were taking him seriously. Paula had been called out, though to what end nobody really knew, and the night started to get longer and longer for everyone involved. His friends received visits, but they found nothing. Old haunts and new, all searched, all empty. Time and tide waits for no man (or child), and as the panic mounted, the only thing that was certain was that nobody had a clue where he was.

Snowball's long, slow, sullen walk had taken him down into the town centre, and towards the Wanderers Football Stadium. He forlornly kicked an empty can around in the car park for a while, imagining he was on the pitch, and had just delivered the decisive through ball to his footballing hero Frank Worthington, who, with a flash of genius, had then gone on to dummy several Tottenham players, before slotting in an inch perfect shot from outside the penalty area, into the top right corner. They celebrated together in front of the Burnden Park faithful, with the final whistle going shortly after, and they left the pitch to the chant of their names ringing in their ears, and the points in the bag. In other games he was standing shoulder to shoulder with big Sam Allardyce, while together they shored up the Bolton defence, with a series of 'do-or-die' last man tackles and headers, which enabled Bolton to maintain their slender lead and go on to win the game. As the crowds chanted, 'Six Foot Two, Eyes are Blue, Big Sam Allardyce is After You', another section of the stadium could be heard to chant, 'and he has Snowball with him', or at least that's how he imagined it happening, before again, the crowds went quiet, as the game came to an end, and the stadium emptied.

He had spent many an afternoon attending Burnden Park to watch his heroes in action, but a realisation that he might never see them again had cast a dark shadow over his goal scoring exploits that night. He had sold prize draw tickets on the club's behalf most weeks during the season, and upon returning ticket money to the club on Saturday mornings, he would be given a free ticket to the next home game. The prize tickets were hard to sell, and you needed to sell a lot of them to earn your match day ticket, but for the likes of Snowball, who would never have seen a game otherwise, it was a great option to have, and also meant that there was no need to participate in the usual match day event of taking a direct run at the turnstile, diving over onto the concrete floor opposite, and dashing, knees and hands grazed into the crowd, before the steward could get out of his box and give chase. It was tactic he had deployed many times, but invariably led to the sorts of cuts and grazes that lasted until the next home game, where the scabs would then be ripped off again. So, it was a case of all things being equal, selling prize tickets was a win-win for both poverty-stricken spectator and financially challenged club alike.

Game's over, points in the bag, and after a last glance over the entrance of the club, he had so often imagined playing for, he moved along Manchester Road, before finally, after what seemed like an eternity, heading into Pendlebury, where he stopped outside a large fish and chip shop, and enjoyed the council estate supper special of scraps in a tray, covered in pea soup (juice from the mushy peas), with a wooden fork (completely fucking useless for eating the pea soup). It wasn't much of a supper, not much of a last meal at all, but in the absence of cold hard cash, the chip shop concession was a welcome treat inside a hungry stomach. He continued his walk along Manchester Road. He didn't really know why, but if he was thinking of dying that night, he wanted to die in Manchester, home to Tommy Docherty's Manchester United, the dream stadium that was Old Trafford, and a place he had heard so much of, but rarely seen.

It held some strange attraction, a weird fascination, given that his experience of the place was limited, but Manchester bound he was, food in stomach, tears in eyes, and pain gripping his heart. His second footballing passion was Manchester City, for whom, alongside the likes of legends such as Dennis Tueart and Colin

Bell, he had scored an outrageous number of prolific goals for, and helped them win numerous titles, long before the real 'Noisy Neighbours' up the road in Trafford Park had even heard what football was. He ran the possibility of visiting Maine Road through his mind, but he had no real idea of how to get there, nor how far away it was, and the chances were it would never live up to the experience of knocking a match-winning pass through to Frank Worthington in front of the home crowd.

He was mid-way between Pendlebury and Pendleton, completely exhausted, soaked to the skin, and limping badly, when the blue light of an approaching police car lit up the sky around him. He had inadvertently strayed onto the pedestrian free section of a small stretch of dual carriageway, as he tried to reach Manchester by the shortest route possible. The rain and cold had bitten him so hard, that he had barely computed the car's presence, when through the flashing blue light, he caught sight of an officer approaching him with his hand outstretched. He knew he couldn't run, and he couldn't think, he was simply too exhausted, and as the officer reached him, and asked him where he was going, he simply fell to the floor with exhaustion.

It was a mixture of relief and anxiety swirling like a tidal wave through his body and emotions. The rear seat comfort of the Rover 3500 was a welcome respite from the harsh weather that had dogged the latter part of his trek, and he took little convincing to get in, as the officer had swung open the door, and pointed firmly towards the rear seats, but in he got. As he slowly began to doze in the furnace like heat of the car, confirmation came over the radio that he was being looked for by police and that he may be in possession of a large quantity of tablets or could possibly have already taken them. His docile state, brought on purely by the elements and fatigue, convinced the officer in the car that it was a case of the latter, but too tired to argue or fight, Snowball had produced the tablets on request, and the entire state of panic fizzled out, as the Rover moved off from the kerbside, before heading slowly back towards a reunion with Mrs Marsden.

"What were the tablets for?" the officer asked, peering up into his rear-view mirror, and attempting to make a sustained eye contact with the wilting child in the back. Snowball remained quiet, but he had noted the tone of concern in his voice, and silently wondered why he even cared. 'All Coppers are Bastards', was a common enough chant, and the majority Snowball had encountered in his short life excelled at living up to that notion. "You can tell me, you're not on your own," he continued. Again, Snowball remained silent, wanting to speak, but wary of this complete stranger who had crafted the art of sounding like he cared. "Why would a young lad like you want to die?" The question came out of the blue, and stunned Snowball with the brutality of a cattle prod. "Why would I want to live?" he fired back, the words flashing from his mouth, before he had fully come to understand what he was about to say, or formulated the feelings behind it. They were talking.

The police car slowly pulled into the next lay-by, and the officer got out, and then sat in the back with a now disconsolate and dejected child. There was mutual silence and a silent, unspoken understanding, as they simply and knowingly stared at each other. For the first time in years, Snowball realised that he was in the presence of someone who did actually care, who wanted to know, and was prepared to listen. It wasn't a trick, there were to be no surprises, no punishment, no brutality. The man cared, and it was just as frightening as all those who didn't. Over the course of the next hour, Snowball laid bare his own personal story, and that of others, and explained in detail what had brought him to this place and time. The act of simply talking about it was a painful exorcism, and fraught with danger. But slowly he succumbed to the need to unburden his load, and over the course of time, the full story was laid out in the open. They continued to talk, as they eventually continued the journey 'home'. The more they drove, the better he felt, and for once, life seemed to be less fraught, less fearful, and with a little more hope than it had ever appeared before.

There was another stop on Manchester Road, as the officer pulled over and bought them both a bag of chips. They laughed and joked as they ate them, Snowball now in the front of the car, and making full use of the sirens and flashing blue lights to warn straggling drunks on their way home of their immediate presence and the need to move on from pissing in the doorway of number 248, and use the toilet at home. It was an all too rare moment of fun, which had alluded him for so much of his life, and he revelled in the attention and warmth. A radio message to control was relayed to Paula, and as the car pulled up outside, Mrs Marsden appeared at the gate, and casually strolled over to the rear door of the police car. She had the devil's own smile on her face. One that spoke volumes of both her relief that the panic was clearly over, and the realisation that she was now free to continue the unashamed abuses once the police presence had disappeared into the darkness of the night. She reached out to take hold of the rear door handle, only for a stunned look to sweep across her face, as the front window came down, and a voice bellowed out, "Leave the door alone, and go back inside, NOW! I will bring him in when WE are ready."

It was the sort of statement, delivered with the type of intonation, that was designed to convey a very clear message, and one that she clearly understood as she wilted away into the darkness. With that one statement, he had simply told her, 'I know what you've done. I believe what I have been told, and you need to be extremely careful from now on'. The brightest of smiles now adorned Snowball's face, as she slowly pedalled backwards towards the garden gate, and into the front garden, with the words, 'Well I never' screeching from her mouth. His face glowed, his teeth shone in the reflecting moonlight. His breathing lightened, and his chest relaxed. Snowball was back, and there was nothing she could do to damage the splendour of his return.

The officer turned to Snowball in the back, and slipped him a small piece of paper, which contained a telephone number. "If you ever feel like you did tonight, I want you to call me, do you understand?" he said. Snowball nodded and smiled. "You find a phone, reverse the charges, and you call me, OK?" Snowball smiled and nodded again. "You need to understand that this isn't forever, you can get through this, and you will get through this." They were strong, inspiring and unexpected words. Snowball completely understood what was being said, and though he wasn't too sure how he would get to use a phone in the near future, he knew that from that moment on, if he did get to one, he had a friend on the other end. He took a cognitive step back and paused. He couldn't help but think that nobody had told him there'd be days like these, but it was turning into a great day very quickly. He felt better. He felt warm, and for the first time in a long time, he felt that he wasn't alone. It would appear all coppers aren't bastards after all.

It wasn't long after this that Snowball found himself on the receiving end of another move, as his leasehold on the bedroom at Mrs Marsden's came to a sudden and welcome end. Mrs Marsden had come to realise the she had gone way too far with her sadistic excesses, and was now juggling the knowledge that she might not only end up in a court of law as a direct consequence of her unbridled abuses, but as Snowball had intimated, she might potentially one day have the death of a child on her hands, and as a consequence, she had made frequent and loud noises to the effect that she wanted him gone, and the sooner the better. Snowball wasn't objecting, and his only regret was that he hadn't had the opportunity to see her stood in the dock, and held accountable for her actions, and those of her pathetic husband. The only downside was that once again, Paula would sit in the car and ask him if he was OK, as they arrived at his new abode, he would once again tell her to 'fuck off' and life in a new home, and the challenges that would bring, would be underway. But he decided he could easily live with that in the general scheme of things, and with that, and Mrs Marsden's departing bile ringing in his ears, he was gone, and a new chapter of institutional life opened up before him.

THE TRUTH DOESN'T ALWAYS SET YOU FREE (CRAMLEY GARDENS)

Hill Road to Cramley Gardens was nothing more than a short hop across town, and the too much travelled Snowball saw nothing new or exciting to look forward to, as the latest development in his troubled and turbulent life began to unfold. They had successfully buried the abuses at Hill Road, the dossier had disappeared for 'safe keeping', and Snowball had been easily enthroned and crowned as the villain of the piece accordingly, by all who should have cared, and those who didn't. It had been a right royal let-down, and all that remained for the Marsdens to return to their unbridled excesses and ritualised abuses, was to have rid of Snowball once and for all, in order that they could put the momentary 'hiccup' behind them. Snowball had rapidly descended from the potential saviour of the many, to just another brick in the wall of abuse victims, of which the Social Services had constructed their fortress.

Another move had been deemed to be in everyone's interest, and after a few hastily convened case conferences, no doubt filled with plenty of finger wringing, painful reflections and sighing, it was decided that Snowball's future lay elsewhere (primarily a large home for criminally delinquent boys on the opposite side of town) and the sooner that a move could be effected, the happier everyone would be. That of course was the 'ROYAL' everyone, as the simple reality was that nobody cared much for whether Snowball was going to be happy or not. The last place a boy like Snowball needed to be, criminal record free, and generally well-suited and receptive to rational thinking, reasoning, structure and education, was to be amongst a group of juvenile delinquents, whose only qualifications, past, present, and potentially in the future according to the much-vaunted scripts, rest in the number of shops they could screw, or people they could rob. But the social workers knew best.

The issue was a political one, and priorities focussed around protecting the social services department, its complicit social workers, the Marsden family, and all the other abusers across the homes that they ran, who had found themselves, vicariously or otherwise, up front and centre stage with Snowball, as his complaints unfurled. It was clear that the golliwog at Mrs Marsden's had to go, the only blessing being that they didn't have to paint him black and curl his hair, before they packed him off to pastures new.

Snowball was in a deep, contemplative and reflective mood on the short journey into the town centre and out of the opposite side, via the Moorcroft Bypass. Both Mrs Marsden and Paula had already been told to 'fuck off' that morning. Mrs Marsden simply for being Mrs Marsden, and Paula for asking the inevitable stupid question that she always asked with regards to whether he was 'OK' or not. He wasn't sure how many times she would require telling to 'do one', and so all he could do was to improvise with the subtle addition of increases in hostility and intonation every time he told her, in the hope that the penny would one day drop, and she'd either stop asking him the question altogether, or she would actually just fuck off as requested, which in this case would have actually made him 'alright', but he would have had nobody to tell about it.

So, the preliminaries to the short journey across town were complete in record short time, and after his few possessions and a plastic bag of clothing had been stowed in the boot of Paula's new Escort, and Mrs Marsden had bid him farewell with a characteristic push from behind, and short sharp slap to the back of the head, he was on his way yet again to pastures new. He was beginning to lose count of the number of homes they had moved him to. It didn't really matter that much, as they were all so much alike, forgetting was often the only comfort he had, but he knew it was many. He was unwanted and uncared for, and he knew it, as each and every move served to simply reinforce the simple fact that nobody really wanted the black kid. It was a cold, harsh and brutal reality, which he had learned to live with. They would never, as they had frequently promised, find him another foster home. He was stuck in the system, and he was likely to remain there until his care order finally expired at sixteen. For Snowball, there was no out.

As early afternoon closed in, Snowball realised that yet again he was now on his own. As naive as Paula clearly was, she wasn't stupid enough to jeopardise her own career and financial well-being, by defending and supporting him publicly, and in the way that he desperately needed. So, like the rest of those who had taken part in the whole debacle as it became, she had abandoned him to an unknown future, and in doing so, had tentatively secured her own, as long as he remained silent. He knew that he was now the only person he could ever depend on, and that his own self-reliance was now the master key to his continued survival. Snowball had been taught a harsh lesson. The truth doesn't always set you free and can sometimes serve merely to enslave you further. He would eventually bounce back and stronger than ever. After all, he was but a few short years away from stepping out into the big wide world, all on his own, free from the brutality, the violence, the heartache and misery that had dogged him for so long, and free to make them all pay one way or another, in his own time.

Cramley Gardens turned out to be another large, sprawling, semi-detached, brickbuilt house, much the same in character as Hill Road, and only a few short miles out of the town centre. Though hardly in an area that you would proudly call the suburbs, it was in fact located in a relatively affluent looking part of town, which aesthetically served to offset the oft felt stigma that came part and parcel with living in a children's home, and being classed as poor. There had been a slow and subtle transition from the council-owned social housing that dominated nearer to the town centre, into the industrialised terraced rows that dominated the close-knit communities in and around the factories and mills and would primarily have been occupied and owned by the shop floor workers.

This in itself had given way to a spattering of mid-management type semis, in private gardens and driveways, of which Cramley Gardens was one, before tapering off further up the road into line after line of neatly manicured gardens, within which stood fabulously presented detached houses that had invariably been occupied by the wealthy upper management types, and factory owners at various points in their history. From there on, it was open countryside, and the residential domain of the 'rich pricks', who, peculiarly enough, found themselves to be just as much an ostracised section of the community, with their real leather shoes, crisp white shirts and proper packed lunches, as the poorer people, with whom Snowball would frequent by virtue of his exalted status as a 'cared for child'.

There was a small garden to the front of Cramley Gardens, and smaller garden to the rear. The house was accessed by a 'front' door, which weirdly was located on the side of the property, with the front garden over-looked by a large bay window, which concealed the staff office behind the grimy, greyed, tatty lace curtains that were draped in the window. There was a small half brick, half wood entrance porch, that led into a small reception area, and then directly into the staff office on the right, which Snowball would later learn was out-of-bounds to 'people like you' as it was so eloquently explained, as were various other rooms in what was now supposed to pass off as his new home from home. The entire outside of the house had been painted black and white, in an attempt to give it the popular mock-Tudor look that was so prevalent at the time, with just about everything faux that could possibly be imagined inside, from the tacky Axminister look carpets, worn and threadbare in places, to the crystal-look plastics so reminiscent of The Manors, all lending itself to a pretension that it could ill-afford, and was ill-advised to aspire to given the criminal demographic of the unwilling and unwanted residents.

Paula had deliberately chosen to drive into the grounds along the short tarmac drive, rather than park on the road like everyone appeared to do, with Snowball assuming this was a gentle nod towards his frequently exercised and well expressed right to go on an impromptu and unhindered walkabout, when things got a little bit too much for him, or someone, usually someone like Paula, had irked him sufficiently enough for him to have to choose between enthusiastically assaulting them, or taking a 'few quiet moments of reflection' as Miss Bradwell had instilled in him, and simply walking away from potential confrontation and trouble. He had no intention of walking away on this occasion, nor was he about to assault Paula; however, he did take a casual stroll to the gate, just to let Paula know that he could have walked off, if he had really wanted to.

They were greeted at the door by a portly lady called Mrs Lynes. She was one of a number of part-time assistants at the home, who, between them, ensured that the house remained clean and tidy, clothing and people were washed in a timely manner, and that food wasn't only cooked, but actually reached the table for which it was originally intended. Mrs Lynes introduced both Snowball and Paula to Karl, who between bouts of alcohol infused stints on duty, defecating in the staff bed, beating his ex-wife, and feeding his gambling addiction at the local bookies, was actually the man deemed to be in charge of the entire home, and the well-being of all who lived there. The joys that Snowball had felt leaving Hill Road for the last time were subsequently numbed by the stench of neat Bell's Whisky, as Karl determined that the best way to welcome someone to the fairground attraction that was Cramley Gardens was to breathe heavily in their direction, before belching out his welcome, and stumbling into the staff room, like something from a Carry On sketch.

The staff room was somewhere that Snowball would soon learn to avoid. It was a place of many abuses, and plentiful misery, not least of which was when the often summoned police were in attendance, and summarily carrying out random beatings and strip searches, which often led to hushed talk in quiet corners, in regard to inappropriate touching, and worse. It seemed hard to believe at first, but as Snowball witnessed the frequent comings and goings, the idle talk began to gain a veracity and momentum all of its own.

Karl's demeanour didn't seem to faze Paula at all, as she simply chose to swiftly bypass the extended hand of the inebriated Foster Brooks impersonator and headed directly into the vestibule, before following him into the office, plastic bags in one hand, and Snowball held tightly with the other. This rare but openly assertive display in front of Karl was pretty impressive, though Snowball found himself slightly less enamoured with her steely grip around his collar. She had finessed a disapproving look, which lent itself to an unspoken but nonetheless implicit 'yes, you twat, it has been noted', which clearly informed Karl that it was perhaps something to be discussed in the absence of others who were currently present. So it was a big old round of applause for Paula from Snowball at that point, however disconcerting Karl's appearance had initially been.

After being passed from Mrs Lynes to Karl, there was no respite for Snowball as he was quickly ushered from the sanctity of the staff offices, along with its noxious whisky odours, and the ever pleasant and diminutive Paula, and sent to see Uncle Bernie Wilson, who was the on-duty burst arsehole for the night, and as it would transpire, a much and frequently reviled man amongst unhappy residents and staff alike. (Where do they find these fuckers?) He wasn't so much an individual arsehole, as he was an amalgam of weirdly constructed arseholes, haphazardly rolled up into one obnoxious, foul-breath, sweat stained individual, with the capacity for any level of critical thinking, self-control, and personal management extracted via a secret lobotomy while he had been eating, before being ruthlessly let loose on the delinquent prey that resided in Cramley Gardens.

He in turn swiftly introduced Snowball to Aunty Jane, who apart from having a much talked about affair with Bernie, and a much admired, and well thought of cleavage and backside, was as unremarkable as a woman, as she was remarkable for her capacity for the inane. It was rumoured that Karl and Bernie had long fought over the sloppy, buttock clenching sexual attentions of Aunty Jane, and that Karl had lost out, having been put to the sword by Bernie, on account of the fact that the whisky meant that he simply couldn't get it up, willing or not, with the frequency that Aunty Jane demanded in return for her favours, and subsequently turned to greater quantities of alcohol to get over his humiliation. It was probably untrue, but nobody really cared. It was a great story, and gave the lads a good laugh, every time they saw Karl sniffing around Jane's bedroom door during the night, as they pretended to need the toilet, every time they heard his door close and his footsteps crossing the landing.

So it was Uncle Bernie who was shagging Aunty Jane on nights, and if you were 'lucky' enough, you got to see a flash of her cellulite dimpled, pock marked arse, as she darted between bedrooms in the early hours of the morning. Snowball originally thought Aunty Jane was a bit of a 'looker', but he soon came to realise that his thinking and his eyesight had been somewhat abused and perverted by the aesthetics of Mrs Marsden, and in time, as his eyesight, and adolescent sexual cravings were realigned to a semblance of normality, he would accordingly re-adjust his thinking towards more appropriate fodder. It's not that he thought Jane was too old for him, she was just too fucking big. As one of the boys often said, great tits, but what the fuck do you do with the rest of it?

From there on in, it wasn't long before Snowball found himself the centre of attention again, as in the early sunset of evening, a slow trickle of juvenile residents began to arrive back at Cramley Gardens. It was a ritual he was now well acquainted with, and one that he knew he simply had to tolerate. Someone would arrive and display complete indifference to his presence. Another would invariably appear in front of him, full of bravado, before calling him a coon, sambo or a 'nigger', whilst others were just glad that he was there, as it meant a degree of respite from the bullying that they often suffered, and would no doubt return to, once Snowball had asserted himself as an 'untouchable'. This was a two-fold message in many ways, as the 'verbals' as they were commonly known, were in the first instance designed to put him in his place, and in the second, establish the abuser as being higher up the hierarchy, and thus deemed as somebody not to be messed with. Snowball had developed a very clear-cut strategy to deal with this introduction, which in effect reversed the psychology and dynamics, and put everyone else into a state of panic and concern. The strategy was simple, and readily executed, though potentially fraught with danger. He would simply stroll over to the abusive little toe-rag and smack him in the mouth. This was then the point where the other child had to put up or shut up, but either way it established Snowball as someone who was willing and capable of defending himself, and sent a clear message to all present, that if they weren't capable of doing the same, they had better stay clear of the new black kid.

As it happens, Danny was the cocky little attention seeking piece of human detritus that decided to test Snowball's mettle that day, and, as expected, he delivered the inappropriate racial slurs, only to be met with a firm black fist that had claret spewing from his nose in a matter of a few seconds. As a worldrenowned boxer would say decades later, 'everyone has a plan, until you punch them in the face'. Danny was just another cocky little no-mark who had nothing of real substance in his personal arsenal when it came to a ruck, but instead had come to depend heavily when things got violent upon the support of his elder brother Peter, who was also resident at Cramley Gardens. It quickly became apparent to Danny that he had bitten off more than he could chew, and although he remained unrestrained in the delivery of expletives and continued his racial abuse, he did so while back-pedalling towards the door with his brother, while delivering a host of threats he knew he couldn't carry out, but which were designed to save face amongst the assembled and somewhat bewildered onlookers.

Gerry Delaney was perched at the head of the dining table, as if he was some kind of mafia overlord surveying his assembled henchmen, with a view to deciding which one had betrayed him, and accordingly how they would meet their fate. He was an obnoxious bully boy, and spent most of the time disapprovingly stabbing at his tea, and shifting it around the plate, as if that would make it taste better, while attempting to fix Snowball in a stare that was designed to intimidate and demean. Snowball had clocked him and the stare, but remained impervious to his intent, as he had long ago come to realise that the only people he had to worry about were the ones who were up on their feet actually doing something.

Delaney was the product of a violent and abusive home like most of them were. He had little to offer in terms of emotional or general intelligence, and instead relied heavily upon a cocky gait, and an illusion to a toughness, most likely gained from watching too many films about prison life and recent episodes of The Sweeney. Snowball knew enough to know that Delaney wasn't going to be a problem. He simply wanted to protect what he felt he had, and as long as Snowball appeared to pose no threat to him or 'his turf', or indeed be seen to be challenging 'his rule', he was the sort of bully who would make occasional overtones towards dominance and aggression, but would always find some feeble reason or other, to back away from the actual confrontation, while saving face, and leaving with reputation intact.

Like so many others, Delaney had evolved to believe that violence was the solution to most things that troubled him and was regularly to be seen involved in violent physical altercations with one boy or another at Cramley Gardens, as he sought to resolve various disputes in the only way he was equipped to do so. Snowball would often come to muse how Delaney, a pale, gaunt and relatively feeble looking boy, could carry off such a persona. Perhaps it was the Indian Ink beauty spot etched into his right cheek, as apparently all the hard cases at the time had one, and he wore his with a certain degree of masculine pride, even though it had been gained through an act nothing more violent or hard than a huddle under a torch-lit blanket, while a friend jabbed away at his face with an ink dipped sewing pin. It was clear to everybody and anybody with an ounce of intelligence or experience, that he was largely incapable of living up to his own hype. But nevertheless, Snowball determined to let it ride, as long as he was being left alone and to his own devices.

Delaney's only redeeming feature in the eyes of the few, was the fact that he was extremely skilled with a table tennis bat. It was probably a small balls thing. This was particularly useful to Karl, as he had entered the home into one of the local leagues, and the regular frequency with which Delaney won his matches served the purpose of adding a certain gravitas to Karl as the 'Head Coach', as he boasted far and wide about the sporting successes of the home he was running. There was even talk of Delaney playing for the county in national competitions, so he rapidly became Karl's poster boy for children under his care.

For Karl, it also served as a very efficient means of detracting attention away from some of the home's more overt failings under his stewardship, and as a result, Delaney found himself very much in the favours of Karl, and thus was able to exploit the situation to his own benefit. This quickly came to mean that Delaney was largely untouchable discipline wise, as he and Karl shared a mutual dependency that relied on the goodwill of the other, if the successes at the table were to continue. Delaney, as expected, took full advantage of the situation, and as a result, his bullying, intimidation and violence knew no real bounds, apart from the limitations of his own cowardice.

The Beak, however, was the complete opposite of Delaney in every regard. A socially awkward and emotionally inept introvert, weak of mind and body, and grossly obese. He was the typical cry-baby of the group, never quite understanding that you simply don't cry out loud, or in public, as it was a sign of weakness that exposed the culprit to further abuse and bullying. He would gorge himself on penny tray sweets and had no cares with regards to his personal health, well-being or personal hygiene. Even by the fashion of deficient standards of children in care, he dressed appallingly, and seemed to just amble through life with an aged shuffle, no aspiration to have or achieve anything better, and little by means of personal character or hope.

Beak was one of life's born and bred victims, and it was easy to see why his parents didn't want him. He had 'hit and abuse me' written across his forehead, and people, parents, relations, staff and residents alike, often obliged, in the knowledge that there would be absolutely no retaliation, attempt to defend, or repercussions involved. Unlike Snowball, who had grown to appreciate the need for mounting an adequate defence, regardless of the odds, The Beak would simply just take it, and walk on by, in the perverse hope that they would at some point tire of hitting him. But as he would unfortunately, and frequently find, there was always someone waiting to have a pop, someone with a status to establish or defend, and life was never going to be as simple as he hoped.

The Beak's entire deportment, gait, physical appearance, and general demeanour were constantly and readily lending themselves to the almost certain unavoidable reality that his life would be spent as the punch bag of some bully. He was also one of those people who appeared to have an intrinsic aversion to helping himself and mitigating his own plight. Whereas most of the weaker boys attempted in some way to fit in, or at least blend into the background, and remain relatively unnoticed, The Beak had a tendency to stroll brazenly into the gladiatorial arena, only to then realise that he was carrying no weapons, and they had closed the gates behind him, having already set the lions loose. You simply can't appease a fucking lion with a bag of penny sweets.

He would, however, become very useful to Snowball, in the context of absorbing much of the bullying, torment and abuse that was generally reserved for the 'nigger' in the house. The Beak was also a self-harmer and was regularly seen with blade marks across his lower arms. The sweets and lack of self-care were in fact another form of self-harm, as was his propensity to put himself at the mercy of violent bullies, who constantly abused him. His own self-loathing appeared to know no bounds, and his chosen method of rehabilitation was to put himself into one form of danger or another, and simply absorb the consequences.

Life in Cramley Gardens wasn't much of an existence. It was another bleak, austere environment in which to grow through his teenage years, and as always, existing as the only black child in this white world was proving problematic. The issue for Snowball wasn't one of whether he could take it or not. He had been taking it all his life. No. The issue was just the sheer relentlessness of it all.

It just went on and on. There was no end in sight, no respite, no safe havens in which he could relax, regroup and come back feeling stronger than before. He just needed some private space, and there was none to be had. Cramley Gardens also provided a veritable feast of things to be casually amused about, but there was nothing salient for Snowball, nothing to grasp hold of, to revere, to hold precious. He simply yearned for a stable environment with loving people around him, but it was all just a distant pipedream, and as he would often be told, people simply don't want to adopt or foster a black child these days.

But he had Uncle Bernie, an overweight, hyper-ventilating, obnoxious, pug-faced, violent bully. He had his Uncle Karl, an out of control chronic alcoholic with a gambling addiction, and a tendency to lash out at women with his feet, when things weren't going his way, and there was always Aunty Jane, a weak-minded excuse for a mothering figure, who, if he played his cards right, might be able to facilitate a quick tit-wank or dalliance or two, in the staff quarters upstairs. There was a host of peripheral comers and goers, with various jobs associated with the care of the boys. So, 'what more could he want'? But there was nothing salient. There never was. No salient relationships, no salient friendships, nobody that he could grow to care for, or who cared for him, and above all, as far as he could see within reason, there was no salient future ahead.

Snowball found immediate life at Cramley Gardens very different to that which he had experienced at Hill Road. The group dynamics were widely in conflict, though he found the overall environment more conducive to his immediate needs as a growing teenage boy, though it was clearly lacking in the intellectual and emotional support and attention that he desperately needed. He had no responsibilities towards others, and neither was he expected to be given any. It seemed that all he was required to do was to take care of himself, and remain free from the burden of care and responsibility for others, and he quickly settled into the daily regimen that typified life at Cramley Gardens. It was a regimen that revolved around repetitive simplicity, and simpler rules. There was an immovable time for rising in the morning and going to bed at night. The morning call was followed by a frenzy in the shower room, as the boys jostled for the best performing showers, or the solitary bath that took pride of place in the corner of the wet room. First boy out of the showers was often the best dressed, as the communal clothing and school uniforms were distributed by Mrs Lynes, who would be in attendance for the early morning shifts and took great pride in turning out at least one appropriately dressed child, in clothes that actually fit him. Breakfast would shortly follow, in a small window of opportunity that often saw wet, half-dressed boys sat at the table, through fear that breakfast would be cleared away, before they had managed to wash and dress downstairs.

Meals times were fixed and never budged. The diet was basic and predictable, with set foods served at set meal times, on set days of the week. There would be two choices at each meal sitting. Take it or leave it. It really was that simple. And whilst most boys took it, Snowball often found that the better option was to leave it, through fear of what he might be doing to his insides, if he was to consume the fodder that Jane or Bernie were turning out.

This, however, would often lead to fierce accusations from Bernie of Snowball 'being too good for his food', or somehow thinking that he was 'better than the others', after which Bernie would frequently attempt to force feed him, before Jane intervened as the proverbial peacemaker (usually as the battle subsided, and always after Bernie had had his bit of fun), and attempt to calm the situation down. Breakfast subsequently turned into a frenzied departure for school buses, which at the end of the day turned into an equally frenzied race home, to ensure that advantage could be taken of the 'first home, best dressed' policy of handing out clothing, as uniforms were ditched in favour of casual wear and training shoes. Tea would turn into supper, supper into night, and everyone would retire to their beds, while Bernie retired on top of Jane, and Karl would have a rendezvous with his best mate Johnny Walker. It was all very straightforward, very easy to learn, and in the main, very effective. But it wasn't long, however, before the ghost of Hill Road came back to haunt Snowball, and it would instigate another cycle of violence, which would continue for months at the hands of Bernie, with a complicit wall of silence maintained by all who witnessed the daily assaults.

It had been just over a week after Snowball's arrivals, and there was a certain amount of stress and tension in the air, every time Snowball and Bernie were in the same space. Snowball took the view that it was a simple lack of knowing each other, and things would pan out shortly, but Bernie seemed forever agitated in his presence, and his fuse appeared to be getting shorter and shorter, as each day came and went. It was as if the lack of confrontation from Snowball was frustrating his needs to simply have a pop at him, and he needed Snowball to respond to him, in order to make that happen. He had made casually sarcastic reference to Snowball's time at Hill Road on several occasions, hinting that he knew the Marsdens, disparaging Snowball, and generally trying to talk down the experiences he had endured, and the information he had collated. It was clear there was an issue brewing, but Snowball figured it was to be expected, and that it would disappear, as quickly as it had arrived, if he remained calm, and didn't rise to the bait that was being laid out in front of him. Of the two of them, only one knew the truth, and what they were talking about, and the other was simply spoiling for a fight.

Bernie had been on a sleepover in more ways than one, as he had shared the night shift and a bed with Aunty Jane, who had also stayed over, despite not being listed to do so. It was clear his sexual exploits hadn't been a raving success that night, as he'd arisen from his slumber in a foul mood, and clearly spoiling for a confrontation, with whoever was prepared to indulge him. Jane appeared in no better a mood as she prepared the breakfast, and as the usual fight for showers, clothing and food ensued, Bernie lost the plot, and launched into an attack that left Snowball bloodied and bruised on the floor of the dining room. It was another case of denying that abuses take place, by abusing the accuser, in the hope that they might then agree with you. The sheer fuckery of it all wasn't lost on Snowball, even if the irony was lost on Bernie and Jane.

It had all started over nothing more than a hotdog sausage. A small, calorie deficient, non-descript hotdog sausage that was probably cold, contained no real dog meat, and cost less than a few pence to produce. Jane had run out of traditional sausages mid-way through the breakfast and resorted to opening a tin of hotdogs as a substitute. She had served them up, alongside bacon, eggs, toast and beans, and Snowball had engaged in some banter, regarding the sudden change to the much inferior offering. Upon hearing Snowball's remarks, Bernie launched into his attack, first pushing Snowball into a corner, before launching a volley of punches to his head and face, that sent him reeling to the dining room floor. "Go and put that in a dossier" were the words than spewed from Bernie's mouth, with a vileness that was matched only by his halitosis. Bernie was closing in on Snowball, who remained on the floor, dazed and in shock, but suddenly found himself confronted by Jane, who had raced from the kitchen, and had now positioned herself between Snowball and the boiling over blob of human waste that she had been shagging the night before. She raised a steadying hand in front of his chest, and delivered the icy glare, which she normally reserved for the boys at times when her patience was running thin, and she was about to go off-piste with her temper control. Bernie took the hint and immediately backed away, mumbling some half-hearted apology to Jane, while completely ignoring the victim of his attack, who by now was bleeding heavily from the nose and mouth.

Snowball rose to his feet wondering what the fuck she had put in them sausages, as he spat a lump of blood from his mouth and wiped the remainder from his nose with the freshly ironed white shirt Mrs Lynes had given him that morning. "Get yourself sorted and off to school," Jane implored him, giving a nod towards the door, as she picked up the chair that had been sent sprawling to the ground during Bernie's attack. "No need," came Snowball's reply. "I need to pop and see my social worker." It wasn't the reply she was expecting, but one she understood the consequences of, as he disappeared towards the front door, bloodied shirt and face remaining in evidence.

School life would prove to be no better for Snowball. There was little expectation of a child in the care system, and expectations of a black child in care, and generally within the wider society, were literally non-existent. There were times when it was clear that nobody really cared. They either didn't have time, or just couldn't be bothered, and yet all the time, it was the children, children like Snowball, who were deemed to be the problem. The only consistent thing in his life were the number of people lining up to tell him what a failure he would be, how he would amount to nothing, and therefore, any effort they expended was simply a waste, and by that virtue there was no point in expending effort on him. He was constantly told how children in child care never did, and never would, amount to anything of any substance. That his future rested in abject poverty and lack of achievement. He was supposed to fail professionally, socially and any other which way, with either a jail cell or a park bench being his only comforts, and his relationships provided by a brown paper bag wrapped bottle of alcohol, or people just like him. It seemed that being black, unwanted and uncared for was a death sentence, in terms of expectations in life. He had nothing, and according to the 'knowledgeable' few around him, the drunks, the wife beaters and child abusers, he would never have anything. It seemed that they were determined to stop him before he started, and there was very little that could be done to stop them.

Against this backdrop, there seemed little point in continuing most days. Mental health was becoming the unquantified issue, and there was nowhere to turn, nobody to talk to, nowhere to run or to hide. There was no help. He was alone with his troubles, and alone with his thoughts. Deep, dark thoughts from the pits of hell, that would suck him into their vacuum, and spin him around, before spewing him out, dazed and unstable, into the harsh realities of a world he couldn't control.

How he cursed the 'mother' that had visited this nightmare upon him. Never had she looked down upon him, and thought, oh 'sweet child of mine'. He cursed the fact that he could rarely sleep at night, consumed by dark thoughts that kept him wide-eyed and over-thinking. Dark thoughts indeed. How often he thought of setting fire to the place, and simply wandering away into the darkness of the night, as the flames of his hate consumed all those who deserved them. He had lain there, night after night, and played through a thousand different scenarios in his head. He knew he would never truly entertain the thoughts in a manifest reality, but they got him through the dead of night on many an occasion, and that was enough. As the darkness of life consumed his waking moments, he began to once again wonder if maybe it was simply time to move on.

There was very occasional and periodic respite from the continued drudgery and mistreatment that dogged the lives of those at Cramley Gardens. On one occasion they had all been taken on a barging holiday, on the Shropshire Union Canal. It had been a long, well anticipated break, and most of the boys were eagerly looking forward to a week afloat, playing at captain, doing a little fishing from the deck, and generally fucking about on the water, as Karl had eloquently put it to Delaney. But as with most things Cramley Gardens, there was always an air of something disruptive imminently about to happen, and the whole thing could be ruined as quickly as it had been planned and implemented.

They had got off on the holiday pretty much on time and without incident. Jane had orchestrated the night before packing. Each boy had a holdall full of clothes and underwear. Enough supplies had been packed to ensure that they didn't go unnecessarily hungry throughout the holiday, and dear old Bernie, having had his goodbye shag from Jane, and conscious of his own propensity towards violence, had even packed a first aid kit, despite the fact that the pre-despatched boat's inventory clearly stated that there was one aboard, which made Bernie a bit of a knob, but at least he was making an effort.

It was a good start, considering the mix of personalities and expectations involved, and The Beak had duly indulged the amass of bullies, by spending his pocket money on a large bag of sweets, only to have them stolen from him on his return from the newsagent's. The trip south was punctuated by a short break at a service station, where free sweets and drinks were secured by some of the boys, before Karl hastily decided it was best they leave while they were ahead, and they subsequently resumed their journey, laden with the cost-free fruits of someone else's labour. Two hours later, and they were rolling into a canal mooring area, where they disembarked and began to unpack the minibus that had transported them south.

There had been plenty of talk about the likely ramshackle death trap, in which they would be spending their week afloat, so they were all beyond surprised and delighted when they found that the 'barge' that had been hired for them, was more akin to an ocean-going cruiser, than a dinghy, with a large living area, room to sleep eight or more in comfort, an enormous retractable roof that terminated just before the cockpit area, which in itself looked like something from a spaceship. It was almost as if someone had made a dreadful mistake, from which they were about to inadvertently benefit, when they hired the wrong boat, as it was noticeable that by a long way, they were in one of the better vessels that could be hired. Snowball couldn't help but think that it was all very strange, very surreal, very abnormal and against the general flow of the waters in which they normally sailed. Here he was with Karl and Bernie. Men who would argue the toss with you over a fucking hotdog sausage or a ten-penny tin of soup, and yet they were about to set sail in an expensive canal cruiser, the likes of which he would never have dreamed about being onboard. This had to be a mistake, and one that would surely be rectified before they set sail.

The boat owner took great delight in explaining the finer points relating to the operation of his vessel. He covered every boring inch of the boat, in minute detail, unaware, or in denial as to the fact that his audience really couldn't give a toss, and just wanted to cast off and start dicking around. Karl had packed a large amount of beer and whisky for the holiday, with the promise that the first night afloat was to be a memorable one, as long as everybody could keep their big mouths shut when they returned home, and so the attempt by 'Captain Birdseye' to explain the finer points and etiquette of life aboard his magnificent vessel, and the canal itself, was falling upon deaf and unappreciative ears, as the longer he talked, the less drinking time was to be had. Snowball couldn't help but wonder that the boat owner must be either completely stupid, or insanely naïve, to believe that he had any chance of having the boat returned in the good order that he was expecting, and in which he was letting it to them, but nonetheless, Captain Birdseye seemed happy with his instructions, and that they would be implicitly followed, and without further ado, had issued the route map (route maps for a fucking canal. Lord give me strength), instructed the boys on the operation of the locks, and bid them farewell, as he headed back to his rather plush looking Jaguar in the car park, amid unheard chants of "You're a knob", before heading home to the suburbs. It would be a trip he wouldn't complete promptly, but he wasn't to know that.

Now free to explore the vast wilderness of the Shropshire Union Canal (well the pubs along its banks, a bookies and chippy in a town called Stone to be precise), the boys eagerly loaded up the boat with supplies, grabbed the bunks they thought best to occupy, and awaited the moment they could set sail. Karl nominated two of the boys to operate the lock that they immediately faced, while stating that he would knock up a rota for future encounters of the lock variety, so that everyone got a fair share of this supposedly hard work. Snowball was nominated to steer the boat through the first tunnel bridge, and into the lock ahead, as he was deemed to be the most sensible of what was on offer, while Karl and Bernie would be needed on dry land, to ensure that nobody came to harm, as the boys' display of exuberance and enthusiasm near open water was clearly worrying them, given that three of them couldn't swim, and one was so unpopular, it was likely he would be sent crashing into the canal, just for a laugh.

Delaney had objected to Snowball steering the boat first, on the basis that he (Delaney) had stolen countless number of cars in the past, and was more than capable of steering in a straight line when it was necessary, though he failed to mention the three occasions on which he had failed to do exactly that, having crashed the stolen cars into roadside obstacles, other cars, and on one occasion a pedestrian, before being arrested at the scene of his crimes by the police. Karl had summarily rejected Delaney's objection, on the grounds that, as Karl put it, he was a 'fucking thick twat', and sent him forward to act as a guide for Snowball, who was now firmly encamped in the Captain's Chair on deck, with a gratuitous smile etched across his face.

IS THAT THE
TITANIC I SEE...?

Cast off went like a dream. With Snowball at the helm barking orders to his reluctant skivvy, lines were loosened, thrown on deck, and the cruiser gently shimmied into open water for the first time, with a full crew of society's misfits, malcontents, drunks, and bullies onboard. Snowball drifted the boat to the centre of the canal, and then back over to the left bank, like a seasoned professional, allowing Karl, Bernie and an assortment of delinquents with lock keys in their hands, and enthusiasm in their hearts, to disembark, and head down the banking towards the upcoming lock. "Meet us on the other side of the bridge," Karl shouted as his feet hit terra firma, adding, "Don't approach the lock, until we've opened the gates, then bring her straight in." Delaney replied by asking who was to be brought in, and in that one sentence confirmed the saliency of Karl's decision to keep him away from the boat's controls. "I think they name boats after women, you thick twat," Snowball shouted to Delaney. "How the fuck do you know?" came the reply from Delaney. Snowball came back faster than a bullet. "School, you should fucking try it sometime." Delaney desisted from further conversation on the subject, and Snowball smugly settled into the long voyage ahead (well, to the first bridge). Having subdued Delaney, Snowball, as buoyant as he was, thought better of the temptation to deliver a hearty 'Aye, aye, Captain' as Karl disembarked and cantered up the canal bank barking further instructions, as he could be an arsey, obnoxious drunk, and while he was in high spirits, and willing to let the lads enjoy themselves, it seemed wise to keep him that way.

Fat Bernie was by now some way behind the others, as they reached the bridge, and as they shimmied sideways along the towpath underneath, he could

272

be heard panting in the background like a man close to coronary heart failure. Karl called out to his belligerent colleague, but was waved on, and told to stay with the boys. The Beak was happily chewing away on the pocketful of sweets that he had hidden after a second visit to the newsagent's and secretly brought along for the ride, and Myers, a pig ugly Pitbull of a boy, was busy emptying the fumes from a tube of glue into his nostrils. Delaney remained at the front of the boat, bleating to anyone within earshot about having 'fuck all' to do, while rolling a cigarette and bemoaning the fact that he was running out of papers. And unbeknown to Snowball, as he enjoyed his recent promotion to Ship's Captain, the boat had continued to drift up the left hand side of the canal, and was now only a matter of feet and seconds away from colliding with the stone bridge ahead, much to the fear and panic of the people stood aloft it, who were shouting frantically in an attempt to attract his attention to the impending disaster, only to have Snowball smile and wave back.

It was Delaney who came to appreciate the full impact of the disaster first, as the boat struck the bridge, and Delaney, fag papers, tobacco, bad attitude and all struck the water with a large splash. This was the definitive point at which Snowball was alerted to the fact there was an unfolding disaster and realised that something was amiss. Like all good captains, he remained with his boat, and took full command of the crew on deck, which at this point comprised him and fat Bernie, who had now taken an almighty departure from the daily status quo, and been seen both running to the boat, and jumping on deck, in a vain attempt to rectify the mishap, before it had occurred. If only the lazy bastard had acted sooner, they could have avoided the extensive damage to the sliding roof, as the boat became wedged at an angle on a cornerstone in the bridge. There wouldn't have been a hole in the front fibre-glass panelling, and there would have been no need to eventually, after much anger and repercussions, limp the boat back the less than three hundred metres it had travelled from the boatyard, before disembarking and awaiting the arrival of the owner, who probably hadn't even arrived home in the suburbs at that point, but at least they had saved him the petrol. It was clearly Fat Bernie's fault, and Snowball wasted no time in telling him that.

From that moment on, the holiday seemed to go from bad to worse. As expected, Karl spent most of the time staring at the bottom of a bottle of whisky, or on his better days, staring at the bottom of a bottle of whisky, while ruefully enthralling the boys with the tale of how his horse almost came in, and almost won him a fortune, if only it had approached the jump in a different fashion, or another much better and more able horse hadn't rained on the jockey's parade, and left him penniless. It was a familiar tale for Snowball and the other boys, who on a frightening scale of frequency were privy to Karl's inebriated verbal excesses, violence, and abuses.

Karl seemed happy enough though. Having got over the initial trauma of the first day calamity, and having resigned himself to the fact that the substantial deposit that had been paid was now lost, he was comfortable enough with the idea that any further damage the boys did was in effect gratis, and so he could relax into the holiday free from the worry of containing the boys, and returning the boat in the condition which they had received it earlier. Bernie was a different kettle of fish altogether. He seemed to take the loss of deposit personally, as if it was coming from his own pocket, which in effect it probably was, as there was a tendency amongst some staff to see the money that was made available to support the boys and the home in general, as their own personal slush funds, which could be dipped into for trips to the bookies, off-licences, chip shops, and all manner of other things, that they knew they couldn't rightly afford, unless it was being funded by the state.

Bernie had hence sought to make Snowball's life as miserable as he possibly could, and had assaulted him on two occasions since, whilst hurling racial abuse, only to be reined in by Karl, although not through some sense of responsibility towards Snowball, but the fact that the boat was tandem tied at a mooring alongside a similar vessel, and everything that was said and done could be heard by the other party in the boat alongside. But Snowball wisely sought safety in his ability to walk the towpaths alongside the boat when things got overly heated, safe in the knowledge that walking anywhere, bar the exception of going to dinner or the bar, was well and truly off fat Bernie's agenda.

The holiday quickly drew to a close, and the boys were returned (minus deposit) to Cramley Gardens, where life continued along its familiar path. Karl spent his time drunk in the office, while making occasional appearances to issue betting slips and money to one of the boys, before sending them down the road to place his bets. Bernie was still shagging Jane, who was still occasionally and inadvertently flashing her dimpled arse on the stairs, as she sneaked back to her own room, unaware that just about every boy in the home knew exactly what she and Bernie were up to most nights. Bernie became more and more abusive, with a particular brand of brutality reserved for Snowball, who he had come to develop a serious loathing for. He would often punch, kick and push him around the house, resulting in one occasion where Snowball was sent crashing down some stairs, and a moment of sheer panic, as he remained motionless at the foot of the final tread, with no visible sign of life.

However, as with most bullies, there is often a price to pay at some point. Bernie had been acting with particularly aggressive vitriol towards Snowball. The racial slurs were coming thick and fast, as were the punches and kicks. He was excelling himself, and enjoying life, safe in the knowledge that there would be little, if any, comeback for his actions, and as the day rolled on, he remained in pursuit of Snowball, making the most of every opportunity he had to confront and harass him. But as the old saying goes, 'the Lord works in mysterious ways', and today was to be no exception.

Lunch had been served, and Snowball had been directed to the kitchen to help wash up. It wasn't his turn on the rota, but Bernie was in that sort of mood, and so Snowball knew better than to challenge it. Bernie had followed him into the kitchen, barking out instructions, and explaining with great delight how he would be checking every plate, knife and fork, and how he would stay there all day if necessary, until the job was done properly. Bernie arrived at the corner of the large wooden dining table, that took centre stage in the kitchen, and called out to Snowball, who upon realising that they were alone, steadied himself in readiness for another violent onslaught. Bernie opened his mouth, chin raised, head cockily perched back, as he confronted his prey one more time. He tried to speak, but for some unknown reason the words wouldn't come out. He just continued to move his lips, silently expressing something, but communicating absolutely nothing. The colour suddenly ran from his face, and there was a large, troubled intake of breath, before he suddenly fell to the floor, vacantly looking up at Snowball, with the look of a man resigned to imminent death, as he clutched his chest, and his eyes bulged.

Snowball took a step closer, stepped over Bernie and closed the serving hatch. There was no need to trouble the others and make a spectacle of what was happening. He could hear the words of Miss Bradwell ringing in his ears, as he looked down on what appeared to be an expiring Bernie, laid out in front of him. 'You have to think,' she would tell him. 'You have to think.' He desperately wanted to leave Bernie on the floor where he had fallen. It seemed like the only fair thing to do given the day he'd had. He was a vile, obnoxious and odious bully, who had brutalised Snowball since the day they had first met, and yet here he was, life apparently hanging by a thread, and completely dependent if he was to live, on the one person he had sought to brutalise and humiliate as if it were some kind of sport.

Snowball desperately wanted to walk from the room, and simply close the door behind him. It would have been simpler for everyone. Nobody would have missed Bernie in all honesty, and Jane would have soon found someone else to shag at night. But of the many things he might rightly or wrongly be accused of being, he certainly wasn't the sort of person who would let a man die in front of him, and he certainly wasn't going to be seen to be helping Bernie on his merry way, however appealing that might have been. And so reluctantly he hastily headed to the office and sought out Jane. She immediately tended to Bernie and his most pressing needs, who on the one hand was no doubt cheered by the fact he was breathing and alive, whilst on the other, clearly saddened by the knowledge that his immediate shagging days were over, for the foreseeable future.

Snowball fleetingly considered offering to step into his shoes, homework and chores rota permitting, but it clearly wasn't the right time, so he decided to let it go. An ambulance was unfortunately called (no you didn't read that wrong), and Bernie promptly found himself on a paid sabbatical, while he recovered from his apparent trauma, and regained his previous state of ill-health. Cramley Gardens descended into a period of relative calm, and a new member of staff in the form of Uncle Mark arrived and began to literally make his mark.

It was Mark who unwittingly signalled loud and clear that some clouds do have a silver lining. His arrival shortly after the potentially fatal, and much craved demise of Bernie, had ushered in something quite new to Cramley Gardens. It was something that none of the boys, Snowball included, had experienced or witnessed in recent years, and was a much-needed breath of fresh air. Mark was, put simply, someone the boys could look up to. He was what they termed a man's man. The sort of man other men wanted to be like, to emulate, to have as a friend. He was a man who garnered respect because of how he personally conducted himself, not how much or how often he brutalised you and then demanded respect. Snowball took an instant liking to him. He had a presence. He seemed to know a lot, in an unassuming way. He could impart knowledge and experience, without the need to raise his voice, or resort to violence. There was an aura around him that Snowball could identify with. He was different, and it was immediately apparent that he was different. He talked in quiet understated tones. There was no inflective edge to his words, and he had a habit of asking, rather than demanding. Snowball appreciated the fact that he was now apparently party to decisions that were being made, even if compliance was implicitly expected. Mark had a respectful way of asking that inspired reciprocal respect, and Snowball was open and receptive to this new guy on the block. Though the preponderance of life at Cramley Gardens continued in the same violently oppressive vein that it always had, it was Mark who brought a degree of respite and calm to the continued onslaught, and infused the home with occasional periods of normality and a semblance of hope. He also had a pretty fit wife, who would occasionally call over, adding a ray of sunshine and hope, where previously only Jane's lumpy arse had existed.

As much of a breath of fresh air as Mark would prove to be, there was always an undercurrent of violence and intimidation in the home, which usurped any and all of the benefits of having someone like Mark onboard the rat-infested ship. As always, and more so in the welcome absence of fat Bernie, Karl being Karl was the primary problem. Drunk, aggressive, abusive and deliberately intimidating, he would prowl the home looking for trouble, and in its absence, create some himself. The absence of Bernie, and the intake of the fresh-faced Mark, meant that Karl was spending more and more time visibly on duty at Cramley Gardens, which was as much an annoyance to him as the children there. Time spent on duty was time wasted in Karl's eyes, as it was clearly the only time that he attempted to constrain his drunken, gambling addicted behaviour, not through any desire to reform, but the ever-present threat that someone in authority may just pay a visit in passing, and as the occasionally solitary social worker on duty, he would be unable to avoid having his dirty little secret exposed.

Karl when sober was a shrewd man. He knew that being caught drunk on duty wasn't the problem. What was a problem, however, was that being caught meant he made someone else party to his drunkenness, and that presented them with an unwanted professional dilemma. Ignore his behaviour and become complicit to it, or report it and be ostracised from your professional network as an undesirable whistle-blower. It was a choice people would rather not make, and in the main actively sought to avoid. As a result of this professional blindness, visits were always announced some days prior, in order to prevent such a dilemma from arising. But when Karl was single staffing the home, that presented him with a considerable problem.

Karl ruled by violence and intimidation. But his behaviour often led to someone absconding in its aftermath, which he was formally obliged to report to the police. The police would be obliged to visit the home, and when confronted with a lone member of staff, who was also drunk and in charge of a largely delinquent group of teenage boys, were professionally obliged to cover their own arses, by taking action. Karl had been caught out by this before and was warned by the police about his future conduct. So, when single staffing the home, Karl was forced to put violence on the back shelf and communicate like an adult with the boys. He had to reason with the boys, and when he had to communicate and reason, he was vulnerable.

This vulnerability came to a head with Snowball, over Karl's favourite subject, food and drink. Well, primarily drink as you know, but he did occasionally eat when his drink ran dry. Snowball had arrived home later than usual, having taken part in a school sports event, and had missed his tea. He had enquired with Karl as to what was available and been told to sort himself out. As it happened, that would be a relatively simple instruction to carry out, as Snowball's favourite comfort food was nothing more complex than tomato soup and tinned hotdog sausages. Chopped, diced or sliced. It didn't matter, as long as they were tinned hotdog sausages, and they were covered in tomato soup. Cold, bedraggled, soaked to the skin, and with a mild shiver setting in, comfort food was exactly what was required. Snowball went to the larder. Soup was on the middle shelf, cans of hotdog sausages were next shelf up. It wasn't much of a tea for a growing teenager, but it was all he wanted, all he needed, and as he had carte blanche to feed himself, it was how he was going to indulge.

The feast was duly prepared, and Snowball sat at the table and tucked in. Though his appetite was voracious, and it would by no means fill him, the satisfaction of the dish itself would keep him going until the morning. It wasn't just about the taste, it was the smell, the texture, the heat that flowed up into his face as he spooned the liquid sustenance in to his mouth. It was everything and anything to do with tomato soup and hotdog sausages.

He was halfway through his feast, when a drunken Karl presented himself at the door of the dining room. He was clearly enraged, and Snowball quickly noticed that he was holding the empty can of hotdog sausages in his right hand. "Have you had all of these?" Karl demanded of him. Snowball, somewhat bemused, replied "Yes". There were only six small sausages in the tin to start with. In reality, that constituted less than three decent sausages in real money, and as they probably didn't contain any bona fide meat, they could hardly be described as sausages in all truthfulness.

Snowball could instinctively tell that trouble was about to unfold, though he remained bemused by the fact that trouble was brewing over a ten pence tin of six scabby fucking sausages. Karl was looking for trouble, and he found it. He hurled the empty tin at Snowball, who, looking down at his food hadn't seen it coming, and as the open end of the tin struck his forehead, he felt the sharp surprise of the lid cutting into his skin. At this point, Karl was now bearing down upon him, though he was unaware that Snowball had just reached his breaking point and was now in the process of rising to his feet, in order to meet the onslaught face to face.

Karl swung a wild right-handed punch, which glanced across Snowball's nose as he shimmied backwards in an evasive action. The force behind the glancing punch spun Karl around, who now found himself with his back facing Snowball, and in a firm bear hug that had taken him completely by surprise. Within seconds Snowball had wrestled his drunk soaked, piss stinking, trouser soiled attacker to the ground, onto his stomach, and was lying full body down upon him, preventing any further punches from being thrown. Karl wriggled, squirmed and cursed, but remained firmly in place.

The boxing and wrestling club was a great example of how the lost children of society could find somewhere that accepted them for what they were, made no judgements, and only demanded that they comply with the rules of the club, when they were in the club. Snowball had found attendance fulfilling, and he knew that with the few skills he had learned, the fat oaf beneath him was not only going nowhere, but within the next thirty to sixty seconds of struggling would be so out of breath that he would pose no threat when he did let him rise. Karl duly obliged the prediction, by wriggling and squirming himself into exhaustion, and as Snowball rose to his feet, Karl wobbled first to the left, then right, before half rising to his knees, and then slumping back down while he caught his breath. Snowball stepped to the side, placed his bowl on the serving hatch, and quietly left the room. The attack was the final straw, and a catalyst. Snowball knew there and then it was time to move on, and if he could drop Karl into the proverbial shit while doing so, then all the merrier for everyone as far as he was concerned.

AU REVOIR BOLTON,
BONJOUR PARIS

It was a cold night for the time of year, but as Snowball sat in the disused portacabin, on the semi-abandoned building site, he knew that by now they would be out looking for him. It was eleven-thirty. He should have returned to Cramley Gardens by nine that night. By now he would have been reported as missing, an absconder, and there was no turning back. Though curled and shivering under the dirty Donkey Jacket that had been left in the rubbish, he felt strangely liberated. It was cold, it was harsh, it was far from ideal, but it had also relieved him of many troubles, troubles that now seemed so far away, so distant, as his eyes had closed, and he slipped into deep, undisturbed sleep.

An extremely cold night turned into a much colder morning, and as Snowball rose, his mind turned to planning his next move. The cold was now compounded by hunger, but he had money in his pocket, and there was a pie shop nearby. His pockets bulged with leftover fruit that he had picked up the night before from the market stalls opposite the bus terminal in the town centre, and he had a small bar of chocolate, which he had left out in the cold the night before, to prevent it from melting if he turned onto it. He had been too cold to bother eating any of it that night, and it somehow appeared far less appealing, after spending the night on the floor of the cabin. But nonetheless he kept it all, just in case it ever became needed.

A visit to the pie shop became a visit to the train station with meat and potato pasties in hand, and before long, a ticket in the other as he headed towards Manchester. The day again quickly turned to night, and as the cold once again began to bite deep, with chips wrapped in newspaper, he crouched beneath a discarded tarpaulin, at the rear of a shop in Piccadilly Gardens, and settled down for the long cold night ahead. It was an uneventful night, that seamlessly rolled into morning. Tarpaulin cast aside, face and hands washed in the underground toilets by the gardens, and before long he was heading back to the train station, and onwards to London. The plan was simple enough. The train would take him to London (free of course, if he played it canny), and from there he would get himself down to Dover. He knew that from Dover, you could get the hovercraft or ferry to France, and from there he could start himself a whole new 'trouble free' life. It really was that simple. What could possibly go wrong?

London came and went in a blur, and he soon found himself on a slowmoving train, heading for the Kent coast and a new life abroad. For Snowball, 'skipping' the train as it was known, was quite an easy affair. The key was in knowing exactly what carriage the conductor was in when you got onboard, and more importantly, when the train stopped. Then all he had to do was execute the off-on strategy, until he arrived at his destination station. Between stops, the conductor would move slowly down each carriage, checking tickets. When the train pulled into the next station, Snowball would get off, and back on again, having looped back around into an area that had already been checked by the conductor, who had also briefly disembarked, in order to usher on the new passengers. On short journeys, he could do this all the way, but Manchester to London was clearly a different matter, and the chances of eventually being caught were high. Plan B, however, never failed. Sit next to an adult, by a window, cover yourself with your coat, and feign sleeping.

Now lady luck hadn't visited Snowball for quite some time, but the morning after another cold night sleeping rough, she graced him with her presence, and was in fine form. He had consumed a hearty breakfast of crisps in a barmcake, polished off a can of Cream Soda, and swift of foot headed down to the Ferry Port. The idea that he might need a passport had never crossed his mind, but as he was to find out, Lady Luck was on point that day, and he simply wouldn't need one. Entering the terminal complex, he noticed a number of coaches had arrived and were forming tidy queues awaiting their embarkation. Two coaches from the front stood Lady Luck herself, in the form of a local grammar school teacher, who was disembarking her eager and excited group of school children, heading on the annual school holiday to France. It was an opportunity not to be missed, and Snowball promptly fell in with the group, as they headed towards the passenger terminal, and casually hung around until they were finally boarding. Never too close to raise suspicion from a teacher, never too far away to attract the attention of the terminal staff. Walking the fine line as always. He had clearly learned many things. As the announcement to board came, and the school kids rose in a display of synchronised conformity, nobody chose to challenge the only black face in the crowd that was tagging along at the rear, and some time later, he found himself onboard, and heading out to sea, the famous white cliffs beginning to fade in the distance, and the smell of fresh croissants and warm baguettes about to make a welcome appearance.

If departing the shores of the Dover were a triumphal success, Snowball soon found that his arrival in France was going to be a cold, harsh and unwelcome reception into the realities of life 'on the run'. Unlike in Rio when Ronnie Biggs arrived, in Calais it was raining, it was grey, it was cold, and it was miserable. There were no dancing girls waiting for him to disembark, and the beach looked cold and uninviting. He had wandered through customs without a hitch. Again, he had remained close enough to the other school children for it to be assumed he was with them, but far enough away so as not to attract a teacher's attention, and the unwelcome questioning that might bring. Out in the wet and cold of Calais, the supreme greatness of his big idea was fading fast. As the other children boarded their waiting buses, which swept them onwards to their doubtless warm and comfortable final destinations, Snowball, head bowed and miserable, began a long lonely walk into the nearby town. He wasn't even sure where he was. He might well have landed in Belgium and he wouldn't have known, but he wasn't home, he wasn't being victimised or brutalised by Bernie or Karl, and so he didn't really care. The cold bit hard, the rain dripped from his unprotected head, down his face and onto his shoes, but he trudged on, shivering his way from Rue to Rue in abject misery. Ca VA? Non, Tres mal, Mme.

'What the fuck is a Boulangerie?' he thought, attracted by the small lantern that hung outside, which cast a faded blue light across the shop front, as the outside light began to dim, as it succumbed to the closing dark clouds overhead. "Aaaahh, funny cakes, long butties with veg in, and weird round bread, why not call it a fucking bakery?" he thought, as the smell of freshly baked produce weaved its way up into his dripping nostrils, and seemed to sedate his increasing levels of anxiety. "Oui?" queried the stout Boulangere from across the counter. Snowball looked puzzled, and simply stared back at the him, imagining he was talking to someone else, who clearly hadn't arrived in the shop yet. "Oui?" repeated the stout man. "Vous-parlez Francais, non?" Snowball stood quietly and alone in the shop and awaited his 'turn'.

The man promptly left the shop, and headed into a back room, returning shortly with a woman, who Snowball assumed was his wife. Gesticulating wildly, he pointed in Snowball's direction, delivered a stereotyped gallic shrug, and wandered into the backroom, from where he never returned. The woman peered in Snowball's direction and gently asked, "What do you want?" in a soft-spoken, unintimidating manner that immediately appealed to the fraught disposition Snowball was finding himself in. There was a calming warmth behind her heavily accented English, adding a distinct sense of mystery to every word she uttered, and as the whiff of cheap perfume permeated the allure of her freshly baked produce, his heartbeat dropped a few beats per minutes. This adventuring lark was going all wrong. Snowball pointed eagerly at one of the long butties he had seen in the window. "Ham Baguette," the kindly woman offered in alluring English. Snowball nodded, unsure what a baguette was, but pleased nonetheless that she was now wrapping it neatly in brown paper (he would have preferred a bag, but when in Rome, and all that bollocks), and was ready to hand it to him.

It was at this moment that Snowball recalled the porcelain faced features of Miss Angelique Natale-Masterson. Miss Natale-Masterson had been his French teacher back in the Manchester-based grammar school he had attended for a short while. She was French born, but married to an English man, whom she had encountered while on holiday in London some years earlier. She was also his calligraphy teacher, but he had never told anybody about that, as in the first instance, most people wouldn't know what it was, and in the second, once you explained it to them, you usually got a punch in the face for being one of those 'Posh School Sissies'. He had no real interest in learning French at the time, although the value of it was becoming clearly apparent to him, as he tried to figure out a solution to his current dilemma. French seemed hard, nobody wanted to do it, but like most of the boys in the school, the attractive face and stunning figure of Miss Angelique Natale-Masterson was enough to ensure that not only was the option selected, attendance at her classes was guaranteed, even if it couldn't stimulate enough interest in a language nobody had reason to believe they would ever need. It was at this point that he recalled Miss Natale-Masterson had once done a lesson on unique differences between English and French money. Centimes and Francs to be precise, and which he now realised in the immediacy of the here and now, meant that he had no means of paying for his long butty.

Wet, shivering, and with a nose running like Niagara, he held up a handful of mixed coins, and offered them to the woman behind the counter. She was still holding his baguette, so he had no option but to await her judgement, and hope beyond all expectation that he could spend what he had. The woman glanced down at the pitiful looking creature in front of her, looked over the handful of coins he had offered, smiled, closed his shivering hand inside hers, and passed him the baguette. She watched as he slowly made his way down the street, and back towards the ferry port, then wisely and promptly picked up the telephone, and called the Gendarmes.

His first night on foreign shores was spent in the office of a customs officer in Calais. He hadn't been arrested, but fortuitously, as the rains continued, and he had become more and more desperate for shelter, he had spotted an office window slightly ajar, as he had wandered the terminal grounds looking for shelter, and with an accomplished shimmy, prised himself through the open gap, and into a rather spartan official-looking office, belonging to a gentleman called Vincent Trudeau. A few pictures on the wall indicated that Trudeau was a family man, dog owner, and had a penchant for shooting shotguns and killing birds. His desk was OCD tidy, and he had set aside a small area in the far corner, where he made his coffee, and stored his lunch, the remnants of which had been tidily resealed in a bag, and set aside for later consumption. There were two cups, two saucers and two teaspoons on a tray. All immaculately cleaned and ready for their next use. The heavy lined coat hanging on the back of the door provided for a meaningful blanket, and as the lightness of the office gave way to the creeping external darkness, Snowball slipped into another deep, relaxed sleep, by the office door, oblivious to the distant sound of the Gendarmes' sirens, as they searched the nearby locale for his presence.

For Snowball, there was no rising to the sound of bird song, and the smell of fresh coffee and warm toast wafting through the house. No, his awakening was rude and painful, as Vincent, returning to work early that morning, had attempted to enter his office, only to find his entrance blocked by the sleeping child on the opposite side of the door. Panic set in hard and fast, as Snowball awoke and realised the predicament he was in. There was a huge man on the opposite side of the glass partitioned door glaring down at him. A colleague appeared to be summoning help on the phone, and an overweight Madame was walking towards him, with a mixture of both shock and amusement registered across her face. For a few fleeting moments, Snowball stood on one side of the glass panes, while three bemused French nationals stared at him from the other. Miss Angelique Natale-Masterson had told him that a polite 'Bonjour' was a typical French greeting at the start of the day, but nobody was speaking, and in all honesty he was feeling a little unwelcome.

It was time to leave. Étape de sortie à droite (exit stage right to you). There seemed little point in hanging around, and after drying himself out the night before by the radiators, the office had served its purpose. He bolted for the window, which he had slipped in through the night before. He could hear the office door open, and Vincent's footsteps closing in behind him, as he slid stealthily through the open gap, head first towards the concrete floor below. Vincent caught hold of his right leg, as the nearly departed Snowball was about to make good his escape. Hanging on as Snowball kicked out, he could be heard calling for help, while he tried to lever him back through the window. "Aidé moi, Aidé moi!" he bellowed to his colleagues, "aidé moi!" Oh shut the fuck up, Vincent! Dangling helplessly, and only a foot from the ground, Snowball could see three Gendarmes rushing towards him. It was now or never. One last effort for freedom, or it was all over, and he was finished. They wouldn't have treated Jacques Mesrine like this, and Snowball wasn't about to put up with it either.

He raised his left leg, and with everything he could muster, kicked out at the grasping hands of Vincent, who simply held on with typically French stubbornness and resolve. Another kick, and still no response. The police were getting closer. The fat Madame had joined the fray and was attempting to raise the window a few inches more, in order to assist Vincent in his efforts. Time was running short, and with one last kick to the hand, Vincent released his grip, and Snowball tumbled onto the concrete floor below. "Merde," bellowed the fat woman from the office window, disgusted by the apparent failure of her colleague to hold on until the police had got closer.

But all had not been lost for the French Fries Hoover. In falling to the concrete floor, Snowball had taken a glancing blow above the eye, as his head had hit the curbing below. He was up and running, but the razor-like pain than traversed across his forehead caused him to screw his eyes together, wince and for a few moments, he was running blind. Moments were all that were needed for the giant like frame of Lessou to close the gap, and take a firm hold of him around the waist, before taking him quickly to the ground, and over onto his stomach. A tactfully placed knee was positioned firmly into the small of his back, and within seconds, as the handcuffs came out and were snapped in place, Snowball's game was up.

It took a few hours of investigation, but before long, Lessou and his colleagues had established who Snowball was, that he was a runaway, and that it would be far easier for all concerned, if they simply returned him to Britain on the next available crossing. Snowball was fed, watered, and held in a locked office at the local Gendarmerie, until a crossing could be organised. Lessou drove him back to the port, escorted him onboard, and waited until departure time arrived. Satisfied all was well, he rose to his feet to disembark. "Bon Chance, Explorer," he proclaimed, patting Snowball on the head, and moving to the exit door. Snowball looked quizzical. "Good luck" Lessou explained. One last smile, and Lessou was gone. It was a lonely sail back to the UK. The pain of failure, mixed with the anxiety of his imminent return to a hostile home, bit harder than the cold ever could. But there might be one last chance as the time to disembark encroached, and he would take that chance if given the opportunity.

WHY iN THE NAME OF KENT SEND HER?

"Who is coming for me?" he had tentatively asked. The housemother's reply was short and sweet. "A lady called Sheila," she said. Snowball's heart sank. The trouble he was in had just got exponentially worse, and there was no getting out of this one. That was the one name that he simply didn't want to hear. He had only asked the question, to ensure that it wasn't her. But it was, and now he was in a whole world of shit, and it was all of his own making. The trouble that was about to descend upon him, was a lovely woman called Sheila. She was the only person he knew who appeared to actually care about him, and as a consequence, the only person that was likely to give him the right royal 'parental' bollocking he richly deserved and had duly earned. There was no doubt at all. Kent to Bolton was going to be a very long drive!

He had arrived on what was the last crossing that evening. He had been met at Dover, by a 'Sweeney' themed sting operation, which saw half a dozen police officers rush towards him as he meandered unescorted through the customs hall, and into the arrivals. The only thing missing was Jack Regan telling him he was nicked, and a bumpy ride in a dodgy Ford Granada by an under-trained and over enthusiastic driver from The Met. The night had been short and sweet. A short ride in an unmarked police car, and he had arrived at a large children's home, lodged in a hillside in Kent. Exhausted, hungry, and 'travel' weary, he had been given a hearty supper, clean pyjamas, a warm bedroom on the second floor with a locked door and left to sleep it all off. Sheila arrived three days later. She wouldn't have sworn in front of him, but he was pretty certain it was an 'Oi You Fucker' moment for her. It clearly wasn't the time for smart quips and witty retorts, so he resolved to play it by ear, and make every effort to endear himself to her, on the long haul back to the North. There would be no Green Avenger moments, no Plan A or Plan B. Just a long, uninterrupted, relatively silent trip from the South, and a polite, dignified and authoritative promise to 'deal with this properly when we get back', as Sheila put it with deadpan clarity.

Snowball had first bumped into Sheila aged about eleven. Neither of them could possibly have realised how deep and meaningful their relationship would eventually become over the years that would ensue, nor how it would endure across time, as they both moved on from that first meeting. It would at times be volatile, riddled with doubt and mistrust on both sides, but somehow against unreasonable odds, it was a friendship that would ultimately stand the test of troubled times and circumstances, so long as he survived the imminent drive home.

In those early days, to Snowball she was just another patronising, faceless wonder, no doubt with a bag (albeit a Gucci one) full of the usual false promises, as she first appeared at his school gates, bedecked in fur, and smelling like the fragrance department in an upmarket store. She had introduced herself as another one of those loathsome creatures that called themselves social workers, and as the person who was about to interject herself into his miserable life. He had grown weary of their forever changing faces, their lies, broken promises and deceit, and wondered in all reality, why she had even bothered to turn up, if all she had to offer was an unlimited amount of the same undiluted bullshit that her predecessors had espoused. She seemed fairly enthusiastic, and certainly up for the then unknown challenge that lay ahead of her, and she appeared to have a bit of clout around the office, being senior to most of the dross who apparently now worked for her. But as a famous general once said, rarely does a plan survive first contact with the enemy. The only upside that he could see in the entire charade, was that she was pleasingly pleasant on the eye (as far as social workers go), and as long as he didn't have Paula asking if he 'was OK', there really wasn't anything to be lost in giving her a chance to fuck it up under her own Chanel-infused steam.

By now, Snowball had cultivated a widely known, but seldom appreciated, strategy of total silence in the face of the 'enemy', and was quite comfortable and content to sit her out in a battle of wills, until she buckled under the weight of the mass of nothingness that he offered her by means of conversation, and accordingly shuffled her well dressed Marks and Spencer's clad backside, and perfectly manicured nails back to the office on the other side of this drab little town in which they lived. But at first glance, and as far as first impressions go, she appeared a little bit different to the previous fodder the department has sent his way, and he couldn't help but feel a little bit intrigued. The likelihood of her having anything to say that he might have the slightest bit of interest in hearing was slim, if not anorexic, but if nothing else, she might constitute a comfy lift home in her shiny car, and there was always the potential to tap her up for some sweets on the way past the newsagent's, if only his endearing charm captivated her long enough to make a positive impression. There was absolutely no end to his fuckery and charm when it was vitally needed.

Sheila was a tall, slim, elegant woman. She oozed a sense of sophistication. Blonde haired, slim figured, poised and somewhat statuesque, in a northern pit town sort of way. The long slim fingers of her left hand were adorned in expensive looking diamond rings, and her slender wrists were home to an expensive looking watch on the left, and diamond studded bracelet on the right. There was a certain amount of grace and elegance, classic sophistication that Snowball immediately tuned in to. If nothing else, he had become adept at spotting everything that was inherently different in people, and Sheila very much presented as being very different from everyone he had previously been associated with, as she strutted around in her fur hat, and erstwhile confidence. It was the complete contrast between expectation and reality that both caught and held his eye and imagination captive. She had a champagne appearance, on lemonade money, and in the full dullness of a town like Bolton, to pull that off was pretty impressive to say the least. 'This fucker will need to be given a chance,' he thought to himself. One of his better decisions as it turned out.

She was clearly a very different proposition from most he had previously encountered or been encumbered with. Beautiful in comparison to the many social workers he had previously been assigned, and it was immediately apparent that the department had moved on from assigning him the ugliest, roundest, most visually offensive social workers they had, in some perverse form of additional punishment for the crime of being in their care, and had decided that after years under their control, it was his turn for the posh looking totty, and it was very much appreciated.

She was intelligent and well spoken, something which he found extremely appealing, and she held herself with a composed dignity, which allowed her to stand out in the seething swell of normality that surrounded her, without appearing too overly strident, aloof or uncharacteristically forward. She was altogether strikingly impressive, and for the first time in a long time, Snowball felt there may be an immediate need to break with his vow of 'Omertà', and actually speak to this intriguing woman who had stepped into his path, albeit uninvited. How the road to Damascus was unveiling its many surprises.

The ride back to the home had been an interesting one. Sheila had introduced herself, and as if it needed explaining, had explained her role, while fortunately refraining from making the sort of pointless promises that Snowball could spot as lies from a mile away through the eye of a needle, and which usually signalled the immediate cessation of meaningful conversation, and an end to any possibility of a constructive or fruitful relationship hence. She spoke in firm positive overtones. She was clear, precise and to the point. It was the kind of unassuming confidence, borne from an understanding of detailed fact, that Snowball liked and appreciated. She appeared to be devoid of the usual bullshit that encumbered the less than average social workers he was accustomed to, and she tended to approach him with a degree of understanding and mutual respect that he found appealing. All told, Snowball found that first meeting to be of great interest, and whilst he would never have admitted it, he was quite taken by this apparently new and peculiar social worker who had arrived on his block, and he was in many ways looking forward to their next encounter, and what intrigue it might bring. Of course, she needed to be tested, but all in good time.

Snowball soon found out that Sheila worked out of the nearby offices not far from his home. They were on the outskirts of Bolton, or in the suburbs, depending on whether you were trying to buy or sell your house at the time, or worked in estate agency. The offices were a slightly longer distance away from his school, but regardless he figured he could pop in occasionally when the school curriculum was not to his immediate liking and grab himself a cup of tea and a quick chat with blondie. Over the coming weeks and months, he would occasionally pop in for unscheduled chats on company time, and while she invariably would find these visits both inconvenient and bloody annoying, given that it bestowed upon her an element of complicity to his truancy, she indulged his eccentricity in the knowledge that he was at least talking to her, which was a huge step forward from his interactions with those whom she had succeeded, and was much to their chagrin, as they shared the large open space of the office, and were privy to the interactive progress she was making, in an area they had clearly failed to master.

He was developing a very distinct mental connection with Sheila, which was finally permitting a two-way dialogue that was serving them both well. She was now in the position of being able to raise issues of concern with him, which had previously resulted in a volatile explosion of anger and rage, followed by weeks of enforced silence and miscommunication. He in return was now sensing that he was with and around someone who cared, had his interests at heart, and was working in those best interests, and he responded accordingly. It wasn't the case that they would agree on everything, but he was beginning to understand that good people came with a small price attached, and if he wanted to reap the benefits of their goodness, he knew he now had to offer goodness in return.

It was small change pocket money, in relation to the benefits he could accrue, but the issue for Snowball was how. How could he rise above the cesspit swell in which he had unwillingly trodden water for so long? How could he escape the violence and abuse that had dogged his very existence, and demonstrate to this woman that he was innately a good and decent person, who deserved a chance? How was it to be, that amongst all that was bad around him, all the hate, violence, anger, the detriment and pain, how amongst all that, was he to rise from the ashes of his own childhood, decent, unscathed and worthy? It appeared to be an almost impossible challenge. A challenge too far. He had no idea where to start, or what to do, but he knew above all else, that it was what he desperately wanted, and above all else, needed in order to survive.

Lady Luck smiled upon him once more. Salvation and solution for his journey would come easier than he ever thought possible, with the simple suggestion that he start with school. Sheila had suggested that all good things in life, job, house, money in pocket, car, holidays, all emanated from education and qualifications, which he could only ever achieve by attending school. Success and life's comforts were not to be found in walking aimlessly around the town centre during school hours or dodging the police and truancy officers around the parks and play areas that he frequented with his friends. It seemed a reasonable enough position to hold, and one which after some thought, he chose to adopt, if for no other reason than ramming her smug little attitude back down her throat, when he demonstrated that he was capable of doing it and stepping up as suggested. He wasn't to know at the time, but she had just beaten him up with reverse psychology, but as long as he thought he was winning, it didn't really matter. He had found no real comfort in his truancy anyway, and only really indulged out of a misplaced sense of loyalty to his mainly glue sniffing pack, and the knowledge that it was something that clearly pissed off those who controlled every other aspect of his day to day existence. He was bright. Very bright. He just didn't have a reason to focus until Sheila arrived.

For Snowball, it was the first time in recent memory that he could remember somebody caring enough to offer him sound, reasonable and believable advice.

There were no lies, no false promises. It was advice that had risen from exposure and experience of life itself. Welcome advice in many respects, however unpalatable it appeared upon first taste. He found himself being forced to sit and reflect. He had to make choices, and they had to be the right choices. He had to ponder his position and evaluate how much he was personally willing to sacrifice in order to achieve all those things he had previously dreamed of. Was he strong enough to stand alone in the adverse and perverse world in which he lived? Could he find the strength he now needed to rise up to the challenge she had presented to him?

Who was this smug fucker, with her blonde hair, and jewellery-bedecked hands, who spoke so much truth that he was left with few avenues of challenge, and fewer options to ponder, if he was serious about his future, and the fulfilment of all his dreams and expectations. Miss Bradwell had told him to trust nobody. It was the only way to stay safe, she had told him, and to an eerily accurate extent, she had been right all along. But he could see that now, at the point he needed her to be most right, she was in fact wrong. Times were changing, and if he was to succeed, he would have to adapt and change with them. He would have to lend his trust to somebody, and pray that against all previous experience, it wouldn't be betrayed. Sheila was the chosen one, and he subsequently invested all he had in her casual guidance, and well-hidden care.

As time moved on, Sheila eventually got around to introducing Snowball to her family and friends. It was the early day equivalent of becoming 'Facebook Official' in that it conferred am element of immediate acceptability amongst people who had otherwise been unknown to you, and likewise, you them. Her husband Eric was a wise, intelligent man, who had an eye for factual detail that Snowball admired. He was a mathematician by trade and nature, and within him, Snowball found a kindred spirit, who relied on that which could be proven, at the expense of that which could not. The absence of conjecture appealed to Snowball, and Eric proved from first introduction to be a man to emulate and follow, the likes of which he had never previously encountered. Sheila's mother was also adorable, and immediately accepted Snowball for all that he was, and could be. He came to love her carefully executed, mature, dignified elegance, experienced insights, and welcoming charm. She was everything he expected and thought a mother and grandmother should be, and he quickly came to love her as if she were his very own.

Snowball began to develop a begrudging, but increasingly deep respect for Sheila, and all that she was bringing to his table. She was becoming the much sought-after parent figure that he had craved for so long. There was the light simmering of something more meaningful developing, which seemed to be serving a functional purpose for them both. On the one hand, Snowball was finally, so many years after being torn from his much-loved foster mother, being presented with something positive he could attach to, and on the other, Sheila who by choice had remained childless, seemed to be comfortable in the maternal role of passing on her worldly experience and insight, to the raw young boy, who had finally found a reason to develop his innate capacity to grow.

Sheila was a woman Snowball found easy to respect. Intelligent, sharp and with a cutting wit that matched his own razor-sharp sense of humour. She was a woman who had stepped into his life, and replaced the brutality of physical and mental abuse, with educated, well thought out words of wisdom that he found thought provoking and inspirational. He watched, listened and followed the positive examples she casually conveyed. He learned to step back and take the helicopter view of what life was placing in his path. Short term perspectives were gradually replaced with the big picture overview and planning. He slowly began to see his abusers as victims in their own perverse right. Trapped in a cycle of self-perpetuating violence from which they couldn't escape, and which they knew would one day catch them up and become their undoing. At last he could see a future for himself, and conversely, no future at all for those who had sullied his life with their abuses, violence and brutality. He was going to be free. Free to grow. Free to roam. Free to be himself. The abusers had lost. The stereotypes were untrue. He wasn't going to be a wasted life, nor end up on sleeping on a park bench, with a brain addled by booze and mental disease, or worse still, alleviated of his personal liberty under the care of Her Majesty's Prison Service. It seemed that Sheila had wittingly or unwittingly shone a bright light into the tunnel of darkness, in which he had walked for so long, and he was steadily walking towards it.

The tensions that were always in the air slowly began to give way to mutual understanding and trust. It was clear Sheila was someone Snowball could trust and confide in, and as Sheila came to realise that he himself could be trusted, an unusual friendship began to develop that would pervade long after Snowball walked away from the care system for the very last time. Between them, they slowly moved from stand-off support and begrudged respect, to a common centre ground that reflected an understanding of where they had both emanated from, and where they were both going. Sheila began to expose Snowball to some of the better things in life. Things he could never have dreamed of experiencing, and introduced him to people he would never have normally met. He responded with the behaviour that was both implicitly demanded by her actions and appropriate to the circumstances, as he continued on the path that she'd placed him upon, as he developed appropriate emotional and socially acceptable behaviours, as his responsibility to himself and towards her grew in tandem.

In many ways for Snowball it was a simplistic endeavour. He simply had to copy her acceptable behaviours and ignore the rest. It wasn't that she displayed particularly abhorrent behaviours generally, but he clearly recognised that when she sat on a colleague's lunchtime sandwiches, farted and then put them back in his lunchbox, it wasn't a behaviour she wanted him to emulate. Nor would she be happy if he mimicked her occasional use of an expletive riddled sentence, in order to make a valid point that she had failed to get across any other way. It was amusing to witness, but chances were, if he indulged in anything similar he would be the unwilling recipient of a sharp slap across the back of the head, or a stern look, the likes of which could freeze a polar bear dead in its tracks. There were clearly boundaries that Sheila wouldn't allow him to cross, but she was bringing a lot to the table, and compliance with her limited, but worthwhile expectations seemed an incredibly small price to pay, for the kindness and hope she brought with her.

On the right path. Something Snowball never thought he would actually experience. Life now looked good. He felt he had prospects, a future, a reason to live. Everything he rightly held in his grasp, years ago in that terraced house in the Fylde, was slowly being returned to him thanks to Sheila. He had a proper friendship, felt valued, and for the first time since he was torn screaming from his foster mother's arms, he felt truly wanted. His very existence, his very presence was being acknowledged and respected. He now dared to dream, and he was dreaming big. Sheila was everything he had ever wanted. She was filling the maternal delta that had stood between himself and the happy fruitful childhood of which he had dreamed so often. He would often wonder if she would eventually foster or adopt him. Would she take him into the heart of her family, and free him from the misery and perpetual heartache that plagued his life in care? It was what he wanted. What he desperately wanted, but he knew he couldn't ask. She had a great life. A loving husband and extended family and friends. It would have been an enormous imposition, and departure from the life she and her husband had both agreed with each other. But still, he dreamed that maybe one day he would finally have a family he could call his own.

Deep love and respect were alien feelings for Snowball. It was an emotional rollercoaster, and Sheila was turning his life and feelings upside down. He was emotionally intelligent, but it was an intelligence borne of and domicile in adversity. This was wholly new territory in which he had never previously trodden. He was becoming strangely compliant to her will, simply because it made sense. Her will ran contrary to everything he was experiencing in life, but it was valid, logical, honest and beyond reproach. He knew if he was to experience anything that remotely resembled a normal life, that he could no longer run with the pack. No more could he build insurmountable walls between himself and the rest of the world. He had to expose his sentient being to scrutiny, to challenge, and become one and at home with the ability to express himself rationally, intelligently and with forethought for the likely consequences that resulted from the words he spoke. Gone were the days of the 'banshee attack', or wrestling staff to the ground as he clung violently to the hair on their heads. No more would it be acceptable to simply tell the likes of Paula to fuck off, and expect to get away with it unchallenged. He had to be better than that. She demanded he be better than that by the example she set, and he knew he had to respond in the way she knew he was capable of doing. It would be a hard path to tread, but Snowball had finally arrived in the human race.

For the first time in his recent living memory, Snowball had someone he was scared of losing. It was ground breaking territory, and as the long-term fear of ever losing Sheila, Eric and all they have become to him set in, he would come to realise and appreciate the value he attached to her, all that she was, and all that she gave him. He grew through all the stages of emotional attachment and ultimately respect, to cherish and love her like he could never have expected to cherish or love, before they met. The primary instinct was to rebel. The instinct was a powerful one. He didn't want to be hurt again, and the heartache, turmoil and mental anguish that had gone before, was an ever-present reminder that he needed to be guarded at all times. He desperately wanted to distance himself from the potential heartache that would inevitably ensue and smother him one day in the future, but equally he knew that this was all part and parcel of human interaction, human relationships and the essence of life itself, and if he was ever to experience and enjoy the multitude of flavours life had to offer, inevitably he had to risk tasting plates that weren't to his palate. As he would come to appreciate in later life, it was better to have loved and lost, than to never have loved at all.

Sheila and Eric would remain an ever present, much loved and respected feature in Snowball's life. They would become the rock on which he could always depend. She would become godmother to his child. They'd share many of life's significant moments, from weddings, anniversaries, to the birth of children, deaths and all that falls in between. Sheila would become the person he turned to first when the conundrum of life held no real answers. She would provide the wisdom and belief that allowed him to move forward, strong, determined and confident. He would never be able to repay her trust, her loyalty, her kindness or faith in him, and all that she had instilled that would turn him into the person he would become. But he would come to appreciate that it wasn't about repayment at all. It was about a growing love and mutual respect. It was about the pleasure that derives from offering a helping hand to a lost soul and turning a life around. It was about the fact that she had pulled him out of a sea of low expectation, and provided focus, hope, aspiration and a future, and above all else, it was about those occasional special moments, when eyes cross, then meet, and above the noise and hullabaloo of everyday life, you can hear each other silently whisper, 'we got there in the end'.

It wasn't much longer after the dust had settled from the unplanned tour to the continent, that Snowball found himself approaching the age to be leaving care once and for all. He had finally settled down from the almighty bollocking Sheila had administered for the French excursion and become content to sit out the remainder of his time, like a low category prisoner awaiting transfer to an open facility. He had served longer in care than most lifers had served in the British Penal System, and the irony wasn't lost on him, having spent most of his life being told that prison was where he was going to end up. It had been a convenient one-liner for many of his carers and social workers, as a means of justifying the abdication of just about all of their professionally imposed responsibilities towards him, and they seemed constructively ignorant to the fact that prisoners in general would have fared much better than he had and been treated with greater consideration and discernment.

But now wasn't the time for those recriminations, as his mind both wandered and wondered, to and at the prospect of his imminent release in the big wide world. Staff had taken every opportunity to try and torment him about how he might expect to fare in this 'big bad world' outside as they termed it, which seemed somewhat ironic, given that the hell they presided over in care could hardly be viewed as a walk in the park in comparison. It was as if they thought they had done a good job, despite the clear and obvious fact that he was being released from their care, ill-prepared, ill-equipped, brutalised, traumatised, filled with hate, anger, and alone, into a cold world that he was supposed to embrace, and which was expected to embrace him. But he took their taunts in a confident stride, and in turn ridiculed them as to their persistent professional, social and personal failures. It didn't go down that well, but as he had come to appreciate, and often been reversely taunted with, the truth has a habit of both hurting and biting, and at this point, he really didn't care about what they liked or disliked.

His sixteenth birthday had been and passed in a completely memorable blaze of nothingness, as had most of his birthdays, and enthusiastic plans were being formulated in some corners for his final preplanned and scheduled departure from the home, and care system for the last time. They were about to wash their blood-stained hands of him, but it was a day that he had grown to welcome, cherish the prospect of, and came to embrace, not so much as the end of one era, but the beginning of another. As time would come to pass, he knew he would eventually reacquaint with his tormentors and abusers on a much more equal footing. He dreamt of the day that he would meet them in the street, and confront them, eye to eye, man to man, and 'discuss' their abuses in some detail. There would be fear, but it wouldn't be his. He had done with fear. He had done with their tyranny, and he had done with their abuse. No, the next time they met, he knew it would be a completely different dynamic that favoured him, favoured the brave, and hindered the weak.

TIME TO LEAVE

Oi You FUCKERS, go fuck yourselves, was the thought racing through Snowball's mind as he awoke for the very last time, under the care of the local authorities that had failed him so miserably, since the first day they had become acquainted with each other. The gentle patter of the rain could be heard on the opposite side of the curtains. The 'sun' had barely risen on the distant horizon, and yet the warmth running through his body, his mind, his spirit, told him all he needed to know. Today was going to be his day. The first day of the rest of his life. The day he walked away from the violence, walked away from the abuse, walked away from the betrayals, the anxieties, the hate, the callous disregard for his well-being, and the lies and misery.

There would be one last glass of water from the calcium stained taps, one last shower in the communal wet-room, one final set of malicious taunts from an uncaring staff, and one final set of goodbyes that he would strive to make permanent, as the lingering thought that he might encounter some of these hideous monsters again, in some formal capacity or other, served to fortify his burgeoning resolve, that never again would he fall prey to their hostilities, their brutality or their hate, prejudices and abuses. Today was the day that his 'Care' Order had finally expired, and they were about to commit their final act of abandonment, their final betrayal, and with a cold, cruel callousness, throw him onto the streets to fend for himself, alone, isolated, ill-prepared, and with a system infused hope that all their Nostradamus-like predictions of his immediate and pointless future would come true. Never had they wanted someone to fail so much. Never had they primed, prodded, kicked and cajoled someone into failing so much, and never again would they live to experience the profound disappointment of their confounded aspirations, as they would on this solitary occasion in their professional lives.

They had created an almost jovial atmosphere, as he sat down one last time to be fed in the large open dining room, that had been the scene of more confrontations and violence than it had enjoyable dining experiences. It was almost as if, on the one hand, they were triumphantly trying to convince him that they had done a great job with his upbringing, and on the other, they were trying to placate the potential devil inside him, that had recognised their litany of abuse, and was about to be unleashed, with who knows what intent, when their iron-like authoritarian grip had finally been prised open. Yes, this was a young man, who, during the course of their care, had transitioned from baby, to child, youth and now young adult. They, and they alone, were responsible for what was about to be unleashed upon society. The child that they had systematically abused, religiously beaten, violated and condemned to the garbage disposal of human existence, was about to walk free from their control, and they had no idea how he intended to use that freedom, nor what he intended to do.

Snowball sat calmly, refusing to eat his last breakfast, and intelligently surveying the scene in front of him. His eyes momentarily pausing on each of the faces that sat around the table. He felt nothing but hate, anger and hostility, as he paused, face by face, and gathered a few final explosive thoughts that would sum up his feelings about each and every one of them. The hate was strong, powerful, insidious, and yet strangely riveting. It could have consumed him there and then, if only he was prepared to allow it. But the faces he was surveying were simply the faces of more victims. The faces of those who had also been subdued by the violence and abuses, into which, they like himself, had been cast through no direct fault of their own. There wasn't a face around that table that he hadn't had an issue with at one time or another, but he knew deep down that whatever they had said to him or others, whatever they had done to him or others, it had all been part of the big game of personal survival, against seemingly insurmountable and brutal odds. The feelings of hate were there, but they channelled towards the system that had created these faces, that had moulded the thinking behind each visage. Deep inside, he knew they were all wishing they were him. His immediate future was almost certainly cold and bleak, but it had to be better than what they faced from within. They had all been conditioned like a Pavlovian Dog to think that way, but each and every one of them knew that what Snowball was walking out to face that morning was infinitely better than the continued abuses and brutality that they were to face when he had gone, and passed into memory. Yes, the hate in him was strong, and yet, as he sat and surveyed, he was consumed by a euphoric calm that signalled somewhere deep inside him that, 'this was now all over'.

He took a few final glances at Karl, the abusive, hard gambling alcoholic who had been charged with his care over the last few years. The man who had brutalised him more times than he could remember and had brutalised every other boy that resided at Cramley Gardens. Alongside him was Bernie. Yes, Bernie, the overweight, violent, abusive ex-rugby playing sociopath, who had taken a regular, almost perverted delight, in inflicting pain upon those who were simply in no position to fight back against his sadistic and calculated onslaughts. How he craved the courage and physical strength to just step across the room and plunge a knife deep into their hearts. Cold, callous hearts that had failed him and them so much, and in all manner of ways over the years. He would have happily stood astride their fading limp bodies, as their last gasps teetered from their lifeless carcasses, and they expired into the afterlife, happy in the knowledge that never again would they hurt and bring misery to a child in care.

But that was now someone else's battle. He knew that he didn't have to destroy his own future, in order to seek the revenge that he craved. He was aware that one day, some day in the future, they would self-implode. It was only a matter of time before they would self-destruct. It was too late for him to reap the benefits, but times were beginning to change in many ways. There was a new breed of social worker and carer entering the system. They were more aware of the issues, and many were more than willing to confront the abuses. There were mounting cases of evidence of abuse, and eventually, that mountain of evidence would become such that it couldn't be ignored. As with most stories and good films, there was generally a good ending to be had. The only question was that of who was around and alive to enjoy it.

The need for revenge was powerful and deep. But that wasn't Snowball. He knew he was better than that, as was every child sat around the table with him. He was simply warmed with the contented knowledge that he could do better for himself, outside of this wretched system. Infinitely better than they, the abusive and the worthless, could ever do for him within it. No, he would sit there, finish his glass of foul-tasting water in peace, and permit them their final acts of control. He would dutifully take dirty plates to the serving hatch and check the 'Job list' to ensure that he wasn't on the washing up rota, and then he was finally and irreversibly done. Never again would they lay a violent hand across his body, torment his mind, and convince him that he had no future. Never again would they be allowed to tell him he had no worth as a child, as a black child, nor would he hear the words nigger, sambo or coon spat vengefully from their lips, with a hateful inflection that laid bare their deeprooted racist ideologies. No, today was the day that all that would cease. Today was the day that Snowball would be re-born. The real Snowball was about to hit the streets, and this time he wasn't running. This time there was nowhere to run.

He was roughly sixteen and a half years old (always remember that the half is important at that age) when that day of departure had finally arrived for Snowball. He had spent all of his childhood in the care of social services, and to his knowledge had received very little care during the entire period. It had been one continuous fight after another. An unrewarding fight for survival that he had endured from an age when most children could barely tie their own shoelaces. One brand of brutality and abuse, replaced by another brand, in a different town, in a different home, inflicted by different people, but all with the same outcomes. But he had arrived at this day as a survivor, because deep, deep within him, in a darkened place where nobody else ventured, there was something extremely strong inside him.

He had been abused, beaten and mistreated in every establishment he had ever been in, and across most of the North West of England. But now his time had arrived. His liberation was imminent. He would step quietly from the pain and anguish of a world he couldn't control, into a world that beckoned him to shape his own destiny. If nothing else, this day would mark the beginning of some calm, some peace, some stability and balance in his life. He would finally be out of the system. Free from the ritualised abuse, and orchestrated neglect. He would rid himself of the daily torment that being a black child in a white institution had inflicted. He was about to become a care leaver. A care-experienced adult, in a harsh, unremitting and unforgiving world. He would, overnight, at least become an adult to all intents and purposes, bar buying himself a celebratory drink to mark the occasion. His abusers were about to become things of the past. Part of an inglorious history, devoid of heroes, role models, safety and security. Devoid of all things sane, and all things stable. He was about to be able to settle. In one place. In his own place, on his own terms. The thought of life, of living, of freedom, of the absence of pain, humiliation and suffering, now consumed his every thought.

Packing the night before hadn't been difficult. He'd emptied his locker into two plastic bags, been handed a clothing voucher for twenty-five pounds that could be spent at a local clothing shop, and informed by Karl that he wasn't their problem anymore. It was nothing less than he expected from Karl, who, after all, had never had a positive word to say about any of the boys, let alone the black one. But Karl was a man on borrowed time, who would, within a few short years of Snowball's departure, be found dead in a congealing pool of his own faeces, kidneys pickled in whisky, and virtually penniless, as a result of his addiction to booze and gambling.

Karl and Bernie – who would eventually go on to marry Jane, in a whale blubber themed registry office wedding, which made their illicit walrus like shags official – had reluctantly conceded to the fact that they had to feed him that night, but seemed to conspire amongst themselves to ensure that it was nothing special. One last, albeit minor, piece of departing abuse that they couldn't resist. But Snowball cared little for the pettiness of their dying gestures, and it only served to embolden him prior to departure, as he sat and drank water in the heat of their full glare. He was out of their claws. They could no longer touch him, no longer control him. Never again could they hurt him. Now it was their time to worry.

He had been assured that a further twenty-five pounds in cash would be given to him in the morning, in order that nobody could steal it overnight, and he was furnished with the address of the bedsit that would become his new home the following day. He couldn't cook, iron, clean a home, wash up, manage money, use a washing machine, get himself out of bed on time, or interact properly with a society that had rejected all participation in his life to date. But he was over sixteen, and in the eyes of social services, 'their job was done', and he was now on his own. They had 'successfully' prepared him for adult life, and could now heartily pat each other on the back, and celebrate a job well done.

A small, single room, barely bigger than a prison cell, in a mid-terrace house was now home. White washed walls. Two-ring cooker hob, combined grill and oven, a single bed, a flowerpatterned set of three pans, two knives, two forks, two spoons, two cups, two plates, two soup bowls, a blanket, pillow, two sheets, and a solitary picture of a green skinned Cuban woman hung on the wall. They had 'handsomely provided' for him. So, he pondered, as he gazed out of the solitary cracked window pane in his room. This was now the life he had.

I am Snowball, and this was my story.

The End

(or is it, you fucker?)

Names, dates and places have been changed to protect some of the guilty!

The word FUCK is under-valued – use it more often.

All you had to do was get me through childhood. What went wrong?

Stick your judgemental attitude up your arse.

No, I do not have Tourette's, you cheeky twat.

NOT FORGOTTEN

"OMG... I've finally tracked you down"

Your timely words seemed meant to be
But you could not have known, how much they'd mean to me
It's 40 years since we last met in that awful place

Where cruelty went unpunished and justice was disgraced
There were fireworks in the attic with confiscated toys
Colouring books were all you had designed to mute your noise
A cold bath if you wet the bed stood barefoot in the snow
Deliveries hijacked food packed to go

When visitors came the scene was set for influential illusion
Bay windowed lounge unlocked children on parade
Reciting party pieces in humiliating charade
With tea and cake to celebrate this perilous delusion

Years later it was no surprise to discover the boy who spoke out
Was stripped and beaten by police 'moved' and branded liar
For time served leaves me without doubt
.... abusers will be reprieved
As long as truth is worthless and vested interest valued higher

Children will be dispersed scattered like it doesn't matter
Ruptured relationships cannot survive uncertainty
Or self-belief is extinguished when trust is shattered
By those willing to collude with crimes against humanity

Amanda Knowles MBE

AFTER THOUGHTS

The problem with institutional childcare, in recent living memory, is that it has always sought to minimise the impact of the children whose care it is charged with, upon the status quo, upon everyday life, and upon society in general. For far too long the attitude has been that these children are the problem, and not the environments and circumstances from which they hail. The impetus has always been to subdue, and subdue by whatever means are deemed appropriate, whether they be fair or illicit. As a direct consequence of this strategy, society has always sought to make use of generic practices, procedures and rules, which compartmentalise children, and strip them of all individuality, dignity, character, and self-identity. There was and is no room or time in the care system, for nurturing children and developing them as individuals. They are expected to be the same, act the same, be disciplined and socialised in the same way, to like and dislike the same things and in equal measure.

As Snowball came to understand, from one home to the next, this rigid and brutal ideology was designed to serve the needs of staff and the department, as opposed to the children in their care. Individuals did not exist; the system existed. The system demanded conformity, and brutalised and abused those who dared to challenge it. Snowball had witnessed the litany of abuse, brutality, violence, self-harm, substance abuse, dependency and suicide attempts, which bore testimony to the rigidity and brutality that the children existed with and strived to contain. Children, alone and isolated, with nothing more than each other, and a dwindling hope, that one day, someone might step through the doors, and rescue them from the institutionalised daily torment that they all suffered. They were the walking dead. The unwanted, undervalued, unacknowledged and uncared for. They were the lost, amongst the lost, the hated amongst the hated.

They existed without rhyme, reason or hope, in a system that had, by design, vociferously, routinely and wilfully failed them.

Given the complexities of human nature, individuality, character, culture, socio-economics, gender identity, society, nature v nurture, race and the whole gamut of societal and group interactions and dynamics, this is an incredibly flawed and fundamentally naive modus operandi, even when applied in what we would describe as a 'traditional' family environment, let alone the hostile, unpredictable circumstances that formed and forms childcare throughout recent decades. When this formula is compounded with the complexities and dynamics of the troubled child, in an abusive, oppressive, fundamentally and dangerously flawed childcare system that does little to care, value or develop children, this strategy is beyond all logical reason and intelligent thinking.

At the finest of times, children are not, and never will be, a one-size-fits-all commodity. Every human cell, every strand of DNA, contributes towards the individual uniqueness of each and every child. Pavlovian theories are not applicable to raising healthy, well-balanced, intelligent, independent, socially aware and responsible children. A uniqueness that the childcare system fails monumentally to both recognise and embrace. The childcare system had traditionally sort to enforce conformity, with brutality. It has physically and mentally damaged thousands of children for decades, in a manner of which leads to long term, and often irreversible, mental and physical damage, and further exacerbates the impacts of the abuse (physical or mental) that the child has suffered in early years.

The truly unbelievable and unprecedented scale of historic child abuse is becoming widely known in society, and society is rightly horrified, and indignant. That horror and indignation, however, should not detract from the stone-cold reality that this abuse has been known about since inception. This is not a novel situation that needs tackling. This is an old problem, with a fresh, guilt-based determination to tackle it. The Social Services, Police, Judiciary, Education System, Charities and society in general, knew of the abuses that were taking place and being inflicted upon abandoned, unwanted and unvalued children, and they purposefully delivered those children, into a childhood of blatant, open and dangerously coercive physical, mental and sexual abuse, whilst often being complicit, and taking active roles in that very abuse. As a consequence, these institutions, in many cases irrevocably shattered the lives, life chances, opportunities, mental and physical health of thousands of children, and all, in the main, because people simply couldn't be bothered to do their jobs.

Cared for children in the United Kingdom have, over recent decades, made innumerable complaints, told their stories, highlighted the abuses, and sought refuge in police stations, social services departments, the church and many other institutions, only to find themselves punished, and returned into the hands of those who were abusing them. Jail cells have, over the years, overflowed with the victims of this abuse. These were not adults that chose to rebel against society, to wander a nefarious path, or to buck the prevailing system. These are often the battered, broken, abused, humiliated and damaged outputs of a system and society, that for their formative years chose to simply abandon them to a fate so unimaginable to most, that it has to be lived in order to be fully understood.

As you read these final paragraphs, be cognisant of the reality that girls in care are being sexually abused as you read, and adults, charged with their care, are aware of this abuse, and have chosen to ignore it. As you read these final paragraphs, children in care are, at this moment, reeling from the physical and mental abuse that has been inflicted upon them by their 'carers'. This very moment, children in care are sat alone, they are self-harming, they are sinking into addictions, they are being manipulated and groomed, and some are contemplating suicide, as a direct and consequential result of the 'care' that they are receiving TODAY.

Society chose to abandon these children, and is currently choosing to resist any attempts to socially integrate them as adults. Children in care have had their social, gender and identity needs neglected. They have had their racial and religious needs neglected, and as a society, we are choosing to neglect their future needs. Unless something salient is initiated and implemented now, children in care will continue to suffer prolific abuse at the hands of those charged with their well-being. The evidence of abuse is widespread. It cannot be disputed, and it cannot be rejected. In the time it has taken you to read this book, another life has been destroyed, another child abused, raped, beaten, and all is hidden behind the respectable wellintentioned veneer of 'social care'.

Surviving as a survivor is a very poignant concept. Understanding the coping strategies invoked by victims, in order that they can come to terms with their histories, is prerequisite to an understanding of where they have been, have arrived, and are destined to go to. The childcare system in the United Kingdom has farmed a vast crop of its own nurtured victims of sexual, physical and mental abuse, under the watchful and complicit eyes of authorities across the country. These victims are both male and female. They are homosexual, heterosexual, trans-gendered and more. They hail from and cover every social spectrum, every walk of life, and they are embedded in every institution and organisation the country has to offer. They all have a shared history, were all told they would be failures, jail fodder, drug abusers, alcoholics, child abusers, criminals, baby producers, and piss-poor council house dwellers. These are the people who were forced to live every day with misplaced guilt, inappropriate blame, mental anguish and a painful history under constant development.

And yet, today, these are your neighbours and friends, your manager at work, and the bus driver on the number thirty-six. They are now the solicitors who process your mortgage paperwork, doctors and nurses who tend your health, the authors you read, and the taxi cab drivers who drop you off at your front door. They are the dentists, the plumbers and the electricians. They are soldiers, sailors and airmen who stand guard over our country. The van drivers and window cleaners, actors, barbers, chefs and businessmen. They are the travel agents, the project managers, train drivers and the factory workers. They are politicians, charity workers, takeaway owners, and shopkeepers. They are the priests, the explorers, the pilots, and the diplomats. The athletes, film stars, poets and the celebrated. These are the children who had no value.

To all those who taught me everything that I needed to know, and extended an experienced and helping hand, when I needed it most, in order that I become the person that I needed to become, wanted to become, and you knew I could become, I say thank you.

To all those who, by their thoughts, actions, complicity and abuses, taught me everything I needed to know, about the type of person I didn't need, nor want to become, I offer you a **VERY SPECIAL THANK YOU. You have no idea just how much you have helped!**

The Challenge:

Sexual and physical abuse in the UK childcare system, has been an ever-present feature since the first formal and informal homes were established. It has been a feature of institutionalised life that has been largely ignored, covered up, and allowed to flourish. Sexual and physical abuse, at the hands of both paid and casual carers, has destroyed a countless number of lives, and it is still happening today. Young boys and girls, placed into the care of local authorities across the country, are being abused as you read this text. Yes, as you read this text, most likely in the comfort of the sort of home and environment that they could only ever dream about, THEY ARE BEING ABUSED.

As you reach the end of this paragraph, another child has just been abused, or had an abusive experience, in a child care home in the UK.

As a direct result of that abuse, some of those children will ultimately take their own lives. The potential for others to succumb to alcoholism, drug abuse and crime, is wholly disproportionate to their peers from 'normal' homes. In terms of statistical significance, and correlative science, this is an indication that the childcare system is the problem, and not the children who are 'cared' for within it. So why are questions not being asked?

As you reach the end of this paragraph, another child has just been abused, or had an abusive experience, in a child care home in the UK.

Prisons and mental health institutions across the United Kingdom are currently acting as 'homes' to many of the past victims of systematic institutionalised abuse that was perpetrated against them, and many more places will be occupied by them in the future, unless active measures are taken to address the abuses, right the wrongs, bring the abusers to justice, and end the endemic and systemic inequalities that we, as a society, confer upon 'looked after children', simply because we haven't learned to value them in the same way that we value our own.

As you reach the end of this paragraph, another child has just been abused, or had an abusive experience, in a child care home in the UK.

It is an unacceptable statement of fact, that paedophiles and child abusers are, by virtue of their employment, being given free access, and unbridled freedom, to perpetrate crimes against vulnerable children, who have been failed by the justice system, social services, their families, schools and society alike. Systemic abuse is destroying the lives of children on a daily basis. Society must stop this practice. This is not something to be considered, pondered, committee'd or appraised. This is something that must be done. The level of historic abuse is staggering. It is unprecedented, and demeaning to any society that has pretensions to calling itself civilised.

As you reach the end of this paragraph, another child has just been abused, or had an abusive experience, in a child care home in the UK.

In October 2017, I attended a residential workshop in Gloucester called, Your Life Your Story. It was the beginning of this book. The workshop was organised by Amanda Knowles (MBE), who some forty years earlier had been a carer in one of the homes I lived in, and with whom I had recently enjoyed a very pleasant reunion, after which we had become good friends. From this newly found friendship came the invite to attend Your Life Your Story, which Amanda organised and we both attended. Amanda has spent over forty years passionately fighting for the rights of 'looked after children' within the care system, and has witnessed first-hand the systemic abuses that have existed within the care system, and the consequences they have reaped. It was a fitting tribute to the wonderful and incredible human being that she is, that the workshop was so well received, and it provided the inspiration, if any were needed, for her to consider hosting future events of a similar nature.

As you reach the end of this paragraph, another child has just been abused, or had an abusive experience, in a child care home in the UK.

There was, however, a very surreal, very frightening, and totally unexpected realisation that came out of the meeting. The age range of attendees spanned the spectrum, from as low as eighteen years old, right up to and including the late fifties. The staggering realisation was that those who had experienced these abuses in recent years, had in fact experienced almost carbon copy abuses, as those who had been in care almost half a century before them. To realise that these unbridled abuses were still being perpetrated against children, nearly fifty years later, was a hammer blow that inspired the writing of this book.

As you reach the end of this paragraph, another child has just been abused, or had an abusive experience, in a child care home in the UK.

These are stories that must be told, because something must change, and somebody needs to be the initiator of that change. People must be held accountable for actions, past, present and future. This book, and many books like it, makes you party to a cold, undeniable truth and set of circumstances, that you shouldn't ignore. Complicity through silence, to the continued physical and sexual abuse of minors by adults who have been charged by the court system with their care, is not an option.

As you reach the end of this paragraph, another child has just been abused, or had an abusive experience, in a child care home in the UK.

Be a part of something that will change lives for the better. Be that person.

Points of Note:

1. Victims (male and female) are being manufactured on a daily basis, by a system that systematically abuses and brutalises them. This is unbridled physical and sexual abuse, free from external inquisition or interference. These abuses are destroying the lives of children as you read. A conspiracy of silence is responsible for each and every one of these victims, and the passive or overt complicity of many, from individuals within social work, to entire institutions such as the police and the church, is allowing the continuation of the abuses and brutality to impact and destroy the lives of the very children who need society's protection the most.

    This is not a gender issue, nor is it a race issue. It is not an issue of education, social class or economic status. This is a humanitarian issue, or indeed crisis, predicated on the belief that children in the care system do not have the same intrinsic value as children living at home with their natural or adoptive parents.

    In a civilised society, this is unacceptable and must change. Go to any prison in this country, any mental institution, homeless shelter, drug or alcohol dependency facility, probation service or halfway house, and research the childhood history of the occupants. It is guaranteed that you will find an unhealthy smattering of adults who, in earlier life, were looked after children in the care system.

    Many of these people are not part of these systems because of who they were, or what they became in life. In many instances they are the victims of what society and the system of child care did to them, rather than for them. They are not intrinsically bad people. They are not the wrong ones we casually talk about, and dismiss as of no further use to society, because of their continued criminality, or inability to conform to any of society's standards and expectations. These are the children, who in many instances were placed into care for their own protection, and unwittingly entered into a cyclic living hell of physical and sexual abuse, from which there was absolutely no escape. They are the adult manifestation of the children who told the police, the social workers, the churches, and the schools of the abuse they were suffering, and then returned to their abusers and were punished for doing so. They are the victims nobody wishes to acknowledge, because the story they have to tell, tells society more about itself than it does about them

2. Guilt complexes are a common trait amongst looked after children who have suffered abuses at the hands of predatory carers and abusers. They commonly believe that they have done something wrong, something to deserve what happened to them, and something to deserve everything that will happen to them in the future. This is a feeling that goes largely unchallenged until later in life, where often it only comes to the fore as part of constructive therapy, trauma and psychological counselling.

But the damage has often been done by that point, and in many instances, is irreversible. The impacts of sexual and physical abuse are pervasive and damaging, and very little, if any, help is being directed to some of the most vulnerable and exposed children and young adults in society, who have been affected most. Many of these people have been ritually abused in one form or another, and often on a daily basis. This would be totally unacceptable in any other walk of life, and it would be rightly condemned, and action demanded, and yet society remains relatively ambivalent to the plight of looked after children, in the formal care system. We need to ask ourselves, one simple question. Why?

Why has it been accepted practice for young, under-age girls to be sexually abused and used by predatory males and females, on an almost daily basis, just because they are in care? Why is physical violence against young boys and teenagers an accepted practice, just because they are placed into care? Why was it acceptable to beat and maim children as young as four years old, with canes, straps, plimsolls, belts, wooden paddles, and the tawse, in the name of child care? Would society have accepted this level of sustained and deliberate abuse, with any other group of children?

3. Societal attitudes towards looked after children needs to change. It is simply not the case that these are not our children. Society has, by court order, made them our responsibility, and we have chosen a set of professionals to execute that responsibility. But our personal responsibilities should not end there. There is a duty of care, and society is a part of that, and must accept that duty.

Children are being abused and sexually exploited by people who are paid with our taxes to look after and care for them. It could be argued that each and every one of us is going to work, and paying taxes, that facilitate the abuses of children in our care. Together, we need to bring that to a halt, and hold people accountable for each victim that the system has produced.

4. Care provider attitudes towards looked after children need to change. Vulnerable children are not the problem that needs to be addressed. Emotionally disturbed children are not the problem that needs to be addressed. Predatory criminal males and females within and out-with the childcare system are the problem, as is the climate of disbelief and corporate cover-up that prevails when allegations and evidence of abuse is both collated and presented.

Unless the attitude of courts, social workers, child services departments and society alike changes, we are condemning generation after generation of vulnerable children to a fate that is incomprehensible and completely intolerable, amongst that which we would term 'normal homes'. It needs to be recognised that looked after children have the same intrinsic value that we place upon our own children, and in that context, we should all be prepared to go to the end of the Earth for each and every one of them. It's a simple concept that we should all understand.

UK Children's Care Homes or Institutions (Over 250), where allegations of physical, sexual or mental abuses have been proven or made: *http://www.abuselaw.co.uk/other-homes-institutions/* [1]

Getting Help:

Name: Simpson Millar.
Address: 100 Talbot Road, Manchester. M16 0PG.
Tel: 0345-357-9217

NSPCC
Tel: 0808-800-5000
Web: http://www.NSPCC.org.uk
Email: *help@NSPCC.org.uk*

Childline
Tel: 0800-1111
Web: *http://www.childline.org.uk*

Special Thanks to:
@OYFtheBook @amandakn0wles @Rosie_Canning @_LisaCherry @CareExpConf and TAZ (my writing buddy).

---

1. List Accredited to: Simpson Millar LLP Solicitors
    (*http://www.abuselaw.co.uk*)

Printed in Great Britain
by Amazon